PEACEMAKING 1919

PLENARY SESSION IN SALLE DE L'HORLOGE AT QUAI D'ORSAY. By courtesy of the *Illustration.*

PEACEMAKING 1919

By HAROLD NICOLSON

The Universal Library
GROSSET & DUNLAP
NEW YORK

UNIVERSAL LIBRARY EDITION, 1965

BY ARRANGEMENT WITH
HARCOURT, BRACE & WORLD, INC.

LIBRARY OF CONGRESS CATALOG CARD NUMBER: 65-13213

ISBN: 0-448-00178-0
1971 PRINTING

PRINTED IN THE UNITED STATES OF AMERICA

CONTENTS

BOOK I

AS IT SEEMS TO-DAY

BOOK II

AS IT SEEMED THEN

BOOK I

AS IT SEEMS TO-DAY

Chapter I

ARMISTICE

Diplomacy as art and science—The element of confusion—The old diplomacy and the new—Scope and purpose of this book—Questions which it leaves unanswered—The Coming of Peace—November 11, 1918 —The pre-armistice agreements—President Wilson's Notes of October 23 and November 5—Was there a breach of contract ?—The 'Pactum de contrahendo'—Colonel House's 'Interpretation'—How the pre-armistice agreements were viewed at the time—The Coupon election and Mr. Lloyd George's 'pledges'—Nature of these pledges—Public hysteria—The charge of ignorance—Actual nature of preparatory labours—The British preparations—Colonel House's 'Inquiry'—The American Mission to negotiate peace—French preparations—Lack of co-ordination.

I

OF all branches of human endeavour, diplomacy is the most protean. The historian and the jurist, relying upon the protocol and the *procès verbal*, may seek to confine its lineaments within the strict outlines of a science. The essayist may hope to capture its colours in the vignettes of an art. The experts—and there have been many experts from Callières to Jusserand, from Machiavelli to Jules Cambon—may endeavour to record their own experience in manuals for the guidance of those that come after. The journalist may give to the picture the flashes and interpretation of the picturesque. Yet always there is some element in such accounts which escapes reality, always there is some aspect which refuses to be recorded or defined.

This uncertainty of treatment arises from diverse causes. There is in the first place the discrepancy be-

tween the recorded protocol and the stages by which
that protocol has been reached. There is the divergence between the apparent and the real development of
negotiation. There is the tendency to attribute manifest effects to causes which only appear manifest.
There is the temptation to simplify mixed motives in
such a manner as to falsify those motives. There is the
difficulty of determining the proportion between personal initiative and mass-drifting. There is the persistent confusion of tongues, temperaments, purposes
and interpretations. And above all there is the danger
of mistaking actual values, of attributing to circumstances which seem significant an importance which
they did not in fact possess, of underrating other circumstances, apparently trivial, which at the time acted
as determinant factors.

I have for long wished to paint a picture of the new
diplomacy as a sequel, or counterpart, to that sketch
of the old diplomacy which I essayed in the biography
of my father. The more I have considered the subject
the less have I come to believe in any real opposition
between the two. Diplomacy essentially is the organised system of negotiation between sovereign states.
The most important factor in such organisation is the
element of representation—the essential necessity in
any negotiator that he should be fully representative of
his own sovereign at home. Such slight changes as
have occurred in the conduct of diplomacy should not
therefore be described in terms of an abrupt severance
between the ethical conceptions of one generation and
those of the next. It is less a question of ethics than
a question of method : in other words, it is the incid-
ence of sovereignty which has gradually shifted and not

the essential principles by which efficient diplomacy
should be conducted. Now that democracy is sovereign of us all, certain obvious changes in the conduct of
diplomacy have been, are being, and will be introduced.
Yet to describe these changes in terms of ethical rather
than of practical values is to misinterpret the whole
function of diplomacy. The contrast between the old
and the new diplomacy is thus not merely an exaggeration, but may prove harmful to the scientific study of
international relations.

Fortified by such a conviction, I have decided that I
shall attempt no such confrontation. I desire, however, to continue in some form or other my previous
study of pre-war diplomacy and to complete it in the
shape of a trilogy, of which this volume represents the
second of three dramas. I hope eventually to complete
my trilogy in the form of another biography, and to
treat of post-war diplomacy as centring round the
personality of Lord Curzon.

In this, the second volume of my trilogy, I have tried
to deal with the transitional phase between pre-war and
post-war diplomacy and to give some picture of the
Paris Peace Conference. I had intended at first to cast
this study also in the form of a biography and to centre
my story around the personality of Mr. Woodrow
Wilson or Mr. Lloyd George. I found, however, that
such a concentration of theme would convey no impression of the appalling dispersal of energy which was
the actual key-note of the·Paris Conference. The sharp
perspective, the personal continuity, given by the bio-
graphical method would have proved inimical to my
purpose. I am well aware that in abandoning my
original intention I have lost immeasurably in construc-

tion, interest, and financial profit. Yet in adopting such a method I should have been simplifying the issues, rather than furnishing a picture of the confusions and complications which actually occurred. I decided, therefore, that I should merely describe the Peace Conference as I experienced it myself.

Here again I was faced with a difficulty. I realised the impossibility at this stage of furnishing any connected narrative of the Conference in terms either of subject, or of time-sequence. On the one hand many vital documents are still unavailable, and on the other hand the consecutive method would create no accurate impression. The important point to realise about the Paris Conference is its amazing inconsequence, the complete absence of any consecutive method of negotiation or even imposition. The actual history of the Conference will one day be written in authoritative and readable form. What may remain unrecorded, is the atmosphere of those unhappy months, the mists by which we were enshrouded. My study, therefore, is a study in fog. The reader should not look for any continuous lucidity. It wasn't there.

I have, I think, read most of the many books which since 1919 have been published about the Peace Conference, some of which are admirable and some the reverse. Yet from all these books I have derived the impression that something essential was absent, and I am convinced that this vital omission was the omission of the element of confusion. It is that element, and that only, which I have endeavoured in this volume to record.

The memory of those congested days is very vivid to me. It has been fortified by reading the diary which I kept at the time. I have decided to print, as the second half of this volume, the major portions of that diary, feeling convinced that in its chirpy triviality it reflects better than any comments of a disillusioned middle age the very atmosphere which it is my desire to convey. My criticisms of my own diary are however implicit rather than explicit. I was, at the time, young and pardonably excited. No special self-excuse is needed for such faults.

Yet my main thesis, I trust, will be apparent. It is this. Given the atmosphere of the time, given the passions aroused in all democracies by four years of war, it would have been impossible even for supermen to devise a peace of moderation and righteousness. The task of the Paris negotiators was, however, complicated by special circumstances of confusion. The ideals to which they had been pledged by President Wilson were not only impracticable in themselves but necessitated for their execution the intimate and unceasing collaboration of the United States. We felt that this collaboration might possibly be intimate but could not possibly be unceasing. It was thus the endeavour of men like Clemenceau and Lloyd George to find a middle way between the desires of their democracies and the more moderate dictates of their own experience, as well as a middle way between the theology of President Wilson and the practical needs of a distracted Europe. These twin gulfs had to be bridged by compromise, and to a later generation these compromises seem hypocritical and deceptive. Yet were they not inevitable? And is it to be expected that human nature, having but recently indulged in the folly of the Great War, could suddenly manifest the calm serenity of almost superhuman wisdom?

I do not answer these questions. I leave them as interrogatives to be answered by some future generation. All that I hope to suggest is that human error is a permanent and not a periodic factor in history, and that future negotiators will be exposed, however noble their intentions, to futilities of intention and omission as grave as any which characterised the Council of Five. They were convinced that they would never commit the blunders and iniquities of the Congress of Vienna. Future generations will be equally convinced that they will be immune from the defects which assailed the negotiators of Paris. Yet they in their turn will be exposed to similar microbes of infection, to the eternal inadequacy of human intelligence.

It is with saddened regret that I look back to-day to that November morning when Mr. Lloyd George announced the armistice from the steps of Downing Street. The scene, to this moment, is impressed indelibly upon my mind. I was working in the basement of the Foreign Office, in a green and violet dug-out which but a few weeks before had provided shelter against the air-raids of the Germans. I was preparing for the eventual Peace Conference. More particularly, on that morning of November 11, I was studying the problem of the Strumnitza enclave.

Having worked for an hour, I found that I required a further map. I went upstairs towards the tower where our map-room was installed. On my way there I called in at the office of the Chief Clerk to order some further tin boxes for my needs at the Conference. I strolled to the window and looked down upon No. 10 Downing Street. A group of people stood in the roadway and there were some half a dozen policemen. It was 10.55 a.m. Suddenly the front door opened. Mr. Lloyd George, his white hair fluttering in the wind, appeared upon the door-step. He waved his arms outwards. I opened the window hurriedly. He was shouting the same sentence over and over again. I caught his words. ' At eleven o'clock this morning the war will be over.'

The crowd surged towards him. Plump and smiling he made dismissive gestures and then retreated behind the great front door. People were running along Downing Street and in a few minutes the whole street was blocked. There was no cheering. The crowd overflowed dumbly into the Horse Guards Parade. They surged around the wall of the Downing Street garden. From my post of vantage I observed Lloyd George emerge into that garden, nervous and enthusiastic. He went towards the garden door and then withdrew. Two secretaries who were with him urged him on. He opened the door. He stepped out into the Parade. He waved his hands for a moment of gesticulation and then again retreated. The crowd rushed towards him and patted feverishly at his back. My most vivid impression of Mr. Lloyd George derives from that moment. A man retreating from too urgent admirers who endeavour hysterically to pat him on the back. Ought he to have gone ? Having gone, ought he to have retreated so boyishly ? That scene was a symbol of much that was to follow thereafter. Having regained the garden enclosure, Mr. Lloyd George laughed heartily with the two secretaries who had accompanied him. It was a moving scene.

So the Germans had signed after all. I returned to my basement and the Strumnitza enclave. When

I again emerged the whole of London had gone mad.

It was in this manner that I heard of the coming of peace.

2

Many years have elapsed since those November days when I, in my green and violet basement, pored over the problem of the Strumnitza enclave. I am to-day aware that during the same period the rulers of the world were preoccupied by problems of even graver significance.

It is necessary, when examining the legal basis of the Peace Treaties, to concentrate at the very outset upon the question whether the triangular correspondence which took place in October between Washington, Berlin and the capitals of the Associated Powers constituted a contract in the legal sense of the term. Before we proceed a page further it is essential to state the following problem ; ' Did the Germans lay down their arms in reliance upon a pledge given them by their enemies that the ensuing peace terms would conform absolutely to the twenty-three principles [1] enunciated by President Wilson ? If so, did the Allied and Associated Powers observe, or violate that pledge once Germany was at their mercy ? '

The problem is so material to any record of the Peace Conference that I feel obliged to repeat the practice of my predecessors upon this thorny path and to recapitulate in my first chapter the main features of the pre-armistice agreement (the ' pactum de contra-

---

[1] These principles (namely the Fourteen Points, the Four Principles, and the Five Particulars) are summarised on pages 39-41.

hendo ') between Germany and the victorious Powers.
The essential documents can be summarised as follows.
On October 5 Prince Max of Baden, after many anxious
telephone messages to German Headquarters, addressed
an official Note to President Wilson in which he begged
him to negotiate a peace on the basis of his own Fourteen Points and his nine subsequent principles and to
facilitate the immediate conclusion of the Armistice.
On October 8 President Wilson replied in the form of
three questions : (*a*) Did the German Government
themselves accept the Fourteen Points as the basis of
the desired Treaty ? (*b*) Would they at once withdraw
their troops from all foreign soil ? (*c*) Could they give
assurance that the present and future government of
Germany would be placed on a truly democratic basis ?
On October 12 the Chancellor replied in the affirma-
tive to each of these three questions. He added that
his ' object in entering into discussions would be only
to agree upon practical details of the application ' of
the 'terms' contained in President Wilson's Fourteen
Points and his subsequent pronouncements. On
October 14 President Wilson again addressed the
German Government. He told them that no armistice could be negotiated which did not ' provide absolutely satisfactory safeguards for the maintenance of
the present military supremacy ' of the Allied and
Associated armies. He added that submarine warfare
must at once be discontinued, and that a democratic
and representative government must be installed in
Berlin. On October 20 the German Chancellor replied
accepting these conditions. On October 23 President
Wilson informed the German Government that, having
now received their assurance that they unreservedly

accepted the ' terms of peace ' embodied in his own pronouncements, he was prepared to discuss with his associates the grant of an armistice on this basis. He repeated that its terms must exclude all possibility of the resumption of hostilities. He hinted that the path of peace would be smoothed by the prior disappearance of ' monarchical autocrats.' He added that he had communicated to the Associated Governments the correspondence which had passed between himself and the German Government and had asked them whether they for their part would be ' disposed to effect peace upon the terms and principles indicated.' On November 5 the President transmitted to the German Government the replies he had received from his associates. The Allied Governments had declared their willingness to conclude a Treaty with the Government of Germany on the basis of the ' terms of peace ' enunciated by the President subject to two qualifications. The first of these bore upon the question of the Freedom of the Seas. The second extended the principle of ' restoration ' so as to cover ' all damage done to the civilian population of the Allies and to their property by the aggression of Germany by land, by sea, and from the air.' The German Government, on the receipt of this assurance at once despatched their emissaries to receive the armistice terms. The terms of this armistice had been drafted in Conference by the Supreme Council at Versailles : they were such as to place Germany at the complete mercy of the Allied Powers by land and sea : they were signed in the Forest of Compiègne at 5 a.m. on Monday, November 11.

In my next chapter I shall describe my own veneration for the Fourteen Points ; I shall summarise those points and their attendant principles ; and I shall show how nineteen out of President Wilson's twenty-three 'Terms of Peace' were flagrantly violated in the Treaty of Versailles as finally drafted.

For the moment I am concerned only with the pre-armistice agreement under which Germany consented to surrender on the explicit understanding that the peace terms thereafter to be imposed upon her would conform absolutely to Wilsonian principles, and would in fact be merely ' the practical detail of application ' of those twenty-three conditions on which alone she had consented to lay down her arms. I have summarised above the exchange of correspondence in which this agreement was embodied. Yet this is not the whole story. Sufficient importance has not, except by Mr. Winston Churchill, been given to Colonel House's ' Interpretation ' of the Fourteen Points which preceded their acceptance by the Associated Powers. Colonel House, at the time, was the Representative of America upon the Supreme War Council at Versailles. It was that body which approved the Armistice Terms as drafted, and through which the Allied Powers accepted President Wilson's ' Terms of Peace.' Colonel House's ' Interpretation ' or ' commentary ' of or on the Fourteen Points is thus a document of very vital importance.

This ' commentary ' was, on October 29, 1918, cabled to President Wilson for his approval. It contained the following glosses upon the Fourteen Points and the New Principles. The expression ' open covenants ' was not to be interpreted as precluding confidential diplomatic negotiation. By the Freedom of the Seas the President had not intended to abolish the weapon of blockade, but merely to inculcate some respect for private rights and property. The President himself advanced the engaging theory that in future wars, because of the League of Nations, there ' would be no neutrals.' Under this double gloss, paragraph 2 of the Fourteen Points became the vaguest expression of opinion. The demand for free trade among the nations of the earth was not to be interpreted as pre-cluding all protection of home industries. Far from it. All that it entailed was the ' open door ' for raw material, and the prohibition of discriminatory tariffs between members of the League of Nations. The point regarding ' disarmament ' implied only that the Powers should accept the theory in principle, and should agree to the appointment of a Commission to examine the details. The German Colonies might, when the time came, be in principle regarded as the property of the League of Nations, and thus be farmed out among desirable mandatories. Belgium was to be indemnified for all war-costs since every expense to which that unfortunate country had been exposed since August of 1914 was an ' illegitimate ' expense. France on the other hand, was not to receive full war costs, only a full indemnity for the actual damage done. Her claim to the territory of the Saar was ' a clear violation of the President's proposal.' Italy, for reasons of security, might claim the Brenner frontier, but the German populations which would thus be incorporated within the Italian frontier should be assured ' complete autonomy.' The subject races of Austria-Hungary should have complete independence conditional upon a guarantee for the protection of racial and linguistic minorities. The mere offer of autonomy ' no longer held.' Bulgaria, on the other hand (a country with whom the United States were not at war, and on whom they had in the past conferred great educational and philanthropic benefits) was to be compensated for having entered the war against us. She was to be given not only the Dobrudja and Western Thrace, but Eastern Thrace as well, as far even as the Midia-Rodosto line. Constantinople and the Straits were to be placed under international control. Central Asia Minor was to remain Turkish. Great Britain was to obtain Palestine, Arabia and Iraq. The Greeks might possibly be accorded a mandate over Smyrna and the adjacent districts. Armenia was to be created as an independent State under the tutelage of some great Power. Poland must have access to the sea, although such access implied a difficulty. That difficulty was the severance of East Prussia from the rest of Germany. Colonel House was careful to warn the President that this solution would not be an easy solution. And finally the League of Nations was to be the ' foundation of the diplomatic structure of a permanent peace.'

I do not wish to imply that Colonel House, in presenting this, his interpretation to the Associated Powers, was guilty of any desire to modify the fourteen commandments. I have the most profound respect for Colonel House—considering him to be the best diplomatic brain that America has yet produced, yet I confess that a most undesirable obscurity hangs over his ' interpretation.' Was it on the basis of that interpretation that the Allies accepted the Fourteen Points, the Four Principles and the Five Particulars, as the basis of the eventual Treaty of Peace ? If so, then the enemy Powers should assuredly have been in-

formed at the time. I write subject to correction, since
the exact documents, the exact exchange of suggestion
and agreement, are not to-day available. Yet it is difficult to resist the impression that the Enemy Powers
accepted the Fourteen Points as they stood ; whereas
the Allied Powers accepted them only as interpreted
by Colonel House at the meetings which culminated
in his cable of October 29. Somewhere, amid the
hurried and anxious imprecisions of those October
days, lurks the explanation of the fundamental misunderstanding which has since arisen.

In any case we, the technical staff, the civil servants,
had no knowledge of Colonel House's ' Interpretation.' We also looked upon the Fourteen Points and
their attendant pronouncements as the charter for our
future activity. As I shall show, a great gap widened
between our terms of reference, and the eventual conclusions. Had we known of Colonel House's glossary,
we might, in April, have seized upon it as a justification
for our backsliding. Yet it was not until many years
later that I even heard of this glossary. And I cannot,
for one moment, pretend that it influenced my attitude
to the slightest degree. I betrayed my own allegiance
to the Fourteen Points. The purpose of this book is to
give some indication, some slight clue, as to the
reasons for, or rather the atmosphere of, that betrayal.

My intention in writing this record is, however, not
to comment upon documents ; my sole endeavour is to
recapture states of mind. I am aware that I can make
no claim to recapture any state of mind other than my
own—a most insignificant capture. Yet I contend
that what I felt at the time was also felt by ninety-five
per cent. of those who, although not politicians, were

actively concerned with public affairs. When I use the term ' We,' I use it as defining the many people who in Paris felt and thought as I did myself. And, as such, we were representative of wide, and not wholly unintelligent, sections of opinion. I think that my own state of mind regarding the contractual basis of the Armistice and the ensuing Treaty did in fact represent an average point of view, which was widely and not wholly unreasonably, held ; and I have no recollection that *at the time* the divergence between our own conception of the ' pactum de contrahendo ' and the interpretation given to it in Germany presented itself in terms anything like so extreme as those in which it has since been stated.

On the one hand we were convinced that with the crumbling of the western defences—with the collapse of Austria, Turkey and Bulgaria—Germany in any case was beaten to her knees. We were relieved when the armistice was accepted, since it meant a shortening of the war : but we were convinced that had Germany refused to surrender it would have been a matter of months only, perhaps only of weeks, before her complete capitulation could have been enforced on German soil. On the other hand, in that autumn of 1918, we honestly believed that only upon the principles of President Wilson could a durable peace be founded. In other words, it never entered our heads that we had purchased the surrender of Germany by an offer of the Fourteen Points. The former seemed to us inevitable in any case : the latter, at the time, we took for granted. To argue otherwise is to attribute to November of 1918 ideas and ambitions which did not emerge into the open until the following March.

3

Such incorrect dating of opinion is in fact an error even more common to the historian than the attribution of false motive. He would, in this instance, observe that a frame of mind, identifiable in March, gave cohesion to a series of public documents exchanged (in a totally different frame of mind) the previous autumn. Inevitably he confuses the one with the other. It is from such confusion that arise errors in historic judgment.

A similarly unrecognised cause of historic misconception is the early, and often fortuitous, fixation of legend. Some picturesque detail, some coloured phrase, catches in the memory of the public. It becomes salient. Inevitably the facts (those gradations of circumstances which we call ' the facts ') arrange themselves behind this picturesque sign-post. One obtains, from such an angle, a perspective : all too often it is a misleading perspective.

Two such sign-posts emerge during the early period of the Conference. The first sign-post is ' We shall squeeze the orange until the pips squeak.' The second sign-post is Mr. Lloyd George's admission that he had never heard of Teschen. Behind the former sign-post is arrayed the whole problem of the khaki election of December 1918. Behind the second, group the innumerable legends that the members of the Peace Conference went to Paris without any previous preparation : that they were, without exception, ignorant and ill-informed. Against each of these legends I should wish to warn the future historian. It is for him that I compose these notes.

The General Election of December 1918 was certainly a disaster : it is questionable whether it was also a mistake. Mr. Asquith described it at the time as ' both a blunder and a calamity.' It was assuredly the latter : it returned to Westminster the most unintelligent body of public-school boys which even the Mother of Parliaments has known : yet it may be questioned whether it was an evitable mistake. The term ' blunder ' is employed these days to signify those actions on the part of statesmen regarding which they have failed previously to consult one or other of our Press Lords. In English, however, it denotes the sort of mistake which, with a little forethought, could easily have been avoided. I do not think that the khaki election of 1918 could easily have been avoided. I prefer to call it a regrettable necessity which was adopted without full realisation of its potent elements of regret.

Mr. Lloyd George has assured me recently that, were he back in November 1918, he would still ' plump ' for the election. His reasons for holding this opinion are interesting, and, to my mind, just. He contends that the Coalition Government were menaced at the moment by conspiracies both from the right and from the left. The former, headed by that ego-maniac Lord Northcliffe, were all for a peace of victors. The latter, backed by a fierce tide of ignorant opinion, were clamouring for immediate demobilisation. Had he proceeded to Paris with both his flanks thus continually exposed, he would have been hampered and uncertain in his every decision. It was essential for him to provide himself with an unassailable mandate. Clearly he could not have foreseen that his coupon election

would saddle him with a House of Commons so unintelligent as to become subservient to such ill-balanced
persons as Colonel Claude Lowther and Mr. Kennedy
Jones.

Nor was this all. Mr. Lloyd George foresaw that if
he were adequately to cope with the tortured nationalism of France, with the mystic and arrogant republican-
ism of America, and with the potential disunity of the
Dominion Delegations, he would need to render his
own *representative* quality assured beyond all possible
challenge. Even as it was, there were moments when
his right to speak for Great Britain was slyly questioned : there were occasions when the statesmen of
other countries endeavoured to mobilise against him
opposition elements at home, when they flirted both
with the Tories, with the left Liberals, and with the
Labour recalcitrants : and throughout the period of
the Conference Lord Northcliffe, incensed at not having
himself been appointed a Peace Delegate, turned upon
Lloyd George a constant stream of boiling water. It
may be questioned whether the Prime Minister could
have survived such onslaughts had he not been backed
by the overwhelming mandate of the British electorate.

The fact remains, however, that it was unfortunate
that a British Liberal should have placed himself at the
mercy of a jingo Commons and a jingo Press.

It is not, however, upon these more general lines
that the coupon election of 1918 will earn the disappro-
bation of the historian. Relying upon the popular
legend, he will perpetuate the contention that Mr.Lloyd
George, on leaving for Paris, was indissolubly bound
by his election pledges. This would be incorrect. In
the first place Mr. Lloyd George is too much of a

realist to be bound by any platform oratory. In the second place he pledged himself to little in his election speeches, which was incompatible with a reasonable peace. It was not he who used that immortal phrase about the orange and the pips. It was one of the less experienced among his colleagues. I have been at some pains to recover the exact terms of Mr. Lloyd George's election pledges and to compare them with the educated opinion of the time. I am convinced from this examination that Mr. Lloyd George was in fact more cautious, more liberal, than were the people by whom he is to-day traduced.

The point is of some importance for my purpose and I propose to press it further. On November 12—'le jour après le fameux jour'—Mr. Lloyd George addressed his Liberal supporters at No. 10 Downing Street. He spoke as follows : ' No settlement which contravenes the principles of eternal justice will be a permanent one. Let us be warned by the example of 1871. We must not allow any sense of revenge, any spirit of greed, any grasping desire, to over-ride the fundamental principle of righteousness. Vigorous attempts will be made to hector and bully the Government in the endeavour to make them depart from the strict principles of right and to satisfy some base, sordid, squalid ideas of vengeance and of avarice.' This sane liberal attitude he maintained (intermittently) throughout the Conference and even during the early stages of the election campaign. He concentrated on reconstruction. At Wolverhampton on November 24 he spoke of his distaste for ' stunts '—he urged as his sole intention the purpose of ' rendering England a land fit for heroes to live in.' It was Dr. Addison, the coalition candidate at Shoreditch, who first struck the more popular note. *The Times*—at that date passing through a deeply humiliating period under the control of Lord Northcliffe—was quick to catch the breeze of popular hysteria. 'The test,' wrote *The Times* on November 29, 'for the simple elector is clearly the position of the Kaiser.' 'This,' it repeated on December 2, 'is clearly one of the test questions of the election.' There was another test question, 'No indemnity,' proclaimed Mr. Austen Chamberlain in West Birmingham, 'which we can get is too high to ask for.'

Inevitably Mr. Lloyd George was affected by such patriotism on the part of his supporters, by such patriotism on the part of *The Times*. We find him at Newcastle on November 30 talking of a 'relentlessly just peace,' of 'terms not of vengeance but of prevention.' We find him accusing the German Emperor of 'murder.' We find him stating that Germany must pay for the whole cost of the war 'to the limit of her capacity.' In the 'statement of policy' which he issued in December, the trial of the ex-Emperor and the 'whole cost of the war' figured as the first two points. At Leeds on December 9 he spoke of the 'fruits of victory' : at Bristol three days later he used the expression 'the loser pays.' As a result of this emotionalism the Coalition was returned with a majority of 262. Mr. Asquith was defeated by Sir Alexander Sprott. Mr. Ramsay MacDonald and Mr. Snowden were overwhelmed. Mr. Horatio Bottomley was returned with a triumphant majority at Hackney. Mr. Pemberton Billing headed the poll in East Herts. 'Pacifists routed' proclaimed *The Times*. The coupons had done their work.

In all this welter of democracy Mr. Lloyd George, it
may now be observed, never completely lost his head.
In claiming that Germany should pay for the costs of
the war he was always careful to subject this welcome
statement to two reservations. He warned his audience
that such payments must be limited in the first place by
Germany's capacity to pay, and in the second place by
the qualification that such payment must not be allowed
to inflict injury upon our own export and internal
trade. He was sharply reproved by *The Times* for these
reservations. ' The only possible motive,' wrote that
journal, ' in determining their capacity to pay must be
the interest of the Allies.'

The ' Trial of the Kaiser ' slogan is, in its turn, an
episode by which the future historian will be much disconcerted. He will be tempted to attribute it to the
recent introduction of the woman's vote and the pre-
sumably increased hysteria of British politics. In this
attribution he will be making unfair deductions. It
may well be a feminine characteristic to attribute to an
individual sufferings which are caused by mass-cir-
cumstance. Dr. Fedor Vergin, for one, has contended
recently that it would have been good for the psychological health of Europe had William II in fact been
treated as a scapegoat, since the sense of guilt amassed
during those four frightful years might thereby have
been ' unloaded ' ; and in truth the desire to punish
Germany in the person of that unhappy victim was not
a desire felt only by the female section of the proletariat. I have before me a report of a speech delivered
on November 11 at the Carnegie Hall, New York, by
Mr. Alfred Noyes. He informed his horror-struck
audience that the ' reactionaries ' among the Allies

were endeavouring to rescue the Emperor from being tried by an International Court of Justice. ' These people,' exclaimed Mr. Alfred Noyes, ' would permit the Kaiser to return to his yacht and his champagne dinners while the twenty million men he has murdered lie rotting in the ground.' Nor, in thus declaiming, was Mr. Noyes alone. The mind of the British people during those post-armistice weeks was tattered with triumph, and gashed by the wounds of fear.

Hatred also survived. Had the Germans behaved with discretion during the weeks preceding the armistice it is possible that British public opinion, the least resentful on earth, would have forgotten its fear-hatred of 1914-1917. The Germans did not behave with discretion. On October 16 (eleven days after their first request for the mediation of President Wilson) they torpedoed, off Kingston, the Irish Mail Steamer ' Leinster ' with the result that 450 men, women and children were drowned. This eleventh hour atrocity was fresh in people's minds. ' A people,' wrote Mr. Kipling, ' with the heart of beasts.' ' Brutes,' said the mild Arthur Balfour, ' they were, and brutes they remain.' I direct the attention of the historian to the moral effects of the torpedoing of the S.S. *Leinster*. They were deeper, more immediate, than is to-day remembered.

4

A second sign-post which may lead the historian along an unprofitable by-way is Mr. Lloyd George's admission that he had never heard of Teschen. Addressing the House of Commons on April 16, 1919, he made the following frank, modest and eminently

reasonable statement · ' How many members ever
heard of Teschen ? I do not mind saying that I had
never heard of it.' Obviously no more than seven
members of the House of Commons can ever have
heard of that remote and miserable duchy, yet
Mr. Lloyd George's admission of that fact struck
horror to the heart of those specialists, such as
Mr. Wickham Steed, who had been familiar with the
Teschen problem for many years. The cry was raised
at once. ' Lloyd George knows nothing of the
problems which he is attempting to solve. From his
own lips we learn it. The whole British Delegation in
Paris, the whole Conference in fact, are ignorant and
unprepared. Disaster is upon us.' This cry was
echoed in the hearts of all who read the *Daily Mail*. It
has to-day become a fixed opinion. Yet in fact it is
erroneous. The trouble about the Paris Conference
was not that there was too little information, but that
there was far too much. The fault was not lack of
preparation, but lack of co-ordination. It was the latter
fault which vitiated the whole system from the start.

The point deserves some further examination.
Clearly it would have been difficult, during the four
years of war, for the Cabinet, or even the regular civil
servants, to elaborate detailed programmes for the
eventual conclusion of Peace. In the first place the
cataract of current business was so overwhelming that
no time, no human energy, was available for such a
task. In the second place it was impossible until the
last few months of 1918 to forecast even approxi-
mately the exact conditions of the final liquidation.
In the third place the rulers of the world were naturally
disinclined to commit themselves to detailed conditions

of peace which, in the event of a stalemate might prove
too rigid, or in the event of complete victory too restrained. This does not mean, however, that no preparatory work was undertaken at all. Far from it. In
each of the three main countries special bureaux were
established for the preparation of material to be used
at the eventual Congress.

In Great Britain a special organisation was created
in the spring of 1917 for the collection of material and
the training of a peace staff. Mr. Alwyn Parker,
Librarian of the Foreign Office, devoted his marked
talents for administration to the elaboration of a whole
Peace Conference in being. He even prepared a
coloured chart of the future systematization of the
British section of the Conference. Upon this reeling
orrery, Prime Ministers and Dominion Delegates
whirled each in his proper orbit, coloured green or red
or blue. Mr. Parker himself could be discerned re-
volving modestly as a moon, attendant upon Jupiter,
Lord Hardinge of Penshurst, the ' Organising Ambassador.' Mr. Parker's planisphere did not, it is true,
play that part in the eventual Peace Conference which
its designer had hoped. Mr. Lloyd George, on seeing
it, laughed aloud. Yet other of Mr. Parker's schemes
came to more happy fruition and were invaluable. It
was due to his foresight and precision that the vast
British Delegation slipped into the Hotels Majestic and
Astoria without a hitch. It was due to his powers of
co-ordination that the War Office, the Admiralty, the
War Trade Intelligence Department and the Foreign
Office were able themselves to prepare material which
did not, at any essential point, overlap. And finally,
the Historical Section of the Foreign Office prepared,

under the direction of Dr. G. W. Prothero, those invaluable Peace Handbooks, which were each written by acknowledged specialists, and which provided the delegation with detailed information upon any subject that was likely to arise. These handbooks have since been published. Should any historian doubt the quality of our preparation, I should urge him to obtain the whole collection from the London Library and to peruse their contents. He will agree that no more authoritative, comprehensive or lucid basis of information could possibly have been compiled.

In the United States a similar organisation was created in September 1917 under the name of ' The Inquiry.' Placed under the general direction of Colonel House, and under the immediate supervision of Dr. Mezes, this group of 150 graduates worked for twelve months in the premises of the American Geographical Society of New York. The amount of material which they collected was astounding ; the *George Washington* creaked and groaned across the Atlantic under the weight of their erudition. This erudition was supplemented by the invaluable reports of Professor A. C. Coolidge, who early in December was in charge of ' The American Commission of Study in Central Europe.' There were moments when that humane and brilliant man was the sole source of reliable information which the Peace Conference possessed. It seems incredible to-day that neither the American Delegates, nor the Conference as a whole, paid much attention to the sane and moderating words of Archibald Coolidge.

The technical staff of the United States Delegation was recruited mainly from this ' Inquiry ' of Colonel

House. The suggestion has been made in America, and notably during the Senate inquiry, that the United States delegation were ill-equipped. Any such suggestion is foolish and unfair. I have never had to work with a body of men more intelligent, more scholarly, more broad-minded or more accurately informed than were the American Delegation to the Peace Conference. On every occasion where I differed from their opinion I have since realised that I was wrong and they were right. Had the Treaty of Peace been drafted solely by the American experts it would have been one of the wisest as well as the most scientific documents ever devised. Unfortunately, and for reasons which will be indicated later, the American Commission, within the first few weeks, lost the self-confidence, and therefore the authority, which should rightly have been theirs.

The preparations of the French Government were less detailed, and as the event proved, less effective. A ' Comité d'Etudes ' had in fact been established under Professor Lavisse, and a subsidiary enquiry on economic questions had for some months been working under M. Morel. At the last moment M. Tardieu himself endeavoured to co-ordinate the resultant labours of these two commissions. This co-ordination does not seem to have gone very far. My own experience was that the United States Delegation were the best informed ; that the British Delegation came a good second : that the French made up for lack of preparation by intelligence and rapidity of assimilation : and that the Italians knew only what it was that they wanted themselves.

It is thus inaccurate to accuse the Paris Conference of

lack of technical knowledge or technical preparation. Yet, as with most criticisms which have obtained wide and durable currency, the accusation contains a substratum of truth. In the first place the information was not fully discussed either between the several delegations, or between the technical members of any given delegation and their own plenipotentiaries. It was little value, for instance, my obtaining all possible information about the Strumnitza enclave, unless I could also obtain from the heads of my delegation some expression of policy in regard to Bulgaria itself. The lack of communication between the plenipotentiaries and their own experts will be dealt with in Chapter IV, when I come to examine the organisation of the Conference itself. It will come under the heading of ' Mistakes.' It might equally well figure in Chapter III under the heading of ' Misfortunes.' Yet before I examine our misfortunes in Paris I must examine the ideas, the hopes and the intentions, armed with which we disembarked that January at the Gare du Nord.

Chapter II

DELAY

Frame of mind on leaving for Paris—The Congress of Vienna—The New Europe—Attitude towards Enemy Powers—Attitude towards the doctrine of President Wilson—Our early faith—The Fourteen Points and attendant pronouncements—How far incorporated in the eventual Treaties—The Hotel Majestic and the British Delegation—Postponement of Conference—Delay in getting to work—Reasons for this—How far President Wilson was to blame for delay—His insistence on inclusion of Covenant.

I

THE history of the Conference of Paris has yet to be written. It will be many years before the complete material can either be rendered available or digested. The documentary evidence (let us say in the year 1953) will be abundant and authentic. The human evidence will, by that date, be silenced or blurred. Yet I am convinced that at any international Congress it is the human element which determines both the development of negotiation and its issue. The purpose of these notes is to crystallise that element before it evaporates upon the wastes of time.

What then was the frame of mind in which, on that 3rd of January 1919, I crossed to Paris? Let me reaffirm that I am under no delusion regarding my own importance in that unhappy drama. I risk the charge of egoism in order to represent the individual point of view. I am profoundly certain that at the Congress of Montreal in August 1965 the expert staff will be composed of young men and women subject

30

to the same emotional impulses, the same vain confidence, which inspired me, as I lunched that morning between Calais and the Gare du Nord, with the conviction that I was embarking upon a task for which I was qualified by protracted study, by high ideals, and by a complete absence of all passion and all prejudice. In this confidence I was tragically mistaken.

Among the ' Peace Conference Handbooks ' which had been prepared for our instruction was one composed by Professor Webster upon the Congress of Vienna. I perused this slim and authentic little volume with great care. I felt, as the train approached St.-Denis, that I knew exactly what mistakes had been committed by the misguided, the reactionary, the after all pathetic aristocrats who had represented Great Britain in 1814.

They had worked in secret. We, on the other hand, were committed to ' open covenants openly arrived at ' ; there would be no such secrecy about proceedings : the peoples of the world would share in our every gesture of negotiation.

At Vienna, again, they had believed in the doctrine of ' compensations ' : they had spoken quite cynically about the ' transference of souls.' We for our part were liable to no such human error. We believed in nationalism, we believed in the self-determination of peoples. ' Peoples and Provinces,' so ran the ' Four Principles ' of our Prophet, ' shall not be bartered about from sovereignty to sovereignty as if they were but chattels or pawns in the game.' At the words ' pawns ' and ' chattels ' our lips curled in democratic scorn.

Nor was this all. We were journeying to Paris, not

merely to liquidate the war, but to found a new order
in Europe. We were preparing not Peace only, but
Eternal Peace. There was about us the halo of some
divine mission. We must be alert, stern, righteous and
ascetic. For we were bent on doing great, permanent
and noble things.

It is with some sadness that I recall to-day a conversation which on December 5, while I was still in
London, I held with Mr. J. L. Garvin. We had, for
some strange reason, been to a theatre together and
we walked back afterwards past St. Martin's in the
Fields. We paused upon the pavement, and continued
our discussion of the impending Conference. I gazed
defiantly down Whitehall and expounded to Mr.
Garvin how high, how immensely high, my principles
really were. He listened with his usual indulgence
toward the follies of the young. ' Well,' he said, ' if
that is the spirit in which you are all leaving for Paris,
I am glad at heart.'

I smile to-day at such exuberance of fancy. Yet at
the moment I was passionately sincere. Let me
analyse the elements of that sincerity.

The Conference, in its essence, was the imposition
by a group of victorious Powers of certain articles of
surrender upon a group of defeated Powers. It was
not in such terms that we younger people envisaged
our task. We thought less about our late enemies
than about the new countries which had arisen from
their tired loins. Our emotions centred less around
the old than around the new. I beg the young men
who will be in attendance upon the British Commis-
sioners to the Conference of Montreal in 1965 to
believe me when I say that the concepts ' Germany,'

' Austria,' ' Hungary,' ' Bulgaria ' or ' Turkey ' were
not in the forefront of our minds.   It was the thought
of the new Serbia, the new Greece, the new Bohemia,
the new Poland which made our hearts sing hymns at
heaven's gate.   This angle of emotional approach is
very significant.   I believe that it was a very general
angle.   It is one which will not be apparent from the
documents in the case.   It is one which presupposes a
long and fervent study of ' The New Europe '—a
magazine then issued under the auspices of Dr. Ronald
Burrows and Dr. Seton Watson with the doctrines of
which I was overwhelmingly imbued.   Bias there was,
and prejudice.   But they proceeded, not from any
revengeful desire to subjugate and penalise our late
enemies, but from a fervent aspiration to create and
fortify the new nations whom we regarded, with
maternal instinct, as the justification of our sufferings
and of our victory.   The Paris Conference will never
properly be understood unless this emotional impulse
is emphasised at every stage.

   I can, I think, recapture with approximate accuracy
my own feelings at the time towards our late enemies.
My attitude towards Germany was a compound of
fear, admiration, sympathy and distrust.   On the one
hand I had liked the Germans before the War even as
I like them to-day.   I was much impressed by the
fortitude with which the civilian population had with-
stood the blockade, and I was equally impressed by the
magnificent achievements of the German fleet and
armies by sea and land.   On the other hand I had felt
alarmed by their bombardments, anxious at their submarine successes, humiliated by their incessant vic-
tories.   I hated them for their practical ruthlessness :

I despised them for their political ineptitude : I distrusted them for their lack of diplomatic reliability.
Yet this compound of feeling left me with no residue
of revengefulness.   It left me only with an ardent
desire that Germany in future might be rendered
innocuous.

In regard to Austria I had a ' de mortuis ' feeling.
My antiquarian interests regretted her disappearance.
My modernist tendencies rejoiced at the new vitality
which would now spring from that exhausted soil.
My attitude towards Austria was a rather saddened
reflection as to what would remain of her when the
New Europe had once been created.   I did not regard
her as a living entity : I thought of her only as a
pathetic relic.

My feelings towards Hungary were less detached.
I confess that I regarded, and still regard, that Turanian
tribe with acute distaste.   Like their cousins the Turks,
they had destroyed much and created nothing.   Buda
Pest was a false city devoid of any autochthonous
reality.   For centuries the Magyars had oppressed
their subject nationalities.   The hour of liberation and
of retribution was at hand.

For the Bulgarians I cherished feelings of contempt.
Their traditions, their history, their actual obligations
should have bound them to the cause of Russia and
the Entente.   They had behaved treacherously in 1913
and in the Great War they had repeated this act of
perfidy.   Inspired by the most material motives of
acquisition they had joined with Germany, and by so
doing lengthened the War by two whole years.   In the
hour of their victory they had behaved in Serbia and
Macedonia without pity and without foresight.   They

had joined our enemies for purely selfish purposes : their expectations had proved erroneous : and they were now endeavouring to cast upon King Ferdinand the blame for what had in fact been a movement of national egoism. I did not feel that Bulgaria deserved more mercy than she would herself have been prepared, in similar circumstances, to accord.

For the Turks I had, and have, no sympathy whatsoever. Long residence at Constantinople had convinced me that behind his mask of indolence, the Turk conceals impulses of the most brutal savagery. This conviction was not diminished by his behaviour towards the Kut garrison or towards the Armenians within his borders. The Turks have contributed nothing whatsoever to the progress of humanity : they are a race of Anatolian marauders : I desired only that in the Peace Treaty they should be relegated to Anatolia.

Such—and I believe my summary to be an accurate representation—were the feelings, as distinct from the ideas, with which I went to Paris. Yet if I am to convey correctly the state of mind which was dominant and average in January 1919, I must also speak of the more precise purposes induced in us by the doctrines, by the arid revivalism, of Woodrow Wilson.

2

One day, in the late autumn of 1913, I lunched with Mr. Henry Morgenthau, who had only recently arrived in Constantinople as Ambassador of the United States. After luncheon we sat upon the terrace looking out between the sparse and fretted cypresses towards the outline of Stamboul. I asked him questions about

Woodrow Wilson, who had just emerged for us
easterners as a flaming planet in the distant west. Mr.
Morgenthau rose suddenly and went into his study.
He returned with a book. He thrust the book into my
hand. ' If,' he said, ' you really wish to learn the lesson
of Wilsonism, then read this book.'

I have no recollection to-day which of the many
publications of Mr. Wilson was on that mellow afternoon thrust into my hand. I know only that the expression ' Wilsonism ' arrested my attention. ' Here,'
I reflected, ' is a man who is something more than a
politician : he is the exponent of a new political theory.
There was something in the Ambassador's tone just
now which was more than partisanship, more even
than veneration. There was a note of religious fervour.
I must study the words and deeds of this new prophet.'
It was from that moment that I began to absorb the
' complete political philosphy ' of Woodrow Wilson.
I could not foresee, that autumn afternoon, to what
peaks of faith, through what valleys of reaction, Mr.
Morgenthau's slight gesture of proselytism was to lead
me.

By the end of 1918 the teaching of Woodrow Wilson
had resolved itself into three main categories in my
mind. There were his major articles of faith, simple
and withal mystic. There was the application of these
beliefs to the great problem of American neutrality.
There were, as a corollary to his proposition, the
' Fourteen Points,' the ' Four Principles ' and the
' Five Particulars.'

In the main tenets of his political philosophy I believed with fervent credulity. In spite of bitter dis-
illusionment I believe in them to-day. I believed, with

him, that the standard of political and international
conduct should be as high, as sensitive, as the standard
of personal conduct. I believed, and I still believe,
that the only true patriotism is an active desire that
one's own tribe or country should in every particular
minister to that ideal. I shared with him a hatred of
violence in any form, and a loathing of despotism in
any form. I conceived, as he conceived, that this
hatred was common to the great mass of humanity,
and that in the new world this dumb force of popular
sentiment could be rendered the controlling power in
human destiny. ' The new things in the world,' proclaimed President Wilson on June 5, 1914, ' are the
things that are divorced from force. They are the
moral compulsions of the human conscience.' ' No
man,' he said, ' can turn away from these things without turning away from the hope of all the world.'

I admitted, of course, that in the weeks which
followed upon this utterance the ' moral compulsions
of the human conscience ' had not proved themselves
very compelling. I admitted also that Wilson, as a
prophet, was a very American prophet—that his
philosophy was in practice applicable only to the proportions of power obtaining in the Western Hemi-
sphere. I was conscious, moreover, that there was in
his pronouncements a slight tinge of revivalism, a
touch of methodist arrogance, more than a touch of
presbyterian vanity. Yet I was not deterred by these
disadvantages. ' The United States,' I read, ' have not
the distinction of being masters of the world '—(Mr.
Wilson was speaking in 1914)—' but the distinction of
carrying certain lights for the world that the world has
never so distinctly seen before, certain guiding lights

of liberty, and principle, and justice.' I was disconcerted neither by the biblical, nor yet by the Princeton
savour of these words.

I like to think also that, with nerves frayed by the
duration of the war, I still retained my faith in Wilson
as a prophet of human reasonableness. My faith was
revived, from time to time, by the privilege of converse
with Walter Page. ' There is such a thing,' I read in
May of 1915, ' as a man being too proud to fight.
There is such a thing as a nation being so right that it
does not need to convince others by force that it is
right.' I did not, as did the majority of my countrymen, regard this as an irritating remark : I regarded
it as consistent, courageous, sane. Nor was I very
deeply estranged, in January of 1917, by the dictatorial,
the almost theocratic, tone which from that date began
to encroach upon the didacticism of Princeton.
' There are,' I read, ' American principles, American
policies. We stand for no others. They are the
principles of mankind and must prevail.' This statement, I felt, might have been more tactfully worded :
yet as a statement it was sound enough. I agreed with
it. Nine days later the Germans in their blindness
published their decision regarding unrestricted submarine warfare. On April 4 the United States entered
the war. From that moment I was not in a minority
in my faith in Woodrow Wilson.

And then, on January 8, 1918, came the Fourteen
Points.

3

Much casuistry, and some wit, has been expended
upon these historic pronouncements. President Wil-

son himself referred to them in 1919 as ' certain clearly defined principles which should set up a new order of right and justice.'   On the very same day we find Mr. Balfour writing of them as ' certain admirable but very abstract principles.'   Yet were they so very abstract ? Considering the date at which they were first issued, the Fourteen Points are precise to the point of recklessness.   It may be well to summarise them as follows :

Speech of January 8, 1918.

' The programme of the world's peace, therefore, is our programme, and that programme, the only possible programme, as we see it, is this :

(1) ' Open covenants of peace openly arrived at, after which there shall be no private understandings of any kind, but diplomacy shall proceed always frankly and in the public view.'

(2) ' Absolute freedom of navigation upon the seas outside territorial waters alike in peace and in war. . . . '

(3) ' The removal, as far as possible, of all economic barriers. . . . '

(4) ' Adequate guarantees given and taken that national armaments will be reduced to the lowest point consistent with domestic safety.'

(5) ' A free, open-minded and absolutely impartial adjustment of colonial claims based upon a strict observance of the principle that in determining all such questions of sovereignty the interests of the populations concerned must have equal weight with the equitable claims of the Government whose title is to be determined.'

(6) ' The evacuation of all Russian territory. . . . ' ' Russia to be given unhampered and unembarrassed opportunity for the independent determination of her own political development and national policy.'   Russia to be welcome, ' and more than welcome ' in the League of Nations ' under institutions of her own choosing ' and to be given every form of assistance.

(7) Belgium to be evacuated and restored.

(8) France to be evacuated, the invaded portions
' restored ' and Alsace-Lorraine returned to her.

(9) ' A readjustment of the frontiers of Italy should be
effected along clearly recognisable lines of nationality.'

(10) ' The peoples of Austria Hungary . . . to be
accorded the freest opportunity for autonomous development.' (N.B.—This point was subsequently modified to
provide for complete independence in lieu of autonomy.)

(11) Rumania, Serbia and Montenegro to be evacuated,
occupied territories to be ' restored.' Serbia to be given
free access to the sea.

(12) Turkish portions of Ottoman Empire to be
assured ' a secure sovereignty.' Subject nationalities to be
assured security and ' absolutely unmolested opportunity
of autonomous development.' Freedom of the Straits to
be guaranteed.

(13) Independent Polish State to be erected ' which
should include territories inhabited by indisputably Polish
populations, which should be assured a free and secure
access to the sea.'

(14) A general association of nations to be formed
under specific covenants ' for the purpose of affording
mutual guarantees of political independence and territorial integrity to great and small States alike.'

To the Fourteen Points themselves must be added
the ' Four Principles ' and the ' Five Particulars.' The
former were contained in an address of February 11,
1918, and were prefaced by a statement that the eventual Peace should contain ' no annexations, no con-
tributions, no punitive damages.' The Principles
themselves can be summarised as follows :

(1) ' Each part of the final settlement must be based
upon the essential justice of that particular case.'

(2) ' Peoples and provinces must not be bartered about

from sovereignty to sovereignty as if they were chattels or pawns in a game.'

(3) ' Every territorial settlement must be in the interests of the populations concerned ; and not as a part of any mere adjustment or compromise of claims among rival states.'

(4) ' All well-defined national elements shall be accorded the utmost satisfaction that can be accorded them without introducing new, or perpetuating old, elements of discord and antagonism.'

The ' Five Particulars ' figure in an address of September 27, 1918. They are less illuminating. The first insisted on justice to friends and enemy alike. The second denounced all ' separate interests.' The third provided that there should be no alliances within the body of the League and the fourth forbade all economic combinations between League members. The fifth ' Particular ' reaffirmed the prohibition against secret Treaties.

Not only did I believe profoundly in these principles, I took it for granted that on them alone would the Treaties of Peace be based. Apart from their inherent moral compulsion, apart from the fact that they formed the sole agreed basis of our negotiation, I knew that the President possessed unlimited physical power to enforce his views. We were all, at that date, dependent upon America, not only for the sinews of war, but for the sinews of peace. Our food supplies, our finances, were entirely subservient to the dictates of Washington. The force of compulsion possessed by Woodrow Wilson in those early months of 1919 was overwhelming. It never occurred to us that, if need arose, he would hesitate to use it. ' Never,'

writes Mr. Keynes, ' had a philosopher held such
weapons wherewith to bind the Princes of the
world.'

He did not use these weapons. He was not (and the
slow realisation of this was painful to us) a philosopher.
He was only a prophet.

3

Such, therefore, were the feelings, such the thoughts,
such the intentions, with which I crossed to Paris. I
had no doubt, as I have said, that upon the basis of
President Wilson's principles would the peace be
founded. My confidence, I feel convinced, was
shared by those of my colleagues who were my equals
in age or status. It may be contended, of course, that
the emotions and the conceptions of civil servants are
of small importance in the solution of great political
events. I question that contention. Had we all, however subordinate may have been our functions, retained our original beliefs, our initial frame of mind,
the influence which we might have been able corpor-
ately to exercise would have been important. Yet in
fact we suffered, as the weeks passed, a loss of confidence, a decline in idealism, a change of heart. It is
the purpose of this memoir to record, and to explain,
that change of heart. It was due largely to causes
beyond our control, even as they were beyond our
immediate consciousness. Similar causes will be
operative at any Congress of equal complexity and
magnitude. It is in order to warn future civil servants
that I have written this book.

Let me anticipate at this moment. Let me leave
myself driving, wedged between despatch boxes and

tin deed-boxes, from the Gare du Nord on that January 3, 1919, towards the Hotel Majestic. Let me contrast the principles enunciated by the Fourteen Points with the extent to which those principles were embodied in the eventual Treaties of Peace.

Our covenants of Peace were not openly arrived at : seldom has such secrecy been maintained in any diplomatic gathering. The Freedom of the seas was not secured. So far from Free Trade being established in Europe, a set of tariff-walls were erected, higher and more numerous than any known before. National armaments were not reduced. The German Colonies were distributed among the victors in a manner which was neither free, nor open-minded, nor impartial. The wishes, to say nothing of the interests, of the populations were (as in the Saar, Shantung and Syria) flagrantly disregarded. Russia was not welcomed into the Society of Nations, nor was she accorded unhampered freedom to develop her own institutions. The frontiers of Italy were not adjusted along the lines of nationality. The Turkish portions of the Ottoman Empire were not assured a secure sovereignty. The territories of Poland include many people who are indisputably not Polish. The League of Nations has not, in practice, been able to assure political independence to Great and Small Nations alike. Provinces and peoples were, in fact, treated as pawns and chattels in a game. The territorial settlements, in almost every case, were based on mere adjustments and compromises between the claims of rival States. Elements of discord and antagonism were in fact perpetuated. Even the old system of Secret Treaties was not entirely and universally destroyed.

Of President Wilson's twenty-three conditions, only four can, with any accuracy be said to have been incorporated in the Treaties of Peace.

4

The British Delegation in Paris were housed at the Hotel Majestic in the Avenue Kléber. This vast caravanserai had been constructed almost entirely of onyx for the benefit of the Brazilian ladies who, before the war, could come to Paris to buy their clothes. Mr. Alwyn Parker, in providing us with this accommodation, had carefully considered the dangers and temptations to which we might be exposed. Under the first heading he had (such was his habit of thought) grouped the two sub-headings of (*a*) espionage and (*b*) disease. As a protection against (*a*) he had charged Sir Basil Thomson of Scotland Yard with the task of organising a ' Security Service.' The result was that, although it was easy enough to get out of the Majestic, it was extremely difficult to get in. Many a foreign statesman was detained on suspicion for daring to press beyond our portals. Mr. Parker went further. He had studied the Congress of Vienna and was rightly determined that there should be no Metternich nonsense about the Conference of Paris. The Hotel Majestic was therefore staffed from attic to cellar with bright British domestics from our own provincial hotels. The food, in consequence, was of the Anglo-Swiss variety, whereas the coffee was British to the core. Yet, as it turned out, our whole work was done in the adjoining Hotel Astoria. It was there that we preserved our papers and kept our maps. The staff of the Astoria were of French nationality. There were moments (generally at breakfast) when we felt that there had been a slight gap in Mr. Parker's logic.

Yet as an organiser Mr. Parker proved himself superb. In order to cope with (*b*) he had engaged an obstetric physician of the very greatest distinction. The female staff were placed under the direction of a chaperon. The atmosphere of the Majestic was in this way one of cheerful and comradely anglicanism.

The British Delegation consisted of 207 persons, of whom the Foreign Office accounted for 12, with 6 secretaries ; the War Office for 28 ; the Admiralty for 22 ; the Air Department for 13 ; the Treasury and Board of Trade for 26 ; and the Dominions for 75.

It has frequently been stated that we were over-staffed. It would be more accurate to contend that the pressure of work was unevenly distributed. Certain members of the delegation, and especially the political and economic experts, were demonstrably over-worked. Certain other members of the delegation, and in particular the staffs of the Dominion Ministers, found the hours hang heavy on their hands. In-evitably, and wisely, they made the best of their some-what feckless position. The great hall of the Majestic was gay with the clatter of tea cups : the strains of dance music echoed from below the stairs. The more critical among our visitors would exaggerate these symptoms of relaxation. The legend spread in London that the Majestic was the resort of idlers : people in Pall Mall would grumble that Lord Castlereagh had been accompanied to Vienna with a staff of only seventeen. I admit myself that there were moments when I would stagger exhausted into that garish foyer and feel sick with resentment at the spectacle of all those happy people who had time upon their hands. *Time, time, time !* It became an obsession with us as the weeks wore on. To observe it dangling and dancing before our eyes was indeed an exacting ordeal. I do not feel, however, that the charge of over-staffing was wholly justified. It was essential to have at hand many specialists who might at any moment be wanted. It was inevitable that the Dominion Ministers should have been accompanied by secretaries and assistants. And it must also be remembered that so soon as the general lines of work were clearly recognised, the more obvious drones were sent back to London.

The internal organisation of the British Delegation was settled within the first few days. Lord Hardinge, as ' Organising Ambassador,' was charged mainly with administrative duties. Sir Maurice Hankey was appointed Secretary to the Delegation, and established his offices in the Villa Majestic across the road. Mr. Clement Jones coped in a spirit of gay fraternity with the Dominion Ministers. And Mr. Lloyd George ensconced himself in the Rue Nitot with Mr. Balfour in the flat above.

Upon the race-course at Auteuil was constructed, much to the fury of the Parisians, our own printing press. The purlieus of the Majestic clattered to the sound of motor cyclists. A fleet of army cars facilitated our movements. An elaborate telephone system linked us with London and the outer world. A service of fast aeroplanes sped daily between Buc and Croydon. Before the Conference opened, the whole machinery of the Majestic, the Astoria, the Villa Majestic, and the Rue Nitot hummed with the frictionless efficiency of a British Department of State.

On Saturday, January 11, the Prime Minister and the Dominion Ministers arrived in Paris. On Sunday, January 12, the first unofficial meeting between the Plenipotentiaries took place at the Quai d'Orsay. On Monday, January 13, the British Empire Delegation held their first reunion, and on the afternoon of that day the Plenipotentiaries met again for the purpose of renewing the armistice, and under the title of the ' Supreme War Council.' It was not, however, until the afternoon of Saturday, January 18, that the Conference was formally opened, and it was not until a week later that the first five committees were appointed to prepare the technical material. The territorial committees, moreover, who were supposed to fix the future frontiers of Europe, were not constituted until the first week in February.

This delay of more than nine weeks between the signature of the armistice and the first serious attempt to get down to business will certainly remain as one of the most unanswerable criticisms of the Paris Conference. It is therefore necessary to consider the causes, psychological and other, by which it was occasioned. Two phases of delay must be distinguished from each other. There was first the delay between the Armistice and the meeting of the Conference. There was secondly the delay, after the Conference had assembled, in getting down to practical work.

5

The grounds on which the postponement of the Peace Conference is usually excused are strange and various. You have in the first place the historical argument. The Congress of Vienna was even more dilatory : the procrastinations of the Congress of Westphalia were infinitely more prolonged. You have in the second place the ethical argument. It was necessary, it was *right*, that the more extreme passions of the war should be allowed to subside before the rulers of the world met together for the purpose of founding a new order of righteousness and equity. You have in the third place the practical argument. The Peace had taken us by surprise. Such was our familiarity with defeat, that victory, when it came, appeared incredible. Many weeks were necessary before we could realise that we had won. It was essential, also, that President Wilson, the protagonist of the Conference, should be allowed time to establish contact with continental opinion : he must see the devastated areas with his own eyes : he must feel with his own dry fingers the warm pulse of Italy, the intermittent pulse of Belgium, the febrile pulse of France, the yeoman pulse of England. Mr. Wilson must be acclimatised to Europe before he could be trusted to establish her future destinies.

Mr. Lloyd George, also, must consult The People before proceeding to Paris with that people's mandate. Dr. Kramarsh of Bohemia, M. Dmowsky of Poland, M. Bratianu of Rumania, Messrs. Pasic and Trumbic of the Serb, Croat and Slovene Union, must each be given time to consolidate the startling changes of status and territory which had come upon their countries : must each be allowed time to appear at Paris as representative of something organised and real.

Germany, also, was a problem. The collapse of the Hohenzollern Empire had, in its gigantic subsidence, raised a cloud of dust. Dimly, through the haze of

fallen cement and scattered mortar, certain figures appeared. Liebknecht ; Noske ; Scheidemann ; the
Spartacists. Which of these figures was central ? We
did not know. It was perhaps better to allow this dust
to settle before advancing further. It was little use
trying to make peace with Germany, until we knew
whether there would ever be such an entity as the
German Reich with which one could make peace.

It was better to wait.

Each of these arguments contained an element of
falsehood and an element of truth. It is possible, with
perfect intelligence, to argue that the Peace Conference
might have sprung fully armed from the Versailles
Council of October and November 1918. Colonel
House, without a moment's deflection, could have
appeared fully equipped (an affable Athena) as the
representative of his absent friend. The others were
already there.

It may be questioned, however, whether the theocrat
of the White House would have consented to such an
arrangement. The President, in spite of all dissuasions
was determined to appear in person. His decision,
once it had been proclaimed, was incontestable. On
December 2 he was booked to deliver his annual
address to Congress. It was thus in any case impossible
for the Conference to assemble before December 15.
By that date the British Elections could easily have
been concluded. I can find no explanation why the
Conference did not open on December 18.

It is established that President Wilson himself had
fixed that date as the day of opening. It is unfair to
blame him for wasting the ensuing three weeks upon
his visits to London and Rome. Those visits were

unnecessary, and were undertaken only to save the President's face. They were more than unnecessary : they were most disturbing. Few men could have resisted such an apotheosis. President Wilson reacted to it in a manner which was characteristic, but unfortunate. He became obsessed by the ' eyes of the dumb people.' Those crowds at Victoria Station, those crowds on the Corso, acclaimed him as the symbol of their own victory. He imagined that they acclaimed him as a symbol of the New Europe. These visits, these regrettable and hysterical visits, convinced Woodrow Wilson that the peoples of Europe were with him heart and soul. Here was a most misleading conviction.

Mr. Lansing, in that conceited book which he composed about the Peace Conference, suggests that M. Clemenceau was anxious to postpone the opening of the Conference until the armistice had been renewed in terms of French mentality, and until he himself had ' got to know the President better.' I question whether such militarist or social considerations entered largely into the mind of Clemenceau, who was a rude but reasonable man. I have consulted many of the important figures at the Conference on this very problem. ' Why,' I have asked them, ' was the Conference postponed from December 18 till January 18 ' ? ' Oh,' they answer, ' there was Christmas, of course : and we wanted a holiday : besides it was necessary to allow emotions to die down : and after all, we had to take stock of the situation. Russia, you remember, was in turmoil : and so was Germany. We thought that if we waited a little things might settle down.'

6

The historian may find among the archives subsequently available explanations more convincing than the above. I am myself unable to provide any more convincing explanation. Nor do I to this day fully understand why, when once they had assembled, they postponed for so many vital weeks the main purpose of their discussion. After all, they knew from the outset that President Wilson would be obliged in the second week in February to return to Washington for the purpose of adjourning the Sixty Fifth Congress. They knew that with every week that passed the allied armies were melting away under the popular clamour for immediate demobilisation. They knew that every day which was not devoted to the central purpose of making peace with Germany was a day wasted—a day which diminished our own power of imposing an eventual peace by force of arms, a day which entailed further starvation upon a blockaded Germany and further danger of a bolshevized Central Europe. In spite of this, six weeks were wasted upon matters, which although urgent, did not contribute to the essential purposes of their reunion. It was not until March 25 that, under the fiery stimulus of Mr. Lloyd George, the rulers of the world really concentrated on making peace with Germany. And during the month of April they worked with a velocity which was vertiginous and most unwise.

Many publicists have since contended that these delays during January, February and the first three weeks of March were due entirely to President Wilson's determination that no Treaty, not even a preliminary

Treaty, should be concluded which did not embody as an integral part of its structure the Covenant of the League of Nations.

It must be admitted, that President Wilson possessed ' a one-track mind.' It is a strange and pathetic reflection that, once established in the Villa Murat, the President became profoundly bored by his Fourteen Points, his Four Principles, and his Five Particulars. No longer did he identify himself with those past and potent passages of English prose. He identified himself with the new, the mystic, charter of the rights of man. It is not possible to understand the character and policy of Woodrow Wilson unless we give prominence to the strong strain of fanatical mysticism which marred an otherwise academic reason. His childish belief in the potency of the number 13 is a symptom of a mysticism which was at moments almost pathological. He believed in all sincerity that the voice of the People was the voice of God. The ' dumb eyes of the people ' haunted him with their mute, their personal, appeal. He felt that those myriad eyes looked up to him as to a prophet arisen in the West ; as to a man chosen by God to give to the whole world a new message and a more righteous order. The fact that he forebore to commune with Mr. Lansing was due to his preference for silent communion with God. The fact that he treated the United States Senate with irritated aloofness arose from his conviction that it was not as their representative that God had despatched him to the Villa Murat, but as the representative of the Great Dumb People. It is not a sufficient explanation to contend that President Wilson was conceited, obstinate, nonconformist and reserved. He was also a man obsessed : possessed. He believed, as did Marat, that he was the physical embodiment of ' la volonté générale.' He was obsessed by the conviction that the League Covenant was his own Revelation and the solution of all human difficulties. He was profoundly convinced that if his new Charter of the Rights of Nations could be framed and included in the Peace Treaties it mattered little what inconsistencies, what injustice, what flagrant violations of his own principles, those Treaties might contain. He was able, as are all very religious men, to attribute unto God the things that are Caesar's : he was able to convince himself, in ardent agonies of soul, that his own principles had not been violated, that he had surrendered no jot or tittle of his original message. He bitterly resented the suggestions of those people, such as Count Brockdorff Rantzau, who failed to share this conviction. 'I do not understand them,' he confessed to his own delegation, 'they make me tired.' Early in January he immured himself within the Ark of the Covenant : no one thereafter, least of all Mr. Lansing, was able to get him out.

On page 186 of his book upon the Peace Conference Mr. Lansing contends that had President Wilson not insisted in this manner upon the inclusion of the text of the Covenant even in a Preliminary Treaty, such a Treaty could have been ' signed ratified and in effect during April of 1919.' On March 20, 1919, Mr. Lansing noted in his diary : ' The whole world wants peace. The President wants his League. I think that the world will have to wait.' It is on evidence such as this that the French and Italians have, among others, contended that the delay in framing the Treaty of

Versailles was due entirely to the egoism of President Wilson.

It must be recognised that the drafting of the Covenant did, in fact, entail a certain delay. When the President returned to Washington in February he found that the Senatorial opposition was more serious than he had at first supposed. Mr. Lowell and Mr. Taft on whom he had relied as intermediaries with the Republican malcontents, informed him that on many vital points the Covenant would have to be revised if it were ever to be ratified by a Republican Senate. This was unpleasant news. The President, before leaving Paris, had announced in Plenary Session that not one word, ' not even a period,' of the Covenant as then presented could be revised. It was now incumbent upon him to return to Paris and himself to suggest emendations of a very vital character. This would enable the Japanese to revive their clause about race equality, and the French to weigh in again with their desire for a League Army with an ' international ' G.Q.G. When the news of this contretemps reached Paris, it was realised that on the President's return the League Committee would again have to be summoned and that their renewed discussions would again take several weeks. M. Pichon, in a moment of impulse, informed the Press that in these circumstances the Covenant could not form an integral part of the final Treaty. This statement, on the following day, was repudiated. So far from shaking him in his attitude, the difficulties with the Senate strengthened the President's stand : his sense of divine mission. He returned, as Colonel House records, ' very militant and determined.' He insisted thereafter that not only the

German Treaty but the whole world settlement should be indissolubly connected with the Covenant. He imagined that the Senate would never dare to reject the whole connexus of the Treaties of Peace, and he was determined to force the Covenant upon them by involving it inextricably within the framework of the world settlement. This determination certainly rendered impossible the conclusion of an early or preliminary peace with Germany.

Such, therefore, is the argument of those who would wish to throw upon President Wilson the whole onus of delay. There is much, however, to be said upon the other side. Wilson knew that the details of the treaties would inevitably be unjust in many particulars : he knew that the temper of the Allied and Associated Powers was not, in that January of 1919, such as to render possible a settlement of true moderation : and he hoped, in the Covenant, to provide an instrument by which, when saner counsels prevailed, the Treaty could be modified and rendered less punitive. He knew also that the League of Nations would not be able completely to fulfil its high mission unless the directive impulse, the ultimate moral, physical, and above all financial, force, were provided by the United States. The means by which he hoped to compel the Senate into acceptance may not have been very adroit or even very honourable. He would have defended himself by contending that the Senate were a reactionary body out of touch with the Great Warm Heart of the People. In his essential determination to make the Covenant an integral part of every Treaty he was, however, certainly justified. There may be some, even, who will contend that such an achievement was worth many weeks' delay : was worth the whole connexus of treaties : I think so myself.

Apart from these considerations, it should be realised that the delay in framing the Treaty of Peace with Germany was also due to other causes. The drafting of the Covenant did not, in fact, materially interfere with the main work of the Conference. The League of Nations Commission worked rapidly ; its sessions took place on almost every occasion after office hours. The emphasis thrown by some historians upon the responsibility of President Wilson is apt to disguise another, and to my mind, more important cause of delay. That cause was the absence of any agreed or unified purpose. This uncertainty of purpose was among the most dominant of the Conference's misfortunes.

Chapter III

MISFORTUNES

Initial disadvantages—Democratic opinion—In the United States—In Great Britain—Responsibility of the Press—Lord Northcliffe and his organs—The 'Daily Mail' and the Conference—Politicians as plenipotentiaries—Resultant duality of purpose—This duality in Lloyd George, Clemenceau and Orlando—Factor of physical exhaustion and of human courtesy—Other misfortunes—The presence in Paris of President Wilson—Nature of this misfortune—Its causes—Its effects—Choice of Paris—Reasons for—Disadvantages of—The French Press and Mr. Wilson.

I

From its very inception, the Conferences of Paris—(as has always been, and as will always be, the fate of every Conference)—laboured under initial disadvantages.

Some of these disadvantages were avoidable, and I shall therefore discuss them in my next chapter under the heading of ' Mistakes.' Others were either wholly unavoidable, or else avoidable only by a potency of vision and direction not possessed by any of the world-dictators of 1919. I shall discuss these in my present chapter under the heading of ' Misfortunes.'

Of our wholly unavoidable misfortunes, the most dominant was democratic opinion. It is perhaps unnecessary to affirm that the temper of the French, the Italian, the Czecho-Slovak, the Jugo-Slav, the Polish, the Portuguese, the Brazilian, the Japanese, the Belgian, the Albanian, the Rumanian, the Chinese, the South African, the Australian, and the Hellenic peoples

was inconsiderate in the extreme. It will be more useful to indicate that the emotions of the two main
Anglo-Saxon democracies were scarcely more intelligent, more reasonable, or more composed.

The United States, having passed through the internecine conflicts of neutrality, having emerged as a
nation united in an eleventh-hour victory, were still
suffering from the psychological impulse which had
flung them into the war; were still ashamed of the
ideology which for so long had kept them out. President
Wilson had long ceased to be a prophet among his own
people. It was not merely the Congressional Election
of November 1918 which produced in the members of
the American delegation a certain hesitancy of manner :
it was the consciousness that when Roosevelt said that
the Fourteen Points bore no relation to popular
opinion in the United States, that superb realist was
saying something which, at the moment, was actually
true. The tragedy of the American Delegation in
Paris was that they represented something which
America had felt profoundly in 1915 and would again
feel profoundly in 1922. They did not, however,
represent what America was feeling in that January of
1919. The consciousness of this gap filled their democratic consciences with a horrid void. The President
alone (alone with God and the People) was unaware
of any vacuum.

In Great Britain, the public mind was passing
through one of the most regrettable phases in its history. It must be admitted that after a war in which
seventy million young men had been mobilised, in
which ten million had been killed, in which thirty
million had been wounded, it would be unreasonable

to suppose that any democracy could regard with un-
clouded nerves the spectacle of four gentlemen sitting
in a guarded room together, discussing the result. Nor
would it be sensible to expect a population which had
been appalled by naval and military defeat, terrified by
aerial bombardment, anguished by the dread of starvation, to behave in the moment of unimagined victory
with the feudal chivalry of the Black Prince. A mind
like that of Mr. Winston Churchill could, it is true, rise
to such patrician altitudes. Let us not forget that on
the very night of the Armistice his thoughts veered
sympathetically towards ' the stricken foe.' Let it be
remembered that Winston Churchill, at that moment,
desired to send six fat food-ships to Hamburg.

For lesser minds it was more difficult. The war had
been a harsh and unremitting business : it would be
unfair to accuse the British Public of lack of civilisation
merely because, during their first few months of con-
valescence, they demanded that the peace also should
be unremitting and harsh. What is astonishing about
the British Public is not their short attack of hysteria,
but the rapidity with which they recovered their nerve.
This remarkable recovery would have been even more
rapid had they been allowed to convalesce in silence.
No such tranquillity was, however, vouchsafed.

It is upon the British Press—that thoughtless and
impervious combine—that the full onus of responsibility must rest. Alone among our great journals, the
Observer, the *Daily News*, the *Daily Chronicle*, *The
Westminster Gazette* and the *Manchester Guardian*, retained some elements of responsibility. The other
newspapers, not excluding *The Times* and the other
equally educated journals, were silly and irresponsible

to a degree. This was not always the fault of their local correspondents. The *Daily Mail* was represented in Paris by Mr. Valentine Williams, who was the equal of Mr. Wilson Harris in intelligence and rectitude. From time to time Mr. Wickham Steed himself would contribute authoritative articles to the pages of that daily, and in its influence, ephemeral organ. The *Morning Post* was represented by the alert Mr. Grant, the informed Mr. Knox. Yet the newspapers of England were, during that period, all too sensitive to their own circulation. And the tone of that circulation was set by the Northcliffe group; was aimed, that is to say, not at the thoughts of their countrymen, but at their emotions. The figure of Lord Northcliffe brooded over the Conference as a miasma.

This point is important. There are many men and women in Great Britain at this moment who will express the facile opinion that Mr. Lloyd George, although he won us the war, lost us the peace. The unscientific nature of such an assertion is distressing. Those very people would, in fact, be quite incapable of defining the assumptions upon which their conclusion is based. They are the very people who, in 1919, absorbed with approval the propaganda of the Harmsworth Press, a form of hysteria demonstrably dictated by the passionate resentments and delusions of Lord Northcliffe himself. I admit that there was a tragedy latent in the psychology of Lord Northcliffe. He realised that he possessed the maximum powers of destruction, and the minimum powers of creation. He could cause a ruin; he could not build. I readily admit that the possession of vast engines of destruction, minus the possession of even a trowel of construction, must lead, in the end, to serious psychological disturbance. Yet let us consider, subject to this sympaethtic reservation, the attitude adopted, both before and after the Armistice, by the *Daily Mail*.

On the fourth of November, 1918, Lord Northcliffe issued his thirteen points. They were published at a moment when he still imagined that he might himself figure among the plenipotentiaries at the eventual Peace Conference. They are in every respect admirable statements of the objects then in view. Their accordance with the fourteen points of President Wilson is indeed striking. There is nothing to be said against Lord Northcliffe's thirteen points.

Nine days after this manifesto we find the *Daily Mail* exuding patriotism. The ex-Emperor, thus they claimed on November 13, must be handed over body and soul to the Allies. Three days later the Northcliffe Press is attacking the desire of a capitulated Germany to be released from the extreme rigours of the blockade. Their headlines were as follows : ' Hun food snivel ' : their leading article contained the following opinion : ' There are still people in this world who are inclined to heed Germany's whines for food.' During the General Election the *Daily Mail* urged its contributors to refuse support to any candidate who showed signs of ' any tenderness for the Hun.' By December 15 their clamour for the full costs of the war had become almost illiterate. ' Germany,' screamed the *Daily Mail*, ' can pay, if there is any ginger in the Allied Governments.' As early as December 11 they began to agitate for immediate demobilisation, without referring to the problem how one could be expected to bully the Hun without a weapon. Immediately after the Election,

there were references to 'ugly rumours' that Mr.
Lloyd George would take to Paris, not Lord Northcliffe, but the 'old gang' in the person of Mr. Balfour,
Lord Curzon, or even Mr. Asquith. During the early
stages of the Conference the Northcliffe Press divided
its energies between 'The impudent Hun' and 'How
to smash Lenin.' They clamoured for the occupation
of Moscow and Petrograd. They at the same time
clamoured for demobilisation. In April they raised
the panic of 'surrender.' 'It is,' they exclaimed, 'not
our business to ask what Germany will think of the
terms. Our duty is to dictate such terms as shall give
a material guarantee for security, and let the Hun think
what he likes about them.' And still they clamoured
for demobilisation. From then on the *Daily Mail* inserted in a neat little 'box' upon the front page the
epigraph 'The Junkers will cheat you yet.' This little
slogan appeared each day at the head of their leading
article. When the Germans actually reached Versailles
this warning was supplemented by another 'box'
which ran as follows : 'Lest we forget. Killed
670,986. Wounded 1,041,000. Missing 350,243.'
And still they clamoured for demobilisation. After the
wholly merited, and extremely witty attack upon Lord
Northcliffe which Mr. Lloyd George delivered in the
House of Commons on April 7, the Northcliffe Press
surrendered themselves gleefully to the propagandists
of the French Ministry of War. To their minds and in
their columns, the German counter-proposals were
merely 'squeals.' The *Lusitania* and even Miss Edith
Cavell were dragged in to their every leading article in
the hope of preventing Mr. Lloyd George from introducing into the Peace Terms some few elements of

wisdom and moderation. ⸢This unintelligent, personal and hysterical attitude was theirs from first to last. Nor did more reputable British newspapers lag behind them in emotional extravagance.⸥

2

The second wholly unavoidable misfortune of the Paris Conference was that the plenipotentiaries of the five Great Powers each occupied a political position, was⟨each representative of some alert but ignorant electorate.⟩ I have already indicated how Mr. Lloyd George, for all his essential liberalism and vision, was hampered and disconcerted by the fact that he had himself created a House of Commons possessed of a *Daily Mail* type of mind. It might be argued that the Prime Minister should not in person have proceeded to Paris, but that he should have despatched as his representative, either some professional economists and diplomatists, or else men of world experience such as Lord Milner or Lord Reading. Doubtless, had such a method of representation been practically possible, a calmer, quieter treaty might have been evolved. More serious is the criticism that Mr. Lloyd George should have taken with him to Paris some authoritative and informed representative of Socialism, such as Mr. Hyndman. Such a delegation or even fusion of authority was, in view of the tremendous nationalist interests involved, a complete impossibility. It was unavoidable that Mr. Lloyd George should attend in person. I am not of those who would describe this necessity as an unavoidable misfortune. I question, indeed, whether any British statesman then alive could, given the state of public opinion at home, have achieved, or rather, have avoided, so much. Yet it must be recognised that a Prime Minister, with his attention diverted, and his absence frequently entailed, by the requirements of domestic politics, does not in fact possess the detachment essential in a negotiation requiring flawless concentration and unruffled placidity of mind.

Inevitably the political present, or past, of the main plenipotentiaries produced a certain duality of aspect. It is difficult to be a great European and at the same time a great party man. The continental Powers desired a solution which should satisfy, not their greed (there was, whatever may be said to the contrary, comparatively little avidity in Paris) but their anxiety. This anxiety, in each case, was composed, so to speak, of a personal and an impersonal element. The delegates of the Great Powers were on the one hand men of experience and wisdom, desiring to found the Treaty upon bases of reason and moderation. They were on the other hand politicians, representing, if not a definite political party, then at least a definite connexus of political ideas. They were bound to adjust their own thoughts, which might be enlightened, to the emotions of their supporters, which assuredly were not. Democratic diplomacy possesses many advantages : yet it possesses one supreme disadvantage : its representatives are obliged to reduce the standards of their own thoughts to the level of other people's feelings : were it not for the time-lag which affects democratic wisdom, this necessity might prove a safeguard rather than a danger : but in circumstances requiring great rapidity and breadth of decision democratic diplomacy does in fact constitute a danger more

insidious, and far less manageable, than the most un-
scrupulous intellectualism of the older system.

M. Clemenceau, it is true, might have claimed that
he was no longer a politician but only a patriot. He
was at the end of his career. He cared little for the
Chamber : he was, in January at least, without further
political ambition : he might assert, with some show
of truth, that politically he was wholly detached. Yet
in fact Clemenceau also was much affected by party
politics : he was affected by the party animosities of
his own past. He hated M. Poincaré with a tigerish
detestation. He was also bitterly opposed to the doc-
trinaires of the extreme left. He had a personal desire
to steer a Clemenceau course—something between the
meticulous nationalism of Poincaré, the vapid opportunism of Franklin Bouillon and the (to him) pathetic
communism of the extreme left.

Signor Orlando was even more encumbered by the
tentacles of the democratic octopus. In order to impress President Wilson with his own representative
character he had injected the Italian octopus with the
strychnine of patriotism. He thus became the prisoner
of his own propaganda. Throughout the Conference
he found himself in a most uncomfortable situation :
his colleague, Baron Sonnino, did not fail to remind
him of these discomforts. Signor Orlando was never
able to rise to the level of his own intelligence.

There was also an impersonal, a purely national
element in their conceptions. Clemenceau (having
seen with his own eyes the Palais de St. Cloud smoking
across the flames of 1871) was, and with every justification, obsessed by the need of French security. Mr.
Lloyd George—hampered, not so much by his own

election pledges, but by the House of Commons which, by these asseverations, he had produced—hoped to combine the *vae victis* which the British Public expected, with the more reasonable pacification which his own instincts desired. And Signor Orlando, exponent of sacred egoism, sincerely strove to provide his unstable country with those spoils by which alone (so he imagined) the demon of socialism could be exorcised.

Is it strange that such mixed motives should have produced some complexity of purpose ? On the one hand these men desired a punitive peace in order to satisfy their own electorates : on the other hand they desired a reasonable peace such as could re-establish the tranquillity of Europe. Is it surprising that, with such ambiguity of intention, they should have viewed with cautious distaste all preliminary definition of their essential purposes. Is it easy to resist the impression that the main reason for the delays of the Conference was a perfectly intelligent hope on their part that the Great God Demos would, within a month or two, quieten down ?

3

The above two misfortunes were, let us hope, peculiar to the Conference of Paris. Yet the directors of that unfortunate reunion were also subject to other disadvantages which are eternally inseparable from discussion between man and man. Full allowance, for instance, must be made for the very limited powers of endurance possessed even by the most muscular of human brains. Under the strain of incessant overwork, the imaginary and creative qualities are apt to flag : more and more does the exhausted mind tend to concentrate upon the narrower circle of immediate detail : less and less does it aspire to those wider circles of vision which, once entered upon, must entail further discussion, further mental effort, and the sacrifice of much labour, many points of agreement, already arduously achieved. These human deficiencies, these weaknesses of human flesh, are bound in any Conference of long duration sooner or later to dominate the general tone. In Paris, these ordeals of exhaustion were more marked than ever before. It must be remembered that the protagonists in the combat had already for many torturing years been exposed to a strain unparalleled in the history of human governance. Their vitality was overwhelming. Yet no human energy could resist such cumulative experience without having acquired an aptitude for the superficial rather than for the essential, for the expedient in preference to the awkward, for the improvised as an escape from the pondered. ‿The Conference of Paris cannot rightly be criticised unless the element of aggregate exhaustion, and consequent insensitiveness, is given full prominence.)

It would be a mistake, however, for the student of diplomacy by conference to concentrate too exclusively upon those weaknesses of human nature which impede the intelligent conduct of discussion. The difficulties of precise negotiation arise with almost equal frequency from the more amiable qualities of the human heart. It would be interesting to analyse how many false decisions, how many fatal misunderstandings, have arisen from such pleasant qualities as shyness, consideration, affability, or ordinary good manners.

One of the most persistent disadvantages of all
diplomacy by conference is this human difficulty of
remaining disagreeable, to the same set of people, for
many days at a stretch. Inevitably if you have obstinately refused on Monday to accord your agreement in
a matter on which the majority are unanimous it is
extremely irksome to show similar stubbornness on
Tuesday when a wholly different subject is under discussion. The very human temptation to avoid unpleasant precisions, to mingle acquiescence with obstruction, to postpone contradiction until at some later
date it can be mixed with the sugared waters of agreement, was all too evident at the Paris Conference. It
might be possible, indeed, to contend that the collapse
of President Wilson was due to little more than the con-
tinual pressure of ordinary human courtesy : he disagreed with almost everything his colleagues suggested:
they were fully aware of how painful to him was this
constant disagreement : and inevitably—they exploited the situation thus created. It is interesting to
reflect what would have happened to the President had
he been (as was Mr. Lansing) a really combative man.
Many of Signor Orlando's troubles were also due to
his temperamental dislike of behaving unpleasantly.
His reservation on Point Nine of the Fourteen Points
was conveyed in a mumbled aside—so irksome was it
to Signor Orlando to embarrass all those charming
friends of his around the table. Yet that unfortunate
mumble all but split the Conference in two. It was
perhaps with justifiable impatience that Colonel House
noted in his diary : (' Much of the time of the Conference was wasted in a grotesque effort not to offend.')

Such quirks of human behaviour are, as I have said,

inseparable from any Conference. (There were certain other, and more concrete, misfortunes, to which the Conference of Paris was particularly exposed. There was the problem of the Secret Treaties, which had been concluded in the heat of battle, to which the United States had not been parties, and of which, in most cases, they had been accorded but incidental knowledge. There was the problem of the Smaller Powers, whose representatives were forced by their own nationalist opinion at home to adopt an attitude of noisy intransigence. These two problems will be discussed in detail at a later stage. In the present chapter it remains to examine two further misfortunes which impeded the work of the Conference from its very inception. The first of these misfortunes was the presence of President Wilson. The second was the choice of Paris as the site of the Conference. Each of these two misfortunes was unavoidable in the sense that almost superhuman vision and obstinacy would have been needed first to envisage, and then to combat, the full menace of these two initial decisions.)

4

The misfortune of President Wilson's personal attendance at the Paris Conference should be considered under two headings. The first question to answer is ' Why did he come ? ' The second question to answer is ' Why, having decided to come, did he attend the meetings in person ? '

I must repeat that it is beyond the scope of these notes to enter into any great detail on matters regarding which I have no first-hand impression. I was at the time conscious, although somewhat dimly, of the.

disadvantages of the President's participation in the Councils of Ten and Four. I can see to-day that much of the demoralisation, the ' change of heart,' which affected us during the months of April and May was due to an almost panic realisation that the Prophet of the White House was not only unwilling to call down fire from heaven, but displayed an equal disinclination to call for memoranda from his own experts. Paris was something very different from Delphi, and when pressed to explain himself our Oracle ended all too frequently by explaining himself away. It is no exaggeration to attribute the sudden ' slump in idealism,' which overwhelmed the Conference towards the middle of March, to the horror-struck suspicion that Wilsonism was leaking badly, that the vessel upon which we had all embarked so confidently was foundering by the head. Our eyes shifted uneasily in the direction of the most contiguous life-belt. The end of the Conference became a *sauve qui peut* : we called it ' *security* ' : it was almost with a panic rush that we scrambled for the boats ; and when we reached them we found our colleagues of the Italian Delegation already comfortably installed. They made us very welcome.

This simile is not unduly far-fetched. Instinctively, and rightly, did we feel that if Wilsonism was to form the charter of the New Europe it must be applied universally, integrally, forcefully, scientifically. Given an America united in the support of the whole Wilsonian doctrine, we felt confident that we could embark on a secure voyage to the Islands of the Blessed. It was only when we realised that we were being given but a patchwork Wilsonism that anxieties assailed us. These anxieties were trebled so soon as it dawned upon us that in the maintenance of this patchwork we should receive no support from the United States. The New World having failed to answer the call of its own herald, we turned back in panic towards the balance of the old. Inevitably we sought to regain the firm familiar ground of the Old Europe which, with all its dangers, was at least a territory which we knew.

The collapse of Wilson meant the collapse of the Conference. It is very probable that, had the President remained in Washington, he would never have collapsed. His presence in Paris thus constitutes a historical disaster of the first magnitude.

There are minor considerations also which would have rendered it more convenient for all concerned had President Wilson not established himself in the Villa Murat. In the first place he would have been obliged, had he remained in Washington, to furnish his plenipotentiaries with some form of written instructions. These in themselves would have provided the Conference with some solid basis on which to proceed. As will be seen in the next chapter (it was the absence of such a solid basis which constituted one of the gravest practical disadvantages of the whole Conference.) In the second place, the President, (had he remained in touch with Senatorial and public opinion, might have been able either to guide that opinion into constructive channels, or else to warn his Delegation in time that the American people were not in the least ready to provide Europe with new lamps for old) And in the third place (the United States Plenipotentiaries would have gained immensely in their discussions with the more nimble wits of Europe by being able to

suspend decision pending reference to the President at
home.) The Americans, with all their great qualities,
are a slow-minded race. It was the actual slowness of
the President's own mental processes which placed him
at such a disadvantage in his conversations with such
men as Clemenceau or Lloyd George. Inevitably it
became irksome for him in every case and on every
occasion to ask that something might be repeated more
slowly, to confess that he had not fully kept pace with
the rapid development of the discussion. This sense
of being always a little behind the others affected the
confidence and the nerves of every American negotiator.) It would have been invaluable to them if a
legitimate pause and breathing-space could have been
achieved by insisting on a reference to Washington.)
Nor would they have gained time alone. They would
also have acquired an alibi. I have already indicated
how determinant in all discussions between civilised
men is the factor of ordinary human politeness. It
would have been far easier for the American plenipotentiaries to throw the onus of incessant refusal and
obstruction upon the shoulders of an absent potentate.
The President himself refrained, throughout the Conference, from adopting any alibi, although on occasion it might have been fitting, and even useful, had
he reserved his judgment pending consultations with
the Senate Committee. Mr. Lloyd George, when
faced with any quandary requiring delay, would always
become acutely sensitive to the opinions of the British
Empire Delegation, to the opinions, even, of the House
of Commons. The President stooped to no such
alias, to no such alibi. Against himself there was no
appeal. He sat there, in that small and stuffy room,

the mouthpiece of the Sovereign People of America. There was no alternative to himself : no escape from himself : no excuse even for his own need of silent reflection. He alone of those four men was armed with the weapon of immediate decision. It was a most lethal weapon.

Enough has been said to indicate that the presence of President Wilson in Paris was a serious misfortune. It remains to consider how that misfortune arose. It is no sufficient explanation to attribute to President Wilson defects of character which precluded him from viewing his own personality from a detached angle. His decision was not unwise merely : it was also deliberate : it was even obstinate. From a Constitutional point of view the presence in Paris of the President unaccompanied by a Committee duly appointed by the Senate was at least open to question. Mr. Lansing and Colonel House have both revealed with what grave preoccupation they regarded this decision. The latter attributes the determination of the President to a conviction on his part that he was the appointed mediator between man and man. On November 12 the Secretary of State begged the President not to come to Paris. The latter ' turned the conversation into other channels.' On November 18 the President, without again consulting his Secretary of State, issued to the Press a statement that he would attend the Conference in person. ' I am convinced,' noted Mr. Lansing in his diary, ' that he is making one of the greatest mistakes of his career, and will imperil his reputation.' It was this disagreement which from the outset embittered the relations between President Wilson and Mr. Lansing.

Colonel House also endeavoured, doubtless with more tact than the outspoken Mr. Lansing, to dissuade his friend from embarking upon so uncertain a venture. His exhortations proved unavailing. The President was annoyed by his discouragement. ' He looked forward,' records Colonel House, ' to Paris as an intellectual treat.' Seldom has any anticipation been so grimly falsified by the event. ' When,' records Colonel House, ' he stepped from his lofty pedestal and wrangled with Representatives of other States upon equal terms, he became as common clay.' And again : ' A sense of helplessness descended upon him.'

It is not to be assumed, moreover, that the decision of the President was the result of exhortations from either Great Britain or France. Mr. Lloyd George has since confessed that he was ' shocked ' when he first heard that the President had decided to attend in person. M. Clemenceau was more than shocked : he was acutely alarmed. He was alarmed lest Poincaré might contend that the presence of the President of the United States in Paris rendered it essential that the Chairman of the Conference should be, not the French Prime Minister, but the President of the French Republic. Having failed to keep the President in Washington, M. Clemenceau devoted all his efforts to securing that he should remain enshrined in the Villa Murat. It is not yet apparent by what stages, or by whom, the President was persuaded to leave his seclusion and to enter personally into the arena of argument. Mr. Lansing contends, and without adducing any evidence, that Mr. Wilson himself was averse from attending the discussions as a delegate and that he was persuaded to do so by Mr. Lloyd George. The latter may, in fact, have felt that once the President had committed the initial mistake of leaving Washington it would be preferable to reap the advantages as well as the disadvantages of his presence in Paris. ⟨ It is probable also that Mr. Wilson was convinced that no one except himself would be able to impose upon a reactionary Europe the bright novelty of the League Covenant.⟩ And M. Clemenceau, so soon as Colonel House had arranged that there would be no question of ousting him from the chairmanship of the Conference, was only too willing that the President should sit as a delegate among the other delegates. Should take his chance.

This indeed was an unhappy decision. In outward appearance, it is true, President Wilson was treated with a deference not accorded to the Prime Ministers with whom he had now decided to compete. His private detective was permitted to sit in the ante-room of the Quai d'Orsay whereas the private detectives of the other plenipotentiaries were forced to remain outside with the chauffeurs. On his arrival, moreover, M. Pichon would flurry out from between his double doors and fluster down the steps which led to the front door. The President (' Good *aff*ternoon—' he would say to us, as we rose in the ante-room to greet him, ' Good *aff*ternoon, gentlemen') was escorted to his seat in the Bureau de Monsieur Pichon by M. Pichon himself. Mr. Lloyd George, on the other hand, would roll gaily into that heated salon in the company of Sir Maurice Hankey. Yet here the honours ceased. Within those hot high walls, beneath those gay and flippant tapestries, Mr. Wilson was no more than the

plenipotentiary of the United States. He was not a
good plenipotentiary.

It had originally been hoped that the Conference
would take place in some neutral city such as Geneva
or Lausanne. Both Mr. Lloyd George and Colonel
House were definitely in favour of Switzerland.
President Wilson, however, inclined to the view that
the Lake of Geneva was ' saturated with every poison-
ous element and open to every hostile influence.' It is
not apparent from what sources he had derived this
unfavourable impression of that mist-enshrouded
littoral. Brussels, again, appeared to the organisers of
the Conference to be open to the charge of nervous
exhaustion. The Hague was also suggested—yet that
again was awkward. As a symbol of a new order the
Hague, in spite of its Palace of Peace, was not extremely encouraging. Then there was the ex-Emperor
at Amerongen—not a very pleasurable proximity.
And, after all, the Dutch. For London, the plenipotentiaries of the Continental, the Transatlantic, and
above all the British and Dominion Governments
showed no inclination at all. And in this way, inevitably, the choice fell on Paris.

In choosing that shell-shocked capital the rulers of
the world committed a grave initial blunder. Since it
was an inevitable blunder, I call it a misfortune. Yet
Paris, in any circumstances, is too self-conscious, too
insistent, to constitute a favourable site for any Congress of Peace. So long ago as 1814, Lord Castlereagh
had noted this unsuitability. ' Paris,' he wrote to
Bathurst, ' was a bad place for business.' This defect,
in 1919, was very marked indeed. ' We were hampered,' records Dr. Charles Seymour in that admirable

compilation, *The Intimate Papers of Colonel House*, ' We were hampered by the atmosphere of Paris, where German guilt was assumed as a proved fact. Everyone was afraid of being called a pro-German.' Subconsciously the shell-shock of Paris affected the nerves of all the delegates. ' Paris,' records Mr. Keynes, ' was a nightmare and everyone there was morbid.' Its very size, its many diversions, in themselves conspired against that intensive concentration which was essential if all that spate of knowledge and opinion was ever to be classified and arranged. We felt like surgeons operating in the ballroom with the aunts of the patient gathered all around.

Even to those who claimed the privilege of understanding Paris, that sombre and authoritative capital appeared, during those barbarian weeks, to have lost her dignity.

The acquired seriousness which broods under the Institut ; the effervescent seriousness which flutters the bookstalls of the Odéon ; the traditional seriousness which echoes on the hushed pavements of the Rue de Lille ; the domestic seriousness which steams from the little houses of Passy or Auteuil ; the physical seriousness which throbs from Ménilmontant to Clichy ; the intellectual seriousness (that shadow on a blind of an arm reaching towards some upper bookcase) which lives behind those myriad balconies ; the moral seriousness which is the under-current to all her iridescence ; the historical seriousness which, unemphatic, waits observant beside her hurried waters ; all these shrank to the glitter of a limousine flashing reflected in the gyrations of a hotel doorway.

Paris, gashed to her very soul, withdrew to lick

her wounds. Her place was taken by the Compagnie des Grands Express Européens, or more accurately by the American Express Company. American military police stood side by side with the Policemen on the Champs Elysées. The uniforms of twenty-six foreign armies confused the monochrome of the streets. Paris, for those few weeks, lost her soul. The brain of Paris, that triumphant achievement of western civilisation, ceased to function. The nerves of Paris jangled in the air.

The French reacted to this barbarisation of their own foyer in a most unhelpful manner. Almost from the first they turned against the Americans with embittered resentment. The constant clamour of their newspapers, the stridency of their personal attacks, increased in volume. The ineptitude of the newspapers published in Paris in the English language has seldom been surpassed. The cumulative effect of all this shouting outside the very doors of the Conference produced a nervous and as such unwholesome effect. Our breakfast tables became a succession of intemperate yells.

The President himself was strangely sensitive to these forms of animosity. He did not mind so much when he was accused of theocracy, when he was abused for not visiting the devastated areas, or when he was openly arraigned as a pro-German or as a prophet obsessed by his Utopias. Alone with God and the People he could withstand, almost without wincing, these assaults upon him. What he minded were the funny little jokes which the French papers would make about him, the persistent cloud, not of incense, but of ridicule with which they perfumed his path. Every incident that occurred (and there were many incidents) was used by the French press to expose the President in a ridiculous light. To the presbyterian, persecution is a crown of glory, and opposition is an opportunity vouchsafed by God. It is the quiet of the constant smile which goads them to desperation. Mr. Wilson suffered most acutely under the gay lampoons of Paris. This addition to his many preoccupations, these bright shavings flaming around the slow fire of his despair, are not to be underestimated as factors in his final collapse. The President had come to Paris armed with power such as no man in history had possessed : he had come fired with high ideals such as have inspired no autocrat of the past : and Paris, instead of seeing in him the embodiment of the philosopher-king, saw in him a rather comic and highly irritating professor. The cumulative effect of these sharp little pin-pricks was far greater than has been supposed.

The choice of Paris, therefore, became one of the most potent of our misfortunes. Yet none of these misfortunes which I have here analysed would have been determining factors in the situation had they not been increased and crystallised by our mistakes.

In the next chapter I propose to examine the mistakes of organisation and method by which the Conference was doomed to comparative failure from the start.

Chapter IV

MISTAKES

The necessity of an agreed basis and a firm programme—Reasons why the Conference evaded both these essentials—The duality of purpose—Conflict of principle versus compromise on detail—Mr. Baker and Dr. Seymour—Inevitability of some divergence—Failure to face this divergence from the outset—The excuses of the Reparation Commission and of Article XIX of the Covenant—How far are these valid excuses? —European necessities as against American desires—Factual imprecisions—No decision whether Treaty should be Preliminary or Final, negotiated or imposed—Analysis of this imprecision, its nature and results—No definite programme—Reasons for this.

I

AMONG the series of ' Peace Conference Handbooks ' with which we had been supplied by the Foreign Office, was one written by Sir Ernest Satow upon ' International Congresses.' In this admirable monograph the greatest living authority upon diplomatic practice had summarised for us the methods and procedure adopted at past Congresses, and had drawn our earnest attention to the mistakes of organisation which had then been made. His little book was much studied by the junior members of the British Delegation and was by them communicated to their American colleagues, who in their turn read it with interest and respect. It may be questioned whether it was examined with equal diligence by the Plenipotentiaries themselves. It might have been useful, for instance, had the directors of British policy, before leaving London, read those trenchant passages in which Sir Ernest Satow insisted upon the necessity of (*a*) some previous agreement as to the ends in view, and (*b*) a definite and rigid programme.

'A Congress or Conference,' wrote Sir Ernest Satow, ' is usually preceded by the conclusion of preliminaries of peace between the belligerent parties. . . . To enter upon either a Congress or a Conference without such preliminaries would be a dangerous course to adopt, as it might lead to attempts to bring about division between the allies on one side or the other. . . . A definite programme of the matters to be discussed between the plenipotentiaries is to be expected. This programme should be strictly adhered to, and if any proposal to introduce other subjects is put forward, it should be carefully scrutinised before acceptance.'

' Experience demonstrates that in order to ensure the success of a Congress or Conference, a distinct basis or bases ought to be agreed upon beforehand, and the greater the definiteness with which the main points of the basis are formulated beforehand, the greater is the likelihood of general agreement being reached. In past history, when Congresses failed to attain a definite result, the failure was generally due to the ground not having been adequately prepared beforehand.'

M. André Tardieu, in his book *The Truth about the Peace Treaty* is conscious that the failure to co-ordinate any preliminary basis of policy lies at the root of the tentative methods adopted in the initial stages of the Conference, of the ensuing delays, and of the final hurried compromises of March and April. He defends this omission upon two grounds. He contends in the first place that it was difficult enough to maintain a united front for war purposes, and that this difficulty would have been seriously increased had a discussion of eventual peace policy been intruded into so delicate an adjustment of national pride and interests. There is something in this contention. He argues in the second place that after the Armistice an attempt at co-ordination was in fact made during M. Clemenceau's visit to London on December 2 and 3, 1918. This argument is fallacious. The London discussions covered only four points, none of which contributed in any essential degree to the smooth working of the ensuing Conference. It was agreed that a Committee should at once be appointed to assess Germany's capacity to pay ; it was agreed that the ex-Emperor should be tried before an International Tribunal ; it was agreed that the Representatives of the British Dominions might attend the meetings of the Conference whenever their particular interests came up for discussion ; and it was agreed that a Committee should be charged with the duty of examining the problem of supply and relief.

It cannot, therefore, be contended that the discussions which took place in London on December 2 and 3 did anything to establish the ' basis or bases ' of the impending Congress.

2

It might be argued with greater justification, that this basis was in fact provided by the Points, Principles and Particulars enunciated by President Wilson and accepted by all the belligerents as the foundation upon which the detailed terms would be constructed. This was, in fact, our own impression at the time. Yet was it a correct impression ? I fear that it was not.

It is important, from the point of view of diplomatic

technique, to examine how far these principles did, in effect, establish a basis of negotiation between the several parties. Such examination discloses a very serious anomaly. For whereas these bases were in theory accepted as the ' pactum de contrahendo ' for a negotiation as between the two groups of belligerents they were not (even when we add the glossary of Colonel House) unreservedly accepted as an agreed basis of negotiation between the Allied and Associated Powers. M. Clemenceau, for instance, must from the outset have made within his own heart reservations as to the ' security ' of France : these reservations, in that they implied some detachment of the Rhineland from Germany, some prohibition of the self-determination of Austria, some intention of obtaining at least the economic resources of the Saar basin—were in direct contradiction to the principles which, in regard to our late enemies, as also in regard to the United States, he had accepted with acclaim. Mr. Lloyd George, also, must from the outset have cherished doubts, which applied not only to his published qualification on the subject of maritime rights, but which applied also to his unexpressed, but certainly foreseen, difficulties in such matters as the cost of the war, and the allocation of German Colonies to Australia and the Union of South Africa. Signor Orlando, again, in spite of his mumbled reservation, must have known very well that the Brenner frontier, to say nothing of the Adriatic encroachments, were not, and could never be presented as, a settlement of Italian claims ' upon clearly recognisable lines of nationality.' Each of the protagonists, therefore, entered the Conference with a clear (or what should have been a clear) realisation that his purposes were not in complete harmony with his professions. To a certain extent this elasticity of intention must be inseparable from any international Congress. Yet, at Paris, the gulf between the alleged and the actual intentions of the participants was too wide to furnish anything approaching an ' agreed basis of settlement.'

It is not my intention to introduce ethical considerations or to apportion blame or praise. My whole contention is that certain existent factors operated in wholly inevitable ways. My present notes are not concerned with what ought to have happened, still less what ought not to have happened. I am describing what was, in fact, not a Conference, but a very serious illness. I am concerned only with recording symptoms and establishing a fever chart. And to this extent the discrepancy which I have indicated is vital to my argument.

Let me state that argument in a different way.

The Conference has been represented, and in particular by American propagandists of the type of Mr. Ray Stannard Baker, as a conflict of the Powers of Light (represented by President Wilson) with the Powers of Darkness (represented by M. Clemenceau). Such a simplified dramatisation of the issues is scarcely legitimate. Irrelevant also, to my mind, is Mr. Keynes' confrontation of a ' Carthaginian ' with a ' Wilsonian ' peace. Nothing—not even its contrasts or its confrontations—was clear-cut in Paris. The whole business, as Mr. Balfour remarked, was, after all, a ' rough and tumble affair.'

Equally misleading, although far more intelligent, is the opposite type of argument which represents the Conference, not as a conflict between two mutually exclusive principles, but as an adjustment of intricate practical details. I admit that this latter interpretation does in fact describe the machinery of the Conference in being. It describes what the Conference was, rather than what the Conference ought to have been, or what we meant it to be. To that extent it is a criticism rather than an exposition. Future students, who study this line of criticism, will content themselves with the reflection that they (being versed in economics) will not make the mistakes that were made by us of 1919. It is for this reason that I regard this argument as an almost equally unhelpful record of that incessant interaction between the elements of hope and exhaustion, of wisdom and expediency, of vast racial needs and tiny personal preoccupations, of knowledge and ignorance, of justice and revenge, of power and cowardice, of thought and emotion, of the immediate and the ultimate, of the past and the future, of the convenient and the desirable, of the practicable and the difficult, of the popular and the scientific—that interaction which arose less from a conflict, than a fusion, of motive, less from a struggle than a muzz : that interaction which, as the weeks passed, shrouded the Conference in mists of exhaustion, disability, suspicion and despair.

Let me provide as a specimen of such a criticism the excellent passage which figures in Volume IV of Dr. Charles Seymour's edition of the Papers of Colonel House.

' Various historians, especially those writing from an American point of view, have presented the Peace Conference as though it were a clear-cut conflict between two ideals, personified by Clemenceau on the one hand and Wilson on the other : a conflict between the evil of the old diplomatic system and the virtue of the new world idealism. Such a picture is attractive to those who will not understand the complexities of historical truth. In reality the Peace Conference was not nearly so simple. It was not so much a duel as a general melée, in which the representatives of every nation struggled to secure endorsement for their particular methods of ensuring peace. The object of all was the same—to avoid a repetition of the four years of world devastation; their methods naturally were different, since each was faced by a different set of problems.

Inevitably each nation put forward a solution which was coloured by self-interest. This was, in a sense, just as true of the United States as of France, Italy, or Great Britain. We sacrificed little in announcing that we would take no territory (which we did not want) nor reparations (which we could not collect). Our interest lay entirely in assuring a régime of world tranquility; our geographic position was such that we could advocate disarmament and arbitration with complete safety. Wilson's idealism was in line with a healthy *Realpolitik*.

But American methods did not fit so perfectly the peculiar problems of European nations, dominated as they were by geographical and historical factors. According to the American programme we ourselves gave up nothing of value, but we asked the European nations to give up much that seemed to them the very essence of security. We might insist that the most certain prevention of war lay in disarmament and reconciliation. The French would reply that the British and Americans, protected by the Channel and the Atlantic, could afford so to argue; France had been invaded too often not to insist upon better guarantee than written promises. We might insist that it was good business to write off German Reparations as a bad debt. The Europeans replied: "Shall we who were attacked, then pay the entire cost and let the aggressor go scatheless? Not until we have exhausted every possible chance of making him pay."

Even if the Allied leaders themselves agreed to the wisdom of the American proposals, they were prevented from accepting them by the force of public opinion. Clemenceau was branded as a traitor because he refused to break up Germany ; if he had yielded on the occupation of the Rhinelands he would have been hurled from power and replaced by a more stubborn Premier. Lloyd George admitted that the public estimate of German capacity to pay was absurd, but he did not care to tell the electorate. Orlando would gladly have accepted a compromise solution of the Adriatic question ; it was forbidden him by the political forces in Italy. The Prime Ministers were far from exercising supreme power. By arousing popular emotion during the war, an orthodox belligerent measure, they had created a Frankenstein monster which now held them helpless. ׀They might compromise, if they possessed the skill, but they would not be permitted to yield.〕

The conception of Mr. Stannard Baker, the theory of Dr. Charles Seymour, each represents an extreme interpretation of the 〔duality of intention with which the main negotiators reached Paris.〕 The former contends that the purposes of the Old and the New World were not different merely but actually antagonistic. The latter tends to explain that these purposes, although dissimilar in degree, were not really dissimilar in kind. I much prefer the processes of thought adopted by Dr. Charles Seymour to the processes of emotion indulged in by Mr. Stannard Baker. Yet I cannot but admit that of the two it is Mr. Baker who more closely approximates to the truth. In other words, the failure of the Conference of Paris to live up to its own early ideals can only be understood if we start from the popular, but not wholly inaccurate, assumption, that (there did in fact exist a conflict of principle ; that this conflict was never faced squarely but evaded by every possible subterfuge ; and that it was the existence of this constant, but never open, divergence which obliged the rulers of the world ' to weave ' (I am quoting Mr. Keynes) ' that web of sophistry and Jesuitical exegesis that was finally to clothe with insincerity the language and substance of the whole Treaty.')

It may be contended that this initial divergence of purpose was wholly unavoidable and should therefore have been classed in the previous chapter under the heading of ' Misfortunes ' and not relegated to my present discussion of ' Mistakes.' I fully agree that to a very large extent a conflict of intention was inevitable. America, eternally protected by the Atlantic, desired to satisfy her self-righteousness while disengaging her responsibility. She was in the extremely ungrateful position of preventing other people doing what they wanted, while being unwilling to do anything herself. France, having achieved victory in circumstances which she well knew would never be again so favourable, was passionately determined to use this short breathing-space in order to create for herself a zone of protection against the day when the German menace would again loom threateningly in the east. Great Britain, shaken and impoverished, desired to replenish her sunken coffers and to maintain her relations with her Dominions on a basis of amicable co-operation. Japan and Italy were frankly out for loot. The Smaller States thought only of increasing their territory and resources at the expense of their defeated enemies.

Such intentions may have been regrettable. That is not the point. The point is that they were wholly inevitable. Had M. Clemenceau abandoned all efforts to obtain the Rhineland, and the Saar ; had he insisted that the Poles, the Czechs and the Rumanians should reduce their claims against Germany, Austria and Hungary within limits strictly reconcilable with the Fourteen Points ; had he made no provision for the unequal disarmament of Germany at least for such a period of time as would enable the new allies of France to consolidate their strength and independence ; had M. Clemenceau done, or omitted to do, any of these things, he would within a few days have been hurled from power, and his place would have been taken by a statesman in closer accord with the prevailing temper of France. Had Mr. Lloyd George openly disavowed his own election pledges ; had he given way to President Wilson in such matters as War Pensions and the German mercantile fleet ; had he, above all, had an open breach with Australia or South Africa upon the distribution of the German Colonies ; had he antagonised Japan by a too overt opposition to their claims at Shantung ; then he also would have had to face a hostile House of Commons, then he also would have been replaced by a statesman of more extremely vindictive views. Had Marquis Saionji, or Signor Orlando, or M. Bratianu, or M. Kramarsh, or M. Pasic, or M. Paderewsky, or M. Venizelos insisted upon a Wilsonian interpretation of the demands of their own electorates, they also would at once have been forced into resignation, and their places would at once have been taken by representatives more in accord with the nationalist emotions of their peoples.

This essential factor cannot be stated too frequently. The plenipotentiaries of the victorious Powers in Paris were the chosen delegates of an informed, if unenlightened, public opinion. It was wholly impossible for them to act in flagrant violation of that opinion. It was wholly impossible for them, in those early months of 1919, to frame the Treaty on any literal interpretation of the Fourteen Points. This, as I have already indicated, was the fundamental misfortune. Yet there was no essential reason why this misfortune should have been approached in such a manner as to render it also a mistake. (The fundamental mistake of the Conference was that nobody possessed the vision or the courage to cope with its misfortunes from the very outset.)

3

The issue should, in December of 1918, have been formulated as follows : ' We are about to meet in Paris to draft the Treaty of Peace. We have pledged ourselves that the terms of that Treaty will be in accordance with the Fourteen Points. Public opinion will not, however, permit us to fulfil these pledges. We must therefore defer the Final Treaty until public opinion is in a saner mood. Our immediate task is thus to frame conditions of a Preliminary Peace such as will enable us to demobilise, to raise the blockade, and eventually to negotiate with our late enemies a Treaty in accordance with the conditions of their surrender.'

I am aware that such a decision would have been overwhelmingly unpopular, and in practice extremely difficult to execute. It should be noted moreover that Mr. Lloyd George did (in effect if not in appearance) provide for this deferred form of procedure. By leaving it to the Reparation Commission to fix the sum which Germany should eventually have to pay, he was able both to satisfy immediate opinion at home, and to secure that the Reparation question could subsequently be dealt with by technicians and in a saner atmosphere without thereby violating the Treaty as signed. For this wise achievement he is but seldom given credit. Nor was this all. The leading statesmen in Paris, not excluding President Wilson, were vividly aware that the Treaty which was being drafted would require revision at a more distant epoch when the hysteria of the war had subsided. They provided for that revision. They inserted into the Covenant of the League of Nations an article which is too little quoted and too often forgotten. I cite it as follows :

Article XIX

'The Assembly may from time to time advise the reconsideration by Members of the League of treaties which have become inapplicable and the consideration of international conditions whose continuance might endanger the peace of the world.'

The cynic, on reading this article to-day, on reflecting how the rule of ' unanimity ' has in the past blocked all such daring gestures of initiative at Geneva, may smile sourly and condemn this article as merely one more of those threads of ' Jesuitical exegesis ' with which the Paris Conference draped the failure of their own Treaty. I am not certain that he would be correct either historically or actually in dismissing Article XIX with such summary decision. From the historical point of view, from the point of view of how decisions came to be taken in Paris, the Article was all-important. By the end of February we were abandoning any hope of making a Wilsonian peace in that year of anguish 1919. It is impossible to estimate how many decisions were accepted, how often obstruction was relinquished, how frequently errors were passed over, under the aegis of that blessed Article XIX. ' Well,' we were apt to think, ' this decision seems foolish and unjust. Yet I shall agree to it rather than delay the Treaty for a few days further. Its unwisdom will very shortly become apparent even to those who are now its advocates. When that day comes, we can resort to Article XIX.' I am convinced that practically all of President Wilson's own backslidings were justified in his own conscience by the thought that ' The Covenant will put that right.'

Even to-day this Article XIX has, or will have, its applicability. Even those who have no further hope that the League Assembly will ever be willing or able to impose its view upon the Great Powers, must agree that it is convenient to possess in this Article an instrument for Treaty revision when once that revision has been accepted by the interested Powers themselves. It would be convenient, if nothing more, to be in a position, on the strength and with the machinery of this Article, to revise certain provisions of the Treaty of Versailles without affecting the validity of the whole. Conversely the Article provides a useful argument wherewith to counter the contentions of those who affirm that the Treaty is an integral unit, and that no part can be assailed without destroying the whole structure.

I quite see that a certain duality of purpose was inseparable from the Conference of 1918-1919. I quite see that to disclose that duality would, at the time, have been difficult and even obnoxious. I quite see that Mr. Lloyd George and Mr. Wilson did in fact regard the Reparation Commission as well as Article XIX as an escape from their misfortunes. Yet, even when I admit all these things, I am left with the pointing finger of accusation. It points at this. It points at the undeniable fact that they did not face this essential duality of purpose from the start. The result was a blend of improvisation and compromise.

For that unhappy collapse between two stools the Americans were less to blame than were the Associated Powers. The latter had pledged themselves in advance to abide by the Wilsonian principles. The former, from the very first days of the Conference, were weakened by internal events. ' The American Delegation,' records Colonel House, ' are not in a position to act fully. The elections of last November in the United States have been a deterrent to free action by our delegates.' It must be remembered, in fact, that during the whole course of the Conference President Wilson and his staff could not rely upon the support, either of Congress, or of their own public opinion. When the essential crisis emerged in Paris Mr. Wilson could only have triumphed by driving Mr. Lloyd George and M. Clemenceau from office. Would even his own country have supported him in such intransigence? Assuredly not. It was the knowledge that the President did not in fact possess the political, as distinct from the physical, power to proceed to the logical conclusions of his own policy, which destroyed his authority in Paris and enabled other statesmen to extract from him concessions of which he profoundly disapproved. What was the lever which enabled them

to move this cemented man from his initial position?
It was this. They *knew* that President Wilson did not,
in the February of 1919, represent America. They also
knew that he would die (as he *did* eventually die) rather
than admit that fact. They knew that his faith in
democracy was the deepest conviction of his sensitive
soul. They also knew that for immediate, as distinct
from ultimate purposes, democracy was a fool. They
knew that Mr. Wilson would never face the fact that
his own American People had let him down. They
knew that in order to disguise that fact from himself,
he would submit to any humiliation. They knew that
the one way to manage Wilson was to threaten to, and
then to refrain from, showing him up. The conceit
and egoism of Mr. Wilson must, of course, be admitted : yet these were but as straws upon the deep
current of his faith. It was his faith which they
exploited. His faith in The People and in God. They
knew that it would be excruciating for him to admit
that neither of these two illusions played any part in the
Peace Conference. President Wilson was destroyed,
not by his faults, but by his virtues.

Yet what has all this to do with the Mistakes, as distinct from the Misfortunes, of the Paris Peace Conference? It has this to do. It is difficult to resist the
impression that the European statesmen were conscious
of the fact that the President, owing to his own mystic
theocracy, was in a false position. It is difficult to
resist the impression that they desired to allow time for
the falsity of this position to emerge. It is difficult to
resist the impression that they wanted the President to
' absorb the atmosphere of war ' before he came to
dictate the provisions of peace. It is difficult to resist

the impression that they deliberately delayed coming to grips with the President until Mr. Wilson had lost his grip.

This decision, on their part, was not so much iniquitous as unintelligent. They should have realised that there was no middle path between a Wilsonian and a Carthaginian Peace. They should have realised that either was better than a hypocritical compromise. And, realising these things, they should have organised the whole Conference upon a basis of greater reality.

Let me illustrate that basic unreality—that marsh of imprecision upon which rested the whole structure of the Conference—by two curious phenomena. The first is the fact that until the very last moment the Plenipotentiaries were themselves unaware whether the Peace they were negotiating was to be preliminary or final, imposed or negotiated. The second was the absence, in fact the rejection, of any definite programme. These two mistakes will strike the future student as inexplicable. Yet in fact they occurred.

4

It might have been supposed that, however anxious the statesmen of Europe may have been to postpone essentials until Mr. Wilson should have become acclimatized to the less limpid atmosphere of the Old World—there were two vital points of procedure upon which they would have been clear and united from the start.

The first of these points was (whether the Treaty should be preliminary or final.) The second of these points was (whether the Treaty should be imposed or negotiated)—in other words whether the enemy should be allowed, at the last moment, to attend and speak at the Conference, or whether all discussion should from first to last be barred.

It is a strange, but indisputable fact, that neither of these two important points of procedure were discussed or decided in the early stages of the Conference. During January, February and the first half of March —for a period, that is of more than ten weeks—the rulers of the world were completely unaware whether the Treaty which they were discussing was to be negotiated or imposed. It may seem strange indeed that this essential consideration should not have been examined from the outset and from the outset decided. Yet in fact the problem was shelved throughout that period as something which was too painful to raise immediately, as something which would settle itself.

The original idea had certainly been that there would be a preliminary Treaty the terms of which would be settled in advance as between the victorious Powers. This Treaty, which would be imposed upon the beaten enemy, was to have contained merely the terms of military and naval disarmament, as well as the main lines of the future territorial settlement. All other details were to be elaborated at a subsequent ' Congress ' at which the enemy would be represented and at which they would have occasion to advance counter proposals.

At a later stage it was suggested that a ' General Act ' should be drafted by the Conference embracing the essentials of all the Treaties of Peace with the four enemy Powers. So late as March 19, President Wilson was still undecided whether he desired a Preliminary or Final Treaty. He was assured by Mr. Lansing and the jurists that even a Preliminary Treaty would have to be ratified by the Senate, and he was thus afraid that they would grasp at this power of ratification in order to refuse acceptance of the ensuing Covenant of the League. 'At this statement,' records Mr. Lansing, ' the President was evidently much perturbed.' During Mr. Wilson's absence from the United States, the idea was mooted that a preliminary treaty might be drafted and signed under the guise of a 'Final Armistice.' On February 22 it was decided even that the main items of such an Armistice might be prepared against the President's return, and the Military and Naval advisers to the Council were instructed to cast it immediately into shape. Yet by the time these clauses had finally been drafted and approved, the President had himself returned to Paris. It was then discovered that the territorial and other clauses had in the interval advanced to a stage at which, with a little further drafting, they also could be embodied in the Treaty of Peace. The whole theory of a Preliminary Peace was thereafter, and as it were by chance, abandoned.

This hesitation between the conception of a Preliminary and a Final Treaty has a direct bearing upon the question of enemy representation. The Germans are to this day convinced that it was from the outset the deliberate intention of the Allies to exclude their representatives from any share in the Peace discussions. In actual fact, this point, as other points of a similar nature, swirled as a small straw upon the gathering waters of the Conference. In November 1918 Colonel House had solemnly allotted five seats at the impending Congress to the Representatives of Germany. At that date, and until March, it was taken for granted by all who laboured in Paris that once the Allies had agreed among themselves as to the terms to be offered to Germany the Conference would cease to be a 'Conference' and become a 'Congress'—or in other words that we should then enter upon the second phase of our labours, namely negotiation on the terms of the eventual settlement with our late enemies, and in the presence of the neutral Powers.

How came it that this estimable idea faded, as the weeks wore on, from our immediate consciousness? History will refuse to believe that we 'forgot about the enemy.' She will attribute to us motives and a state of awareness which were certainly not ours at the time. It is difficult to explain the exclusion of our enemies from the discussion except in terms which will appear incredible, or at least far-fetched. Yet I seriously believe that the following were the stages by which the necessity of consulting with our enemies receded into the background of our minds.

Subconsciously we thought in terms of a 'Conference' of Allies, followed by a 'Congress' of all belligerents and neutrals. The former conception became identified with the expression 'Preliminary Treaty': the latter took the word-form of 'Final Treaty.' The 'Preliminary Treaty' would be imposed by force upon the defeated enemy: the 'Final Treaty' would be a matter of world negotiation and world consent.

As the Conference progressed, as more and more of the technical Committees produced their recommendations in the form of articles which were ready for immediate insertion in a final document—the conception of a Preliminary Treaty merged gradually into the conception of one final Treaty covering the whole. It had always been assumed that the essential articles—such as those providing for German disarmament and the main territorial cessions—would figure in the Preliminary Treaty and would therefore be, not negotiated, but imposed. It had also been supposed that what might be called the secondary articles—and especially the economic if not also the financial clauses—would be a matter for discussion. Yet when the Preliminary Treaty was abandoned, and the Final Treaty took its place, the latter inherited from the former this original idea of imposition versus negotiation. And all this happened before many of us had realised exactly what had occurred.

I do not contend that we drifted into imposing, rather than negotiating, a Treaty in a mood of complete unawareness. Obviously there were certain deliberate factors which impelled us to that decision. In the first place President Wilson's insistence upon the inclusion of the Covenant, in any form of Treaty, delayed our deliberations beyond the moment when a Preliminary Treaty was either sensible or necessary. In the second place the absence of the President and Mr. Lloyd George, coupled with the attempted assassination of M. Clemenceau, entailed at a vital moment the suspension of the supreme direction of the Conference, and an accumulation in the interval of much completed material. In the third place Marshal Foch feared that the conclusion of the Preliminary Treaty would lead to even more rapid demobilisation on the part of Great Britain and the United States, after which there would be little hope of negotiating any peace at all. And in the fourth place the acute disagree-

ments which, during those weeks, developed as between the Allies themselves produced a feeling amount-
ing to terror lest the presence in the divided counsels
of Europe of so disruptive an element as our late
enemies would lead to even more alarming disintegra-
tion.

The fact remains, in any case, that throughout the
early stages of the Conference the directing Powers
never allowed it to be known whether the Treaty
which was being prepared was a final text to be
imposed upon Germany, or a mere basis of agreement
as between the Allies for eventual negotiation with
Germany at a final Congress. This omission on their
part was most serious and has not, except by Mr.
Keynes, been sufficiently stressed. Many paragraphs
of the Treaty, and especially in the economic sections,
were in fact inserted as ' maximum statements ' such as
would provide some area of concession to Germany at
the eventual Congress. This Congress never mater-
ialised : the last weeks of the Conference flew past us
in a hysterical nightmare ; and these ' maximum
statements ' remained unmodified and were eventually
imposed by ultimatum. Had it been known from the
outset that no negotiations would ever take place with
the enemy, it is certain that many of the less reasonable
clauses of the Treaty would never have been inserted.

5

I have by now indicated what were the two fundamental mistakes committed by those who were responsible for the initiation and conduct of the Paris
Peace Conference. I have contended that their failure
to recognise their own duality of purpose placed the

Conference in a false position from the outset, and led to excessive falsity in the end. (I have contended that their failure to decide from the beginning whether the Peace was to be Preliminary or Final, negotiated or imposed, was the cause of much subsequent muddle, misunderstanding and injustice.) The minor errors of organisation which impeded the work of the Conference will be referred to in later chapters as they occur. It remains to discuss in the present chapter what was a major, and in fact fundamental, error in initial organisation. (I shall now consider the omission of the Conference to provide itself with any definite programme in advance.)

I have already recorded the judgment of Sir Ernest Satow upon the necessity of a rigid programme. That necessity was all the more insistent at a Conference in which the leading delegates were from the outset confronted with a duality, if not a discordance of intention. The cynical observer may conclude that they desired deliberately to occupy a month or two in beating about the Wilsonian bush. I do not exclude such a possibility ; yet I hate to admit it. I prefer to imagine that, as with most of the business dependent upon our rulers, we were at the mercy of improvisation. The members of the Supreme War Council had fallen into the habit of leaving the initiative either to the Germans or to Marshal Foch. They had learnt that the march of events, or perhaps the march of the Germans, was a factor more determinant than any of the elaborate plans which had been put before them. They had come to distrust all paper plans. It is not surprising that when the members of the Supreme War Council transformed themselves within the space of two days into the Supreme Peace Council, this habit of improvisation, this distaste for initiative, this preference for meeting events which had already occurred rather than foreseeing events which might (or might not) occur in the future, became for them the very tissue of their thoughts. So many things which they expected had never happened : so many things had happened which their advisers had never, for one instant, led them to expect. Is it surprising that they should have distrusted the expected, the advised, the preconceived ? It is not surprising.

A programme had, in fact, been prepared by the French. This programme was handed to President Wilson by M. Jusserand, French Ambassador in Washington, on November 29. It provided in the first place for a set of preliminary terms which should be imposed upon the enemy without discussion. It provided in the second place for a subsequent Congress at which both enemy and neutral Powers should be represented. It provided in the third place for a regular time table under which the Supreme Council would discuss the urgent questions first and would leave less urgent questions for subsequent deliberation. And above all it provided for the immediate cancellation of all secret Treaties. In spite of these eminently reasonable proposals the programme submitted by M. Jusserand was not a wholly tactful document, It spoke of the ' Federalisation ' (*i.e.* disruption) of Germany. It suggested that the fate of the Ottoman Empire should be decided by the Great Powers themselves. And it referred in language which was far too realistic to be flattering to the League of Nations, and the Points, Principles and Particulars of Mr. Wilson him-

self. ' Those principles,' thus ran this document—
' of President Wilson which are not sufficiently defined
in their character to be taken as a basis for a concrete
settlement . . . will resume their full strength in the
matter of the future settlement of public law, and this
will remove one of the difficulties that might obstruct
the Allies.' ' The fourteen propositions '—thus continued this sincere but unconciliatory document—
' which are principles of public law, cannot furnish a
concrete basis for the labours of the Conference.'
This at least was intelligent, honourable and frank.
Yet the President was displeased. The French programme found its place among his most unfrequented
files.

{ The great fault,' writes Colonel House, ' of the
political leaders was their failure to draft a plan of
procedure.') M. Tardieu for his part throws the onus
of that fault upon the Anglo-Saxon temperament. He
attributes our rejection of the French programme
to our congenital distaste for the logical precisions of
the Latin mind. He may be right. I think he is. Yet
the fact remains that Mr. Wilson (because of the rude
precisions of the Jusserand memorandum) and Mr.
Lloyd George (in view of his amazing predeliction for
the unexpected) both rejected, and indeed resented,
any written formulation of what, or how, or when,
they were supposed to discuss.

The effects of this disinclination on their part were
deplorable in the extreme.

Chapter V

DISORGANISATION

Contact with the American Delegation—Early unanimity and subsequent misunderstandings—Faults of organisation in the British Delegation—The work unevenly apportioned—The Military Section—Internal co-ordination—Interdepartmental rivalry—Relations between the Plenipotentiaries and the Delegation staff—Lack of central focus or control—Lack of central instruction or supervision—Haphazard allocation of function—Defects of organisation in Conference as a whole—The Council of Ten as the successor of the Supreme War Council—The problem of the Small Powers and the compromises by which that problem was met—Effect of these compromises—M. Clemenceau as chairman—M. Dutasta as Secretary General—The inadequacy of the agenda papers—The problem of the Press—The Territorial Committees—Faults of constitution, terms of reference, and procedure—The atmosphere of their decisions.

I

UNTROUBLED for the moment either by these mistakes or these misfortunes, I found time, during the first few days of the Conference to go hunting on my own. My preparatory work had now been completed : there was little more that I could learn from books, from maps, or from statistics. I decided that the interval which must elapse before my immediate services would be required could best be utilised in establishing contact with my United States colleagues. I snuffed around like a spaniel in the bracken, importantly busy, busily important. I had received no instructions whatsoever from my official superiors : I seldom did : I hunted happily, waiting for the whistle which would call me to heel.

I was aided and inspired in this pleasant diversion by Mr. Allen Leeper, my immediate colleague in that section of the British Delegation which had been charged with Central and South Eastern Europe. Mr. Leeper, at that period, was not as yet a regular member of the Foreign Office, but had reached us through such devious channels as the British Museum, Mr. George Mair's press bureau, and the later Ministry of Information. Having been born in Australia he was able to approach our problems from an antipodean rather than an insular point of view : having been educated at Balliol he had learnt that knowledge is of small value unless interpreted in terms of understanding, that intelligence is but a gaudy thing unless translated into terms of creative action : having never suffered from the routine of a large Government office his eyes shone undimmed by the dust of civil service files : being a citizen of the New World, he could approach the Old with the romantic zest of a scholar on his first visit to the Parthenon : being unimpeded by the trammels of an English public school education it never occurred to him that a passionate interest in the work before us might be regarded as bad form. He was a man of high ideals, the purest Wilsonism, some philological ambition, intermittent health, unfailing energy, and unashamed curiosity. He made no secret of the fact that he really wanted to know what Také Jonescu thought about the Banat. He quite frankly wanted to see whether King Nikita of Montenegro (living exiled, subsidised and indignant in the Hotel Meurice) was really as horrible as we had all supposed. And above all, he realised that our most useful function at the moment was to establish with our opposite numbers

of the American Mission relations of confidence and
mutual understanding.

He was assisted in this laudable purpose by the
chance circumstance that Mr. Rhys Carpenter, a subordinate member of the American Mission to Negotiate Peace, had been a Balliol friend. Mr. Carpenter,
who subsequently became Director of the American
School at Athens, was above everything a scholar. He
had lisped in Greek particles for the particles had come.
He was a shy and charming man. He was of inestimable service to us in smoothing the path of approach towards the diffident, the suspicious, the well-
informed, the amiable, the rather alarming, the often
inarticulate, the sometimes slow-minded, the invariably attentive, the wholly admirable pundits of Colonel
House's 'Inquiry.' It was through him that I was introduced from the outset to Dr. Charles Seymour, Dr.
Lybyer, and Dr. Clive Day. Mr. Alan Dulles, with
whom in the later stages of the Conference I established
co-operation of durable harmony, was, if I recollect
aright, a somewhat later arrival. We compared notes.
Our opinions on every one of the subjects within our
particular orbit appeared to be identical. It seemed
to us that the drafting of peace would be a brisk,
amicable, and hugely righteous affair.

I was not so innocent as to suppose that the United
States Delegation would be permitted openly to associate themselves with their British associates. I felt
indeed that any too ostensible identity of view between
the Anglo-Saxons would be resented by our foreign
colleagues. I aimed only at secret covenants secretly
arrived at. Our unanimity was indeed remarkable.
There—in what had once been the *cabinets particulier*

of Maxim's—was elaborated an Anglo-American case covering the whole frontiers of Jugo-Slavia, Czecho-Slovakia, Rumania, Austria and Hungary. Only in regard to Greece, Albania, Bulgaria and Turkey in Europe did any divergence manifest itself. And even here the divergence was one of detail only, scarcely one of principle.

True it is, that in the weeks that followed this un-expressed covenant was not always adhered to. At some points I extended my demands, at other points they withdrew their concessions. Throughout the duration of the Conference, we would find ourselves obliged to discuss all over again points which we sup-posed to be already settled between us. Yet the prin-ciple of frank and direct discussion, established during those first few days as between the British and American delegations, was never abandoned. Mr. Ray Stannard Baker may say what he likes. The understanding be-tween the Crillon and the Astoria was closer than that between any other two delegations in Paris.

I confess, of course, that in spite of Rhys Carpenter's optimism, I never obtained their unreserved confi-dence. There was always in their minds that dark barrier between the Old World and the New. As the Conference progressed our relations were darkened by the wrangles of our respective chiefs—*quidquid delirant reges*. . . . Yet I, to this day, retain for the members of Colonel House's Inquiry that warm respect which was born during those early discussions in the Place de la Concorde. Their knowledge was greater than mine : their power was infinitely more impressive : their scope was wider. Yet I was a professional diplomatist and they were professors of history. An absurd conflict of vanities was thereby introduced. It was not long before our initial frankness, our initial confidences lost something of their morning freshness. We of the Majestic became impatient of their well-meant hesitations, irritated by their sensitiveness to the falsity of their own position. We were floundering in a bog of secret treaties and looked to them to pull us out : they remained on the bank, agreeing, with ready sympathy, that bogs were cumbersome and filthy things. They of the Crillon were disheartened and confused by the rush and clatter of the Conference in action : they were so determined not to be duped by the diabolical cunning of the Old Diplomacy that they suspected tricks where no tricks had been intended : and as it dawned gradually upon them (as upon us) that America was asking Europe to make vital sacrifices for an ideal which America herself would be the first to betray, a helpless embarrassment descended upon both of us. The ghastly suspicion that the American people would not honour the signature of their own delegates was never mentioned between us : it became the ghost at all our feasts. Yet had our early collaboration with the American Mission been consistently and whole-heartedly maintained, had it been throughout regarded as the unalterable basis of our every procedure, the Treaties of Peace would assuredly have been marred by fewer errors.

In this, when I look back upon it all, lies the point where I feel the deepest regret.

2

I have already stated that the internal organisation of the British Delegation was a masterpiece of precision and ease. So far as human ingenuity can provide for unforeseen conditions of extreme mobility, the machine created by Mr. Parker and controlled by Sir Maurice Hankey was a triumph of administrative efficiency and prevision. It should serve as a model for any future organisation of similar magnitude. It is thus in no spirit of criticism that I indicate the points at which this scheme, so admirable on paper, proved insufficient to mitigate the weaknesses of human nature.

The absence of any fixed programme of Conference procedure, the long delay in appointing technical committees, rendered it in any case inevitable that many of the most able members of the Delegation should not be utilised in the earlier stages. Yet even when we make full allowance for this perhaps unavoidable circumstance, the fact remains that from the start the Delegation fell into certain fortuitous categories, which, as the pressure of work became overwhelming, tended to crystallise into water-tight compartments. These categories, as I have said, were largely, although not wholly, due to chance. Mr. Lloyd George relied in all such matters upon Sir Maurice Hankey. Mr. Balfour relied almost wholly on Sir Eyre Crowe. It was natural that the latter should choose as his assistants those members of the Foreign Office with whom he had been most closely associated during the War. The time was too short, the risk too great, to make any experiments in personnel. As a result, the Foreign Office section were from the outset given perhaps undue prominence, and perhaps too great a share of labour. The Military Section which included men of such marked ability as General Thwaites, Colonel Cornwall, Colonel

Meinertzhagen, Colonel Heywood, Colonel Kisch, and Professor Webster, were in the early stages practically excluded from our deliberations. It must be confessed also that a certain element of departmental and professional jealousy entered into this discrimination. It was a regrettable factor, and Professor Webster is justified in alluding to it in his contribution to Professor Temperley's standard history. (To a large extent the lack of co-ordination between the several sections of the Delegation was due to actual lack of time : yet to a small extent it was also due to an element of rivalry, to a regrettable but perfectly human fear lest too detailed consultation with other experts would lead, not merely to an increase of work, but to the danger lest others might start poaching on one's own preserves.)

In theory, of course, co-ordination was maintained by the constant circulation throughout the Astoria of the minutes and memoranda of every Committee and Section, as well as of the *procès verbaux* of the Supreme Council. Yet in practice there was little time to study these congested documents, nor would it have been wholly welcome were a member of one section to intervene in the preoccupations of some other section merely because he had come across a document with which he disagreed. A similar jealousy precluded smooth communication between the Delegation and the Embassy in Paris. It is quite true that there was no time for much consultation : it is also true that there was little desire.

I do not wish to exaggerate this aspect of faulty co-ordination. Obviously the relations between the various sections of the Astoria were amicable and courteous to a degree. Obviously also, during those endless meals at the Majestic, much detailed inter-communication was. assured. I merely refer to this element of personal or departmental rivalry, since it does in fact constitute a bar to perfect co-ordination, and since it is a fact inseparable from any organisation containing sections recruited from different services and different departments. It is a factor which participants in any future Congress will have to guard against, or at least to bear in mind.

Such faults as may be noted in respect of co-ordination between the several sections of the Delegation were, however, as nothing compared with the haphazard methods adopted for co-ordination between the Plenipotentiaries and the Delegation as a whole. We were seldom told what to do. We were never told what our rulers were doing. This, in the early stages of the Conference, was wholly inevitable. In the first place, our rulers had not the time to instruct us regarding their own policy : in the second place they did not know that policy themselves : and in the third place, had they known it, they would have been very careful not to disclose it in advance. Nor can I contend that my own work in the political section was in any way hampered by ignorance of our main purposes. I assumed that what was required was a territorial settlement as closely in accordance with the principle of nationality as economic necessity would permit. I also assumed that this requirement was, within reasonable limits, subordinate to the necessity of avoiding any serious breach with the United States or France. Within those limits I was perfectly happy to guide my little skiff without instructions. Yet in other sections of the Delegation this lack of co-ordination between the plenipotentiaries and the technical experts was harmful to a degree. It led to water-tight compartments : it precluded any focussing of responsibility : it led to overlapping : and it led, in extreme cases, to a complete divergence of intention. The economic section, for instance, worked hard at rendering it impossible for Germany to pay those very sums which the reparation section were, with equal industry, preparing to extract. As a result, it was only at the very last moment that our Plenipotentiaries were able to read the Treaty *as a whole*. And it was only then that it dawned upon them that, in the aggregate, the terms were far more Carthaginian than they had ever desired or supposed.

In the later stages of the Conference, Mr. Balfour did in fact hold a regular morning council, at which the heads of the several sections or committees presented reports and obtained instructions for the day. It is my experience of the value of those short meetings which increases my regret that some such system could not have been devised in the earlier stages. The fact that the Bulgarian Treaty, for instance, is less un-intelligent than the German Treaty is largely due to the fact that its main lines were continually discussed, under Mr. Balfour's chairmanship, by those responsible for drafting its various sections. No such co-ordinated and technical discussions preceded the framing of the Treaty of Versailles.

Fortuitous also, and haphazard, was the allocation to the various experts of the subjects with which they were charged. I had myself, for instance, specialised for ten years upon the problems of the Balkans and

South Eastern Europe. Yet I was appointed to the committee on the Czecho-Slovak frontiers, a subject for which I was totally ill-equipped. At a later stage I became concerned in the future of both European and Asiatic Turkey, a subject which should certainly have been left in the more scientific hands of Mr. Arnold Toynbee. Nor am I to this day fully aware how it arose that I found myself so deeply involved in the claims of Italy in the Adriatic, or in the compensations in Asia Minor wherewith we endeavoured to bribe that esurient country into a more moderate frame of mind. These things just 'occurred': a certain official would by chance become convenient, recognisable, available : Mr. Lloyd George did not care over much for 'new faces' : Mr. Balfour liked people who could draft resolutions very quickly. It was owing to such haphazard causes that I was given an amount of work greater than my capacity, and a degree of responsibility wholly unsuited to my experience or my years. Such things ought not to have happened.

3

More important, and more destructive, than any defects of organisation or procedure within the British Delegation, was the structural insufficiency of the main Conference itself. I have already drawn attention to the lamentable result of the rejection by President Wilson of the French proposals of November 29. M. Clemenceau seems to have been unduly discouraged by this rejection, and to have made no further attempt to substitute for the original programme another less realistically worded. It will be difficult

for the future historian to explain the tentative nature
of the Conference in its earlier stages, and he will inevitably be tempted to attribute exaggerated importance to the consideration (which existed but was not
predominant) that the European Powers were ' man-
œuvring for position ' as against the United States. It
is undeniable, and I do not see that it is discreditable,
that the leaders of the Conference desired to avoid
committing themselves on any crucial point until they
had tested President Wilson in minor matters, and
ascertained whether the House interpretation of the
Fourteen Points was really identical with his own. Yet
the real nature of the disorganisation of the Conference
is to be sought for in other directions.

In the first place the Supreme Council of the Conference had inherited the status, and with it the
methods of thought, of the old Supreme War Council.
They had fallen, as I have already said, into the habit
of supposing that their agenda would be imposed by
events and not evolved by processes of their own forethought and selection. A good illustration of this
method of approach is furnished by their relations
with the smaller Powers. They realised, and quite
rightly, that discussions between the whole twenty-
seven States represented in Paris would degenerate
into a farce. They saw from the first that the Five
Great Powers would have to constitute their ' Council
of Ten ' as representing a force of twelve million fully
armed soldiers and sailors. They realised that the
smaller Powers would for this reason have to be excluded from the direction of the Conference. They
recognised the fact that these smaller Powers would
resent such exclusion. And they decided, therefore,

that something should be done to salve, not only the personal feeling of the minor Representatives in Paris, but the nationalist expectations of their Chambers and electorates at home. From the very outset, therefore, a method had to be devised such as would enable the delegates of the smaller Powers to pretend that they were in fact playing some sort of part in the deliberations of the Supreme Council. This method took two forms. In the first place the delegates of the smaller or the succession States were asked to put in writing the territorial and other concessions which they desired to obtain from the Treaty of Peace. In the second place these delegates were each invited in turn orally to expound before the Supreme Council the arguments upon which their claims were based. This entailed a wastage of time and a falsification of proportion. There were in fact fourteen such 'auditions' in February alone, and each absorbed many hours. Inevitably, also, the smaller Powers produced memoranda of claims which were far in excess of their real expectations. Inevitably in expounding these claims orally before the Council they merely repeated what had been written in their Statements, and diminished the powers of resistance which those old gentlemen, in that hot and stuffy room, were able to maintain. This initial wastage of time and energy is a point to which any historian should direct his attention. It gave to the members of the Supreme Council the impression that they were doing valuable and constructive work. Yet in fact they were doing nothing more than suffer, with varying degrees of courtesy, an exhausting and unnecessary imposition.

This particular method, this particular phase of

improvisation had results more important than mere
wastage of time.   By taking as their starting point the
'claims' of the smaller and succession States, from the
very start the Council of Ten falsified the focus of their
attention.   By allowing Greece, Jugo-Slavia, the
Czechs and the other smaller States to inaugurate the
Conference by a statement of claims, they introduced
into the earliest stages of the Conference the problem
of Austria, Hungary, Bulgaria and Turkey.   The
obvious programme would have been to deal suc-
cessively with the Treaties of Peace, taking our late
enemies in order of importance.   We should thus have
concentrated (1) upon the Treaty with Germany,
(2) upon the Treaty with Austria, (3) upon the Treaty
with Hungary, (4) upon the Treaty with Turkey, and
(5) upon the Treaty with Bulgaria.   Yet owing to this
initial muddle about representation all these five
Treaties became confused at the outset.   The claims of
each of the smaller Powers touched, in various degrees,
the territory of each of our late enemies.   It thus arose
that the early weeks of the Conference were occupied
in endless discussions of solutions which would only
become operative in the later treaties.   And that instead
of concentrating their energies and material upon the
essential problem of concluding peace with Germany,
the Supreme Council dissipated their forces in a
simultaneous attempt to provide articles of settlement
with our less important adversaries. This mistake was
one of our major causes of delay, confusion, overlapping and eventual improvisation. This vital error
arose, it must be repeated, from the lack of any agreed
programme.   The proportions of the Conference were
thus vitiated from the start.

Nor is this all. The chance circumstance that the Conference approached its problems in terms, not of the enemy Powers, but of the respective ' claims ' of the succession and smaller States, accounts for much of the overlapping and lack of co-ordination to which I have already alluded. Had a central ' German ' Committee, a central ' Hungarian ' and a central ' Turkish ' Committee been appointed, it is possible that these committees would have approached the problem with a greater realisation of what, in the aggregate, was being taken from our late enemies and a lesser insistence upon what, at separate points, was being given to the succession States.

I shall have more to say about the territorial committees in my final section of this chapter. In my next section I shall consider other aspects of the organisation of the Peace Conference as a whole.

4

It was, as I have said, inevitable and right that the Conference should from the outset have been directed by a Committee or Council of the Five Great Powers. It is regrettable only that this essential necessity was not stated and accepted before the Conference assembled. It was unavoidable also that the time of the Conference should be much occupied by what might be called purely executive matters. This was a further cause of very serious delay, yet I fail to see how it could wholly have been avoided.

There was in the first place the Russian problem. It is beyond the range of these notes to examine whether the Supreme Council dealt wisely with Russia during these months or whether such proposals as that of the Prinkipo Conference were ill-considered and impulsive. The fact remains that Russia was a grave problem which had to be considered from the outset and that this problem could only have been discussed by the leaders of the world in common conference.

There were other executive matters, however, which might well have been referred to some subsidiary body such as the Interallied Council of Versailles. Such matters were the hostilities still existent or threatened in Galicia, Teschen, Carinthia, Poland, and the Baltic States. The observance of the several armistices and the renewal of the German armistice. The repatriation of General Haller's army. The continuance of the Blockade, and the provision of supply and relief to those ex-enemy countries who had now become our allies. The time of the Supreme Council was inordinately wasted by considerations of such subjects, secondary to making peace with Germany. It was not till March 26 that this wholly simple fact seems to have dawned upon M. Clemenceau and President Wilson. ' Instead ' wrote Colonel House, ' of drawing the picture with big lines, they were drawing it like an etching.' This etching process continued through several weeks.

The fact that the Conference was held in Paris rendered it necessary that M. Clemenceau should be the chairman and that the Secrétariat Général and the central bureau should also be under French direction. It has frequently been suggested that M. Clemenceau was, as a chairman, uncontrolling and uncontrolled : that he roused himself from long intervals of somnolence only when the interests of France were affected or when some opportunity arose to bully the Representative of some smaller Power. This accusation is unjust. True it is that the President of the Conference was apt, for long periods at a stretch, to close his ivory eyelids below those surprised, those questing, those interrogatory and those sceptical eyebrows. Yet he did not sleep. True it is that on occasions he would insult the Prime Ministers of the less important Powers with a virulence of attack which brought blushes to the cheeks of all beholders. Yet in fact this rude but sensible octogenarian displayed a faculty of alertness, a power of control, which lesser men, faced with such preponderant personalities, might have hesitated to exert. The fact remains none the less that M. Clemenceau was more concerned with controlling what happened, than with planning how the subjects for discussion should be grouped in the most valuable order. His control was more than adequate, more than merely alert : it was his planning and initiation that were so defective.

This fault on the part of the President of the Conference was reflected in the personality of the Secretary General. By some mischance M. Dutasta—a weak, flustered, surprised but not unamiable man—was chosen for this high position. It was said that he owed his appointment to the intimate relation in which he stood to M. Clemenceau : it was indeed apparent that M. Dutasta would stand from M. Clemenceau a greater degree of abuse and insult than might have been expected from any person more detached. Yet it was a misfortune that a brain such as that of M. Philippe Berthelot was not at the full disposal of the Conference from the start. M. Berthelot, at that moment, was under one of those clouds which from time to time have drifted across his Olympian and sunlit career. He was allowed to suggest : he was not allowed to organise. That supreme capacity for secretarial organisation, which is a by-product of the French genius, was not apparent at the Conference of Paris. The compelling precisions of a Berthelot or a Massigli were reserved for later reunions. At Paris we suffered from the anxious timidity of M. Dutasta, from the fumbling, the owl-like obstinacy of M. Pichon.

This defect in the Secrétariat Général was gradually remedied by the hearty British efficiency of Sir Maurice Hankey. Yet in the early stages it constituted a serious drawback. And for this reason. A really brilliant Secretary, a Gentz or a Massigli, might have remedied the omission of an agreed programme by the constant preparation of intelligent agenda papers. M. Dutasta was too flurried for any such acts of vision or responsibility. He took subjects in their order of temporal urgency, not in their order of actual importance. As a result, the first six weeks of the Conference were wasted in the discussion of *actualités* and were not devoted to the central purposes for which it had been convoked.

The detailed work, the ' tactics,' of the General Secretariat, was admirable in the highest degree. It was the absence of secretarial strategy which failed to provide the Conference with an alternative to their rejected programme.

The Conference of Paris is condemned to-day for ignorance and inefficiency. I question whether that will in fact be the main onus of criticism on the part of posterity. According as the foot-hills of immediate

Conférence de la Paix

Quai D'Orsay

Secrétariat Général

Paris, le IX Juillet 1919

Le Secrétariat Général de la Conférence
de la Paix a l'honneur de faire savoir à L'Hon.
H. NICOLSON que la prochaine réunion du Comité
Central Territorial a été fixée à Mardi prochain
15 Juillet à IO h. du matin.

Ordre du jour : Audition de M. VENISELOS

Lecture du rapport au Conseil
Suprême./.

Monsieur NICOLSON
    Secrétariat de la Délégation
        Britannique.

difficulty subside into the mists of time, the peaks of actual error will emerge more clearly. I have a feeling that the judgment of posterity will concentrate, not upon the errors of the Conference (which were comparatively slight and which are already being remedied) so much as upon its appalling hypocrisy. The causes of this basic insincerity have been indicated in previous chapters : its effects will be referred to in the chapters that follow. Yet under the heading of organisation it is necessary to refer to the highly ingenuous, if not hypocritical, methods by which the problems of the smaller Powers and of the Press were evaded.

I have already indicated how the desire to mitigate the somewhat artificial resentment of the smaller Powers at being excluded from the supreme direction of the Conference led to a falsification of approach, and to a consequent confusion of secondary with major purposes. I now come to the farce of the Plenary Sessions. The smaller Powers were given to understand that the recommendations of the territorial and other Committees of the Conference would be submitted to a Plenary Session at which they would have the opportunity to state their views. In practice, the representatives of these Powers were too intelligent to take this promise very seriously. Yet we of the Committees were less sceptical. We believed that our recommendations would, in the last resort, be submitted to some final form of discussion, in which the interested parties would have their say. We were never for one instant given to suppose that our recommendations were absolutely final. And we thus tended to accept compromises, and even to support decisions, which we ardently hoped would not, in this last resort, be approved. I do not believe that it would in fact have been possible to revise the recommendations of the Committees either in the Council of Ten, nor yet in that of Four, nor yet in Plenary Conference. Mr. Lloyd George's revision of the recommendations of the Polish Committee, although wholly justified, produced in itself an outburst. Yet the fact remains that *we* should have been told that our recommendations were likely to be approved without further discussion, and the smaller Powers should have been told that in effect the Committees would constitute the final court of appeal. Here again was an imprecision of function which produced unfortunate results. It is one to which I shall recur later.

The handling of the Press was also vitiated by a timid compromise of a similar nature. Some 500 special newspaper correspondents had been sent to Paris at very great expense. From the outset, they protested that the covenants which were being negotiated were being secretly arrived at. The Supreme Council were much perturbed by this protest. They decided that the Press should be admitted to all Plenary Meetings. As a result, only six Plenary Meetings were held and, of these, only that which dealt with the Covenant of the League was of anything more than a purely fictitious character. In order to assuage the indignation of their own national correspondents, the plenipotentiaries were thus forced to provide tit-bits of information on their own. This led to mutual accusations of 'leakage' and to much bitter recrimination. Yet here again was an instance of timidity in facing facts. The Press should have been warned before the Conference opened that it would not be worth their while to send special correspondents to Paris. They should have been told that the discussions would have to be conducted in secret, and that only agreed communiqués would be issued for publication. There are only two ways of dealing with a democratic Press. The best way is to tell them everything ; that bores them stiff. The second best way is to tell them nothing, which at least provides them with the glory of a ' secrecy ' stunt, which provides a highly pleasurable form of news value. The worst method is to tell them half-truths in the form of conciliatory leakages. It was this flabby method which was adopted by the Conference of Paris.

Such, among many others, were the errors of organisation which might have been avoided by a little forceful thinking in advance. I draw attention to them, since they are all concerned with difficulties which will arise at any future Congress, and since a future Secretariat might have the foresight and the determination to extract from their plenipotentiaries a definite opinion on these problems before the Congress actually assembles. I now pass to the organisation of Committees, which must always form the working basis of any conference. I deal with the Territorial Committees, since it was as a member of such committees that I had most experience.

5

The Congress of Vienna, after a delay of two and a half months, appointed eight Committees. The Conference of Paris, with equal retardation, appointed fifty-eight. They sat for some six months and held 1646 meetings. Their conclusions were verified by

26 local investigations, and were discussed at 72 meetings of the Council of Ten, at 39 meetings of the
Council of Five, and at 145 meetings of the Council of
Four. I take these figures from M. Tardieu's *Truth
about the Peace Treaty*. They are very impressive. I
do not question their accuracy. Yet in practice the
Committees of the Conference were not so organised,
so supervised, so verified, so magnificent as all that.

In the first place there was much unnecessary delay
in their constitution. It is true that on January 25 five
Committees were appointed to deal with War Guilt
and War Criminals, Reparation, Ports, Waterways and
Railways, Labour and the League of Nations. Yet the
Territorial Committees were not fully constituted till
well on in February, and even then their efficiency was
diminished by the nature of their composition, as well
as by the imprecisions and reservations of their terms
of reference.

These Committees consisted of ten delegates, each
of the Five Great Powers having two representatives
apiece. One, at least, of these two representatives was
what was called a ' technical expert,' or in other words
a person who was supposed to have specialised on the
particular area with which the Committee was appointed to deal. The term ' expert ' has been much
attacked on the ground that in many cases these unhappy specialists had little or no first-hand knowledge
of the countries whose fate they were called upon to
determine. I do not feel that this line of criticism is
wholly justified. On the one hand we had the opportunity to consult people who had either lived all their
lives in the countries which we were regrouping, or
who had devoted years of study to the problems which

we were called upon to solve. Allen Leeper and myself, for instance, never moved a yard without previous consultation with experts of the authority of Dr. Seton Watson who was in Paris at the time. On the other hand I question whether life-long familiarity with a country is always an advantage when it comes to framing decisions which should be wide, impartial, unprejudiced, and adjustable to needs and proportions outside the particular area under discussion. ' A decision ' writes Dr. Day, ' on the merits of alternative frontiers involves not merely a knowledge of details, but also a judgment on the relative importance of different human interests, and a prophetic insight into the future of man's development.' This width of vision is not always found in people who since childhood have lived in Tirana, or whose life's work had been devoted to the problem of the Koutzo-Vlachs. I consider indeed that the charge of ' ignorance ' is but a red herring which distracts attention from what were the essential faults and errors of these Territorial Committees. [It was not knowledge that was lacking : it was guidance, precision, co-ordination, principle and scope.

' To create new boundaries,' writes Colonel House, ' is always to create new trouble.' Obviously the new frontiers of Europe caused intense local indignation and wide-spread inconvenience. Yet the point is that these frontiers *had* to be drawn. Nor do I believe that an informed and objective critic would, if he took full account of the difficulties of the time, come to the conclusion that these new frontiers were, on the whole, unscientific. It must be remembered that we were obliged to operate upon the living flesh of what was still an organism : it was inevitable, and foreseen, that the scars which we created would take some time to heal. The whole economic and transport structure of the Austro-Hungarian Empire had, for instance, been devised to cut across the lines of nationality : the whole purpose of the Conference was to re-establish those lines of nationality : many economic sinews, some arteries even, had thus to be severed : yet this necessity was unavoidable, and amply realised at the time.

It is on far other grounds, therefore, that I should myself criticise the constitution and working of the Territorial Committees. In the first place, as I have already explained, they were appointed *ad hoc*, or in other words they were nominated from day to day, not to deal with any general principle, but to deal with the incidental occurrence that some Ally or some New State had presented a memorandum to the Conference demanding certain territory. The main task of the Committees was not, therefore, to recommend a *general* territorial settlement, but to pronounce on the particular claims of certain States. This empirical and wholly adventitious method of appointment produced unfortunate results. The Committee on Rumanian Claims, for instance, thought only in terms of Transylvania, the Committee on Czech claims concentrated upon the southern frontier of Slovakia. It was only too late that it was realised that these two entirely separate Committees had between them imposed upon Hungary a loss of territory and population which, when combined, was very serious indeed. Had the work been concentrated in the hands of a ' Hungarian ' Committee, not only would a wider area of frontier

been open for the give and take of discussion, but it
would have been seen that the total cessions imposed
placed more Magyars under alien rule than was con-
sonant with the doctrine of Self-Determination. True
it is that, at the last moment, a ' Co-ordination Committee ' was appointed to remedy just this sort of overlapping. Yet by that time it was difficult to revise
decisions arrived at after weeks of exhaustive and exhausting argument, and the members of this Committee, although they effected much, were not in fact
able to introduce any very sweeping revision of the
terms as already contrived.

A second error in the method of appointment, in
the terms of reference, was that the Territorial Committees did not receive from the outset any indication
that their recommendations would in fact be final and
determinant. I have already referred to this point, but
it is so important as to require elaboration. Let me
quote the terms of reference under which the Rumanian
Committee were appointed. They were as follows :
' It was agreed that the questions raised in M.
Bratianu's statement . . . should be referred for examination in the first instance by an expert committee. . . .
It shall be the duty of the Committee to reduce the
questions for decision within the narrowest possible
limits and to make recommendations for a just settlement. . . . The Committee is authorised to consult
the Representatives of the people concerned.' Like so
many resolutions of the Supreme Council these terms
of reference were vague and exclusive to the point of
evasiveness. Moreover, all political questions affecting
any of the Allies (questions such as Klagenfurt and the
Trentino) were withdrawn from the scope of the Com-

mittees, who were naturally led thereby to suppose that their functions were advisory only and in no sense executive. That this was, in fact, the initial intention of the Supreme Council, I have no doubt whatever. Yet, with the sole exception of the Polish Report, all unanimous reports of the Committees were adopted without further discussion, and in cases where the reports were not unanimous the Committees were asked to discuss the matter further with the hope of reaching unanimity. I do not say that the decisive importance in this way acquired by the Committees was either unfortunate or mistaken : I say only that it should have been foreseen from the start, and that the members of each Committee should have been chosen with a previous recognition of the very great responsibility which would inevitably be theirs. They were not so chosen.

A third error was that the Committees were from the first discouraged from expressing any view upon ' principles' or ' politics.' The Greek Committee, for instance, were, under their terms of reference, asked to examine the actual claims of M. Venizelos. They were asked, for instance, to decide whether the area claimed by Greece in the Smyrna region was one which accorded with the zones of Greek population : they were not asked whether it was a wise or an unwise thing to allow the Greeks into Asia Minor at all. No guidance was, moreover, given us as to the inevitable conflict between ' self-determination ' and ' economics.' The French were always insisting that our main duty was to render the New States what they called ' *viables*,' or in other words to provide them with those essentials of security, transport and economic resources without which they would be unable to establish their independence. We were never told how far we were to accept this argument. Nor was any guidance accorded on the point whether 'historical' claims should be admitted (the Italians, for instance, showed a marked predeliction for the Empire of Hadrian), or whether the principle of the 'Sanctity of Treaties' (generally the Secret Treaties) was in fact to be maintained. As a result, all these principles were cited together to justify our recommendations. In their counter-proposals of May 29 the Germans were fully justified in contending that the territorial settlement was at one moment based on the principle of self-determination, at another on that of economic necessity, and at another on that of 'immemorial historic right'—and that 'in every case the decision is against Germany.' It was in this manner, by a succession of tiny compromises, by an accumulation of incidental arguments based on false principle, that the structure of Wilsonism was, brick by brick, undermined. Here again the process was the result, not so much of evil intention, as of persistent vagueness of purpose.

The fourth error, and one which lies at the root of the whole failure of the Conference, was that we were not obliged in every case to have our recommendations vetoed by the economists. True it is that, in moments of acute difficulty, we would privately consult individual experts on such subjects as rail and water transport. I can recollect how General Mance was able, in one instance, to prove to me how, with very little expense, an alternative railway could be constructed in Slovakia whereby many thousand Magyars would be saved from incorporation. Yet in general we did not take economic considerations into sufficient account. And our omission to do so caused much suffering to many millions.

I do not say that the Supreme Council were wholly to blame for these our shortcomings. The fault lay rather with the inadequacy of our own vision and mental equipment. (I contend only that here also was a point at which the ' absence of a central focus ' threw our labours out of proper perspective and marred the entirety of the plan.) In all peacemaking the provision of such a ' central focus ' is absolutely essential. Let it be hoped that a similar error will not be made again.

It is with horror that I look back to-day upon those endless Committees in the high hot saloons of the Quai d'Orsay. A group of little men at the end of a vast table : maps, interpreters, secretaries, and row upon row of empty gilt chairs. The great red curtains are drawn, scarlet and enclosing against the twilight sinking gently upon the Seine. The chandeliers blaze with all the emphasis of the Latin genius. To the adjoining banqueting hall we adjourn for a few minutes, for tea, brioches and macaroons. It is a large, slim room, and the tea-urn gutters in the draught. Then back again to our long table. ' *Messieurs, nous avons donc examiné la frontière entre Csepany et Saros Patåg. Il résulte que la jonction du chemin de fer Miskovec-Kaschau avec la ligne St. Peter-Losoncz doit être attribuée . . .*' On returning to the Majestic the sounds of dance music would reach us from the ballroom.

Chapter VI

QUARREL

The Secret Treaties—The Rumanian Treaty of 1916—History of Rumanian entries and exits from the war—M. Také Jonescu— M. Bratianu—His unfortunate behaviour at the Peace Conference— Digression regarding the nature of secret treaties, the danger of ethical assumptions, and the proper equipment of Peacemakers whether young or old—The lesser Secret Treaties—Conflict between our promises to the Arabs and the Sykes-Picot agreement—Resultant Anglo-French disputes in Paris—The Syrian and Mosul questions—Shantung— President Wilson's false position—Other inter-allied quarrels—The case of Montenegro—Self-Determination—Scenario of the Peace Conference.

I

THE Secret Treaties concluded during the war with our actual or potential Allies were, as I have already said, among the major embarrassments which restricted liberty of action at the Peace Conference. The most encumbering of all these Treaties was that by which, in April of 1915, we had bribed Italy to desert the Triple Alliance and to adhere to the cause of the Western Powers. That Treaty, which is known as the 'Treaty of London,' will be discussed in the next chapter when I come to consider the effect upon the principles of Mr. Wilson of the 'sacro egoismo' of Orlando and Sonnino. In the present chapter I wish to examine the difficulties and delays created by the other, and perhaps less central, disputes which arose between the Allied and Associated Powers in Conference assembled. In order that these disputes may be appreciated in their proper proportion, it will be necessary to make some reference to the secondary Secret Treaties in which we were also entangled.

I shall take these Treaties and their resultant complication in ascending order of importance, beginning with the most negligible, and concluding with those which, if we except the Italian Treaties, caused the greatest degree of trouble.

I shall thus begin with the Rumanian Treaty of August 17, 1916. The story of this Treaty is as follows: On October 30, 1883, a Treaty had been concluded between Count Andrassy and the elder M. Bratianu whereby Rumania adhered to the Triple Alliance between Germany, Austria-Hungary, and Italy. Although this Treaty had never been ratified by the Rumanian Parliament, King Charles of Rumania, being a Hohenzollern and a man of honour, was desirous, at the outbreak of the European war, to fulfil his Treaty engagements and to join forces with Germany. For this purpose he summoned a Crown Council to the pine-clad recesses of Sinaia. M. Carp, the leader of the Conservatives agreed with King Charles. The younger Bratianu, the leader of the Liberals, adopted an unfilial attitude, and contended that the Treaty with Germany should be ignored. M. Také Jonescu, the leader of the Conservative Democratic Party, urged immediate intervention on the side of the Entente. It was decided, in view of this divergence between the political leaders, that an attitude of 'watchful neutrality' should be followed. M. Bratianu, maintained this expectant attitude for two years. The successful offensive of General Brusiloff in June of 1916 persuaded him that the moment for intervention had at last arrived.

Negotiations were opened with the Entente Powers and Rumania's price was stated in no modest terms. She was to obtain the whole of Transylvania and the whole of the Bukowina south of the Dniester. She was also to obtain the whole of the Banat of Temesvar, as far as the Theiss. Under Article VI she was to enjoy ' the same rights as her allies ' in regard to negotiation and discussion at the eventual Peace Conference. Under Article V the parties to the Treaty pledged themselves not to conclude a separate peace.

On August 27 Rumania entered the war, and with triumphant foolishness advanced far into Transylvania. The retaliation of the Central Powers was short and sharp. The Germans entered Bucharest on December 6. The Rumanian army retired to Moldavia, and under the guidance of General Berthelot, maintained a very courageous defensive for twelve months longer. The outbreak of the Russian Revolution destroyed all further hope of resistance. M. Bratianu, having endeavoured in vain to induce his Allies to release him from the obligations of Article V, was obliged to conclude an armistice on December 9, 1917, and to sign the separate and capitulatory Peace of Bucharest on May 7 following. Under this Treaty Rumania was forced to cede practically the whole of the Dobrudja and to place herself under the economic protectorate of the Central Powers. This Treaty was never ratified by the Rumanian Parliament.

On November 9, 1918, two days before the final armistice, Rumania repudiated the Treaty of May 7, and again declared war upon Germany. The grounds of this renewed declaration were an alleged violation on the part of Germany of the Treaty of Bucharest.

By adducing these grounds the Rumanian Government committed themselves to the admission that that Treaty, although still unratified, was yet a valid instrument. This was for them a most unfortunate admission.

The resultant situation was typical of the sort of problems which the Peace Conference had to face. M. Bratianu contended that the secret Treaty between Rumania and the victorious Allies of August 1916 remained fully valid. He therefore claimed not Transylvania only, but the whole of the Banat. He also claimed, under Article VI of the Secret Treaty, to be accorded the status of equality with the Representatives of the Great Powers. The latter relished none of these contentions. They did not mind so much about Transylvania and the Bukowina (which belonged to the enemy), but they minded terribly about the Banat which was claimed, and with considerable justice, by the Jugo-Slavs. Moreover the thought of Rumania, and especially of M. Bratianu, aspiring to the status of a Great Power was an agony to the soul. They thus made it abundantly clear to M. Bratianu that, by concluding a separate peace with Germany in May of 1918, Rumania had violated Article V of the original Treaty of August 1916 and had thereby rendered that Treaty null and void.

M. Také Jonescu, it must be admitted, being a man of European discernment, had foreseen from the outset that this would be the attitude of the Conference and that against such an attitude, which was justified in law, it was useless to protest. He had in November hurried off to London and Paris and had succeeded, with the help of M. Venizelos, in negotiating with

M. Pasic a very sensible line by which the Banat would be partitioned between Jugo-Slavia and Rumania on a basis of nationality. He had gone further. He had sketched the lines of a Balkan agreement, under which the four Balkan States would compose all their own differences and pledge themselves to support each other against the anticipated dictation of the Great Powers. Such a Balkan bloc would in fact have drawn Czecho-slovakia, and perhaps even Poland, into its orbit and have constituted a very powerful element at the Peace Conference. M. Bratianu, however, refused to share M. Také Jonescu's view. The latter was not included in the Rumanian delegation to Paris. He remained at the Hotel Meurice shaking his neat head over the follies, the vanities and the obstinate blindness of M. Bratianu. And the latter so mishandled the Rumanian case at the Conference that he estranged the most ardent friends of Rumania and in the end had to be dismissed from office by what amounted to an ultimatum on the part of the Supreme Council.

The above little story is, from the point of view of this record, more important than it may seem. It has frequently been contended that the members of the Supreme Council were all too sensitive to personal considerations, and that the charm and genius of M. Venizelos (to cite an obvious example) obtained for Greece concessions which a man of less supreme diplomatic ability could scarcely have secured. Far be it from me to diminish in any way the legend of M. Venizelos' consummate mastery of diplomatic technique, or in any way to underestimate the triumph which the personal magnetism of that statesman achieved. It must be observed, however, in justice to the Supreme Council, that their decisions were not in fact wholly governed by subjective emotions. The Bratianu incident is valuable as a proof of their objectivity. No man could have been more foolish, unreasonable, irritating or provocative than Ion Bratianu. And yet the almost universal antipathy which he inspired did not, in fact, prejudice the claims of his country at the Peace Conference. Rumania obtained ' all and more than all.' And she obtained this on wholly impersonal grounds.

2

I assume, and hope, that the future student of the Peace Conference will rid himself in advance of all emotional or ethical affects which the term ' Secret Treaties ' may induce. He will, I believe, be sensible enough to realise that in the heat of belligerency statesmen are apt to grasp at any bargain such as may minister to the successful prosecution of war. They have done so in the past ; they will continue to do so in the future. Nor is it sensible to suppose that any statesman would commit his country to joining in a war upon the side of an already existing coalition, without having first obtained in writing from that coalition such pledges as would ensure that he would, if victorious, obtain some proportion of the spoils. Still less is it reasonable to demand that the terms of such a contract should be broadcast from the outset. In fact the objection to the Treaties concluded with our Allies during the course of the War is not that they were secret, but that they were unscientific and in many cases mutually contradictory.

People who study the past under the conviction that

they themselves would automatically behave better in the present are adopting a dangerous habit of mind. They are importing the ethical standards of tranquillity into the emotional atmosphere of danger. It would be better were the student of international affairs to concentrate less upon comparative ethics and more upon the problem of human behaviour at periods when humanity is strained. Highmindedness, once it becomes involved in the machines of human necessity, is not strong enough. Other reinforcements, when it comes to peacemaking, are also required. The elder statesman will need foresight, planning, rigid programmes, time, obduracy, independence, method, and a faculty for insisting upon the most inconvenient precisions. He will also require a trained and numerous staff of expert assistants. What qualities should these experts possess ? They should possess the following qualities : health, rapidity of understanding, patience, comparative sanity, great physical endurance, charm, no class-prejudice either up or down, immense curiosity, a neat manner with maps and papers, industry, accuracy, the power to ask inconvenient questions at the wrong moment, no very outstanding physical disadvantages, intimacy with the Private Secretaries of their own Plenipotentiaries, the good taste to disguise that intimacy, some acquaintance with the more obscure press correspondents (N.B. The less obscure correspondents will tend to reject that acquaintance), the habit of looking upwards and not downwards when they don't know the answer, courtesy, being able to type and affix carbon papers, a slight but not obtrusive acquaintance with economics, cleanliness, sobriety on all fitting occasions, cheerfulness, statistics derived from sources even more recondite and anonymous than those possessed by their foreign colleagues, some proficiency in the literature or architecture of at least one very oppressed nationality, a capacity for enduring long dinner parties, honesty, a faculty of speaking rapidly and well such languages as their foreign colleagues do not speak rapidly or well, no consummate belief in the immediate wisdom of the People or the Press, a good memory, truthfulness, and above all, a complete sterilisation of all human vanity. Only if he possess all the above qualities can a young man hope to be of real assistance to his superiors in the negotiation of a peace of justice, equity, and duration.

I return from this digression to the subject of the Secret Treaties and the resultant disputes between the Allies themselves. It is not possible, within the scope of these notes, to indicate the exact proportion of time and energy which was absorbed by these internecine quarrels. I should say that some 30 per cent of the total energy of the Supreme Council was taken up by executive functions, that some 10 per cent was wasted on unnecessary detail, and that some 40 per cent was devoted to preventing a breach between one or other of the Allies. The remaining 20 per cent was expended upon the task of making peace.

Of the other Secret Treaties, that under which we promised Constantinople to Russia had been denounced by the Soviet Government. The Franco-Russian Treaty of March 11, 1917 (by which, in return for a free hand in Poland, Russia guaranteed to France not only Alsace-Lorraine and the Saar Valley, but also an independent Rhineland garrisoned by a French Army), had also lapsed. Apart from the two Italian Treaties of

London and St. Jean de Maurienne (which will be dealt with in the next chapter) there remain our agreement with the Arabs, the Sykes-Picot agreement with the French, and our undertaking to Japan that we should support her claim to inherit all rights possessed by Germany in the province of Shantung.

It is not my purpose to deal in any detail with these treaties, and the complications which they produced, since I was in no way personally concerned with any of these developments. It is necessary, however, that they should be mentioned, since it was largely through them that an atmosphere of discord and disorder was introduced into the Conference, and since it was in the tense and hectic atmosphere thus created that all our later negotiations were carried on.

Our pledges to the Arabs, conflicting as they did with the promises we made to France in the subsequent Sykes-Picot agreement, produced a triangular situation of great embarrassment as between the French, President Wilson and ourselves. The main factors in this situation were as follows. Between October 1914 and November 1915 messages had been exchanged between the British High Commissioner in Cairo and the Sherif of Mecca, subsequently King Hussein of the Hedjaz. These communications were shrouded in the ambiguity inseparable from all oriental correspondence, yet the impression left on the mind of King Hussein was that Great Britain had assured him support in the foundation of an united Arab Empire with its capital at Damascus. It is true that in the course of the correspondence the British Government (who were bound by an understanding with France dating from 1912 to ' disinterest themselves ' in Syria) had made some vague

reservation about Damascus. This reservation, however, had not been studiously precise, and it is significant that the subsequent Sykes-Picot agreement was
not communicated by us to the Arabs, even as our
pledges to King Hussein were not, until March of
1919, disclosed to the French.

With the outbreak of the Arab revolution in May of
1916 the French Government became anxious lest what
they regarded as their prescriptive rights to Syria and
Cilicia might be jeopardised. In order to quieten them
an arrangement was negotiated and signed between
M. Georges Picot and Sir Mark Sykes on May 16, 1916.
This agreement provided in effect for the partition of
Asia Minor, as well as of the Arab portions of the Ottoman Empire, between Russia, France and ourselves.
We were to obtain Mesopotamia, the French Syria, and
the Russians Armenia and Kurdistan. The territory
between the French and British slices was to be left to
the Arab Empire, but was to be subdivided into French
and British zones of influence. The Italians were
excluded from any share in these partitions.

On October 3, 1918, the Amir Feisal, accompanied
by Colonel T. E. Lawrence, galloped into Damascus
at the head of 1,500 Arab cavalry and hoisted the Arab
standard. This was an extremely awkward thing to
have happened. The wires buzzed between London
and Paris and a series of joint communiqués were
issued. The matter was also raised during M. Clemenceau's visit to London. Yet by the time the Conference
assembled French public opinion was already ' partant
pour la Syrie ' and the British Government were faced
with the alternative of breaking either their vague
promises to the Arabs or else their more explicit

engagements to the French. The matter in fact narrowed itself down to the Homs, Hama, Aleppo line, the attribution of Mosul, and the eventual destination of Palestine. These details need not concern us. What is interesting from the point of view of this chronicle is that the Arab question involved Mr. Lloyd George, M. Clemenceau and President Wilson in three different but extremely unpleasant predicaments. Mr. Lloyd George did not see why we, having conquered Syria, should hand it over, with increased frontiers, and in violation of our implicit promises to the Arabs. M. Clemenceau did not know how he would be able to still the clamour of the French Colonial Party without causing a breach with Great Britain. And President Wilson, who was informed by Dr. Howard Bliss and others that the Syrians did not in any sense desire even a French ' mandate,' was much exercised how to reconcile this disinclination on their part with, on the one hand, the doctrine of self-determination, and, on the other hand, the undoubted fact that France and Great Britain had pledged themselves by treaty to a solution by which that doctrine would be flagrantly violated.

The controversy smouldered during the months of January and February. The Emir Feisal was granted an ' audition ' before the Council of Ten. ' His voice,' records Mr. Lansing, ' seemed to breathe the perfume of frankincense.' And Colonel T. E. Lawrence the while would glide along the corridors of the Majestic, the lines of resentment hardening around his boyish lips : an undergraduate with a chin.

The dispute culminated at a meeting which took place in the Rue Nitot on March 20, 1919. Mr. Lloyd

George stated that if Damascus, Homs, Hama and Aleppo were included in the sphere of direct French administration, then the British would have broken faith with the Arabs. Lord Allenby, who was also present, went further. He expressed the view that if the French were imposed upon an unwilling Syria, ' there would be trouble, and even war.' M. Pichon said that France could not release Great Britain from the terms of a solemn agreement merely because these terms conflicted with previous obligations entered into with a third party, of which obligations France had not been informed at the time. President Wilson (and it was almost the last occasion on which he stood by his principles) said that it was a matter of complete indifference to him what France and Great Britain had decided in the form of Secret Treaty : they had since then accepted the Fourteen Points : they were thus obliged, whatever their previous engagements, to consider only the wishes of the populations concerned : there was some doubt about these wishes : according to M. Chukri Ganem (a Syriac poet of Paris, who, although he had not set foot in Syria for twenty years, had been produced by M. Pichon as the spokesman of the Syrian Arabs) the whole heart of Syria was pulsating with but one hope—that of a French mandate : according to the Emir Feisal the Syrians had no partiality for anything other than their own independence : these divergencies could only be reconciled by an ' Enquiry.' Somewhat reluctantly the assembled delegates agreed to a Commission of Enquiry. Mr. King and Mr. Crane were, in fact, despatched to the Middle East in the month of July. Their report, when eventually received, was a highly inconvenient document. But by that date President Wilson had left Paris for his final collapse. And the King-Crane report was buried under the dust of subsequent diplomacy.

Although President Wilson was in this way able to shelve the Syrian problem without any overt breach between France and Great Britain, and without ostensibly violating the Fourteen Points, no such possibility of evasion was open to him in the matter of Shantung. That also is an episode which must be explained.

In the early months of 1917 the British Admiralty were finding it increasingly difficult to provide surface vessels for the convoy of troopships and food ships through the Mediterranean. They applied to Japan for a flotilla of torpedo boats to assist them in discharging that duty. The Japanese Government replied that they would only furnish such assistance to their Ally on condition that they were promised not only the German Pacific Islands north of the Equator, but also all rights possessed by Germany at Kiao Chau and in the Chinese province of Shantung. A Treaty promising them our support in obtaining this booty was signed on February 16, 1917. The French subsequently adhered to this Treaty in return for a withdrawal on the part of Japan of the veto which she had hitherto maintained against China being allowed to enter the war upon the side of the Allies. The situation was further complicated by the ' Twenty-One Demands ' which Japan had enforced on China in January of 1915, as well as by the Sino-Japanese arrangements of May 25, 1915, and September 24, 1918. I am less concerned, however, with the details of this dispute than with its effects upon the Peace Conference. These effects were damaging in the extreme.

Let us state the issue in its simplest terms. The Japanese desired to obtain from a fellow-ally, namely China, certain privileges which that ally was determined to refuse. Japan, in her insistence upon these demands, claimed the support of France and Great Britain on the basis of the Secret Treaty. China, in maintaining her refusal, based her case upon the unquestionable fact that the demands of Japan were a flagrant violation of the principles of President Wilson. Japan then threatened to withdraw from the Conference unless her demands were accepted. What was the President to do?

Mr. Wilson's position was complicated by two considerations. In the first place he had, in the early stages of the League of Nations Committee, been faced by a most awkward dilemma. On February 13 the Japanese had suggested that in the clause providing for religious equality the words ' and racial ' should be inserted between the word ' religious ' and the word ' equality.' They were persuaded to drop this painful amendment for the moment, but they again revived it on April 11. Mr. Wilson then found himself in a grave difficulty. On the one hand the Equality of Man, as enshrined in the Covenant, implied the equality of the yellow man with the white man, might even imply the terrific theory of the equality of the white man with the black. On the other hand no American Senate would ever dream of ratifying any Covenant which enshrined so dangerous a principle. On that occasion the President had, by the skin of his teeth, been rescued by Mr. Hughes of Australia. The latter insisted that no such nonsensical theory as the equality of races should figure in the Covenant. Lord Cecil was instructed by the British Empire Delegation to support Mr. Hughes' contention in the League Committee. The Japanese, however, were not prepared to allow Mr. Wilson this providential alibi. They put the matter to the vote. They gained their point by eleven votes to six. Mr. Wilson, as chairman, was faced with the unpleasant necessity of having to decree that the Japanese amendment had ' not been adopted ' since it had failed to secure ' unanimous approval.' That incident had left even him with an uneasy feeling inside.

In the second place the Japanese had timed their stand upon the Shantung settlement with exquisite cunning. They had chosen the very moment when Italy had abandoned the Peace Conference because of the alleged intransigence of President Wilson. Could the President afford (for the wind of criticism was already howling dismally around his ears) to permit a further defection from the Conference when the Germans were already waiting behind their spile fences at Versailles ? He was in a minority of one. He surrendered. A compromise was achieved which, in effect, gave to Japan everything that she desired. Of all the defeats of President Wilson, the Shantung settlement was the most flagrant. How bitterly must he then have regretted that he refused to accept, or perhaps even to read, the scheme of procedure which had been handed to him by M. Jusserand on November 29. However much that programme might have jarred upon his vague but authoritative mind, it contained one clause at least which, had it been adopted, would have been a boon of inestimable blessing. It provided that all Treaties concluded before the Armistice should be regarded as null and void. Yet to the memorandum of M. Jusserand the President had omitted even to return an answer.

It is almost pathetic to read in the pages of Mr. Stannard Baker the terms in which Mr. Wilson himself justified his palpable surrender over Shantung. He evolved in his mind the theory that if Japan had been forced out of the Conference she would at once have concluded a military alliance with Russia and Germany. ' I know,' he said, ' that I shall be accused of violating my own principles. Yet nevertheless I *must* work for world order and organisation against anarchy and a return to the old militarism.'

3

In discussing the Shantung settlement I have anticipated tragedies which might more conveniently figure in the last chapter of this book, in which I shall deal with the collapse of America. The Shantung incident is, however, so illustrative of the effect upon the Wilsonian doctrine of these incessant and complicated quarrels, that I have felt bound to include it in the present chapter which deals predominantly with the extreme difficulty, not so much of making peace with the enemy, as of maintaining peace between the Allies.

Apart from the divergence of opinion upon such central problems as French Security, the Rhineland, Reparation, the Saar Valley, the disposal of the German Fleet, the Blockade, Conscription, and the Polish frontier, the energies of the Supreme Council were incessantly being tapped and wasted by petty problems arising from disagreements between the smaller Powers.

These lesser difficulties did not all owe their origin to the Secret Treaties. Some of them represented disputes of long standing : others were created by the sudden emergence of New States or the sudden extension of Old States, each claiming sole occupation of such areas of former enemy territory as contained populations of mixed nationality. There was thus the dispute between Rumania and Jugoslavia in regard to the Banat. The dispute between the Poles and the Czechs in regard to the Duchy of Teschen. The difference of opinion between the Rumanians and the Czechs regarding the Carpatho-Russians and the Ruthenes. The germs of a very serious dispute between the Poles and Lithuania. The wary uncertainty with which the Great Powers skirted the question of the future of Constantinople and the Straits. The problem of Armenia. The problem of allocating Mandates among the several Powers and Dominions. The difficulty between Greece and Jugoslavia on the subject of Albania and Salonica. And in addition the endless inter-allied difficulties which centred around the Italian problem and which, for this reason, will be considered in the next chapter.

As an illustration, or type, of these secondary problems I shall take one which is interesting in itself and which has already been forgotten. I shall take the question of Montenegro. Few of the smaller problems caused us such heart-searching and left us with so durable a sense of dissatisfaction.

Montenegro before the war had constituted a small, independent and impoverished principality under the patriarchal rule of King Nikita of the Petrovic dynasty. Her one national aim had been to secure union with

her Serb brethren from whom she had been separated
by Austria and the Sandjak of Novi Bazar. On the
invasion of Serbia and Montenegro by the Austro-
German armies King Nikita had transferred himself to
Neuilly where he lived in a modest but not uncom-
plaining fashion upon subsidies provided by the French,
Russian and British Governments. At the same time
he despatched his second son to Vienna with the intention, it was said, of reinsuring his own position, and the
future of his dynasty, in the event of the victory of the
Central Powers. King Nikita, although the father-in-
law of the King of Italy, was not a sovereign who
inspired very universal respect. It was said that at the
time of the first Balkan War he had risked upsetting
the whole scheme of the Balkan alliance by anticipating
by twenty-four hours his declaration of war upon
Turkey. It was also said that his reason for this impulsive gesture was a ' bear ' operation upon the Vienna
bourse. It was suggested that during the Great War
he had not accorded to his Serbian brethren that energy
of support which they had the right to expect, and the
willing surrender of the fortress of Mount Lovcen was
by them attributed to the financial rather than the
military aptitudes of ' The Peasant King.' The fact
remains that on the withdrawal of the Austrian forces
from Serbia and Montenegro a Government was
established in the latter state which summoned a
' National Assembly ' at Podgoritza and obtained a vote
for immediate union with Serbia, and the deposition of
King Nikita and the whole Petrovic dynasty.

When the Paris Conference assembled there were
thus two Montenegrin delegations, each claiming the
right to represent their country. The one, headed by

M. Radovic, claimed to have been duly constituted by the Podgoritza Assembly. The other, nominated by King Nikita (who had by then in indignant trepidation transferred himself from Neuilly to the Hotel Meurice), contested this claim and contended that the Podgoritza Assembly was a packed body, and that it had voted under the menace of Serbian bayonets. M. Radovic was loud in his assertions that all that Montenegro now desired was complete absorption in Jugoslavia under the rule of the Prince Regent Alexander. King Nikita, on the other hand, contended that the Montenegrins did not desire absorption within the bosoms of their Serb, Croat and Slovene brethren, but merely some loose form of federation, such as would enable them to retain their independence and, what was most important, their Petrovic dynasty, in the person of Nikita himself.

Now although we of the British Delegation had small sympathy for King Nikita, and although we felt that it was an economic necessity for Montenegro to enter the Jugoslav Union, yet we had a suspicion that the Podgoritza Assembly had in fact been convoked by the Serbian gendarmes, and that it did not, in fact, represent the wishes of the Montenegrin people as a whole. We went so far in our anxiety as to despatch Count de Salis to Cettinje to ascertain the facts. He reported that the Podgoritza Assembly was in fact a farce, and that although the Montenegrins were quite willing to enter the Jugoslav Union they would prefer to do so, not under the persuasion of Serb bayonets, but on their own conditions and as a free people.

In view of this quandary the Conference hedged in a manner which was highly characteristic. Montenegro

was, it is true, represented at the Plenary Sessions of
the Conference, but she was represented only by an
empty gilt chair and a white card on the blotting pad.
' Montenegro,' thus ran the communiqué of the Supreme Council of January 15, ' shall be represented by
one delegate, but the rules concerning the designation
of that delegate shall not be fixed until the moment
when the political situation of the country shall have
been elucidated.'

There, in so far as the Conference was concerned, the
matter remained. The cause of Montenegro in the
shape of King Nikita was, however, espoused in England by Mr. Ronald McNeill. For years the argument
continued. We sent out Professor Temperley to in-
vestigate. We sent out Mr. Roland Bryce. And in the
end, not without some lingering qualms, we accepted
the ' union ' of Montenegro with Jugoslavia on the
basis of the Montenegrin elections to the constituent
Assembly. And on March 1, 1921, King Nikita died.

The story of the submergence, or as Lord Cushen-
dun would say, the suppression, of Montenegro, is not
a very pleasant story. I record it not merely because it
furnishes a good instance of the type of minor problem
with which we were continually faced, but because it
raised in my own mind a very serious conflict of
motives. I disliked and distrusted King Nikita, yet I
felt he was almost in the right. I had a passion for the
Jugoslav State, and yet I felt they had behaved badly
about all those bayonets and that Podgoritza Assembly.
I knew that it would be better in the long run, for
economic and political reasons, were Montenegro in
fact to be absorbed by Serbia, or, as we then preferred
to phrase it, ' admitted into close union with the Serb,

Croat and Slovene State.' Yet I felt extremely uncertain whether such a solution was in fact that desired by the Montenegrin people themselves. Here was a case in which dynastic interests on the one hand, were balanced against the union of a fine and liberated people. It was awkward to reflect that the balance of right inclined towards the dynasty, and the balance of wrong towards the Serbian liberators. It was in connection with this problem of Montenegro that my early faith in Self-Determination as the remedy for all human ills became clouded with doubts and reservations.

4

It is not easy, when using the silent machinery of printed words, to reproduce the double stress of turmoil and time-pressure which in Paris constituted the main obstruction to calm thinking or planned procedure. One writes the sentence : ' It was a period of unremitting strain.' The sedative notes of such a sentence, as applied to the scurrying cacophony of the Peace Conference, forces one to smile. Only through the medium of a sound film could any accurate impression, that sense of riot in a parrot house, be conveyed.

Were I to sketch such a scenario of my own impressions, the result would be something as follows. As a recurrent undertone throughout would run the rumble of Time's winged chariot : incessantly reiterant would come the motif of this time-pressure—newspapers screaming in headlines against the Dawdlers of Paris, the clamour for demobilisation, ' Get the Boys back,' the starving millions of Central Europe, the slouching queues of prisoners still behind their barbed wire, the flames of communism flaring, now from Munich, and

now from Buda Pesth. Through this recurrent grumble
and rumble of the time-motif would pierce the sharper
discordances of other sounds : the machine-gun rattle
of a million typewriters, the incessant shrilling of telephones, the clatter of motor bicycles, the drone of aeroplanes, the cold voices of interpreters, ' le délégué des
Etats-Unis constate qu'il ne peut se ranger . . . ' the
blare of trumpets, the thunder of guns saluting at the
Invalides, the rustling of files, a woman in a black
woollen shawl singing ' Madelon ' in front of a café,
the crackle of Rolls Royces upon the gravel of sump-
tuous courtyards, and throughout the sound of foot-
steps hurrying now upon the parquet of some gallery,
now upon the stone stairway of some Ministry, and
now muffled on the heavy Aubusson of some overheated saloon.

These sound-motifs would be accompanied by a
rapid projection of disjointed pictures. The tired and
contemptuous eyelids of Clemenceau, the black button-
boots of Woodrow Wilson, the rotund and jovial
gestures of Mr. Lloyd George's hands, the infinite
languor of Mr. Balfour slowly uncrossing his knees, a
succession of secretaries and experts bending forward
with maps, Foch striding stockily with Weygand
hurrying behind. The silver chains of the huissiers at
the Quai d'Orsay. Such portraits would be interspersed
with files, agenda papers, resolutions, *procès verbaux*
and communiqués. These would succeed each other
with extreme rapidity, and from time to time would
have to be synchronised and superimposed. ' The
Plenipotentiaries of the United States of America, of
the British Empire, of France, of Italy and of Japan, of
the one part . . . It is resolved that subject to the

approval of the Houses of Congress the President of
the United States of America accepts on behalf of the
United States . . . Si cette frontière était prise en
considération, il serait nécessaire de faire la correction
indiquée en bleu. Autrement le chemin de fer vers
Kaschau serait coupé . . . These coupons will be
accepted in settlement of the table d'hôte meals of the
hotel, the whole ticket is to be given up at dinner. . . .
M. Venizelos told me last night that he had concluded
his agreement with Italy in the following terms :
(1) Italy will support Greek claims in Northern Epirus.
. . . From the point where the western boundary of the
area leaves the Drave in a northerly direction as far as
the point about one kilometre to the east of Rosegg
(Saint Michael). The course of the Drave downstream. Thence in a north-easterly direction and as
far as the western extremity of the Wörthersee, south
of Vlelden. A line to be fixed on the ground. The
median line of that lake. Thence eastwards to its
confluence with the river Glan. The course of the
Glanfurt downstream. . . . (1) Audition de M. Dmo-
sky. (2) Rapport de la Commission Interalliée de
Teschen. (3) Le rapatriement des troupes du Général
Haller. (4) Rapport de M. Hoover. (5) Prisonniers de
guerre. (6) Répartition de la marine marchande alle-
mande. . . . From the coming into force of the present
Treaty the High Contracting Parties shall renew, in so
far as concerns them, and under the reserves indicated
in the second paragraph of the present Article, the con-
ventions and arrangements signed at Berne on
October 14, 1890, September 20, 1893, July 16, 1895,
June 16, 1898, and September 19, 1906, regarding the
transportation of goods by rail. If within five years of

the coming into force of the present Treaty . . . Le traité concernant l'entrée de la Bavière dans la Confédération de l'Allemagne du Nord, conclu à Versailles le 23 novembre 1870, contient, dans les articles 7 et 8 du protocole final, des dispositions toujours en vigueur, reconnaissant. . . . A meeting of the British Empire Delegation will be held on Tuesday the 14th instant at the Villa Majestic at 11.30 a.m. . . . Dr. Nansen came to see me this morning. He represents the urgent necessity of inducing the Supreme Council . . . An entertainment will be held on Saturday next at 9.30 p.m. in the Ball Room of the Hotel Majestic in aid of the Dockland Settlement. Miss Ruth Draper has kindly consented to give us two of her well-known character sketches. Tickets may be obtained from the hall-porter—Le Baron Sonnino estimait qu'il y avait lieu d'établir une distinction entre les représentants des Soviets et ceux des autres Gouvernements. Les Alliés combattaient les bolcheviks et les considéraient comme des ennemis. Il n'en était pas de même en ce qui concernait les Finlandais, les Lettons. . . . Telegram from Vienna. Count Karolyi has resigned and according to telephone message received by Mr. Coolidge this morning from his representative at Buda Pesth communist government has been formed under leadership of Bela Kun. Fate of Allied Missions uncertain. . . . Wir wissen das die Gewalt der deutschen Waffen gebrochen ist. Wir kennen die Macht des Hasses, die uns hier entgegentritt, und wir haben die leidenschaftliche Förderung gehört, dass die Sieger uns zugleich als Ueberwundene zahlen lassen und als Schuldige bestrafen sollen. . . . '

A rapid succession of such captions, accompanied

by the whole scale of sound which I have indicated, would furnish a clearer picture of the atmosphere of the Peace Conference than any chronological record in terms of the printed word. Could colour, scent and touch be added, the picture would be almost complete. The dominant note is black and white, heavy black suits, white cuffs and paper : it is relieved by blue and khaki : the only other colours would be the scarlet damask of the Quai d'Orsay curtains, green baize, pink blotting pads, and the innumerable gilt of little chairs. For smells you would have petrol, typewriting ribbons, French polish, central heating, and a touch of violet hair-wash. The tactile motifs would be tracing paper, silk, the leather handle of a weighted pouch of papers, the foot-feel of very thick carpets alternating with parquet flooring, the stretch of muscle caused by leaning constantly over very large maps, the brittle feel of a cane chair-seat which has been occupied for hours.

And behind it all the ache of exhaustion and despair.

Chapter VII

COMPROMISE

Italy before the Conference—Her negotiations in 1914 *in Vienna and London—The Secret Treaty of April* 26, 1915*—Italian understanding with the Jugoslavs—The Pact of Rome—The Fourteen Points and Italy—The Italians on arrival in Paris—Self-determination versus Imperialism—The Tyrolese and the Jugoslavs—Orlando and House—Sonnino—President Wilson's blunder about the Brenner—Effects of this—Instances of Italian claims under Treaty of London—Albania—Dodecanese—Weakness of America—The Adriatic question—Methods and principles by which it was approached—President Wilson's appeal to public opinion—Its failure—Effects of this on general tone of the Conference.*

I

THOSE writers who have ventured upon complete records of the Paris Peace Conference have tended to adopt one or other of three methods of treatment, striving thereby to find, through all that inchoate confusion, some clue to continuity, some consecutive thread of narrative. A few of them have chosen the chronological system and have sought to tell their story in terms of time. Others have divided their account under the headings of subjects, and have discussed each particular issue as a problem in itself. Others again have dramatised the whole negotiations in the form of a conflict of wills, and have achieved thereby a readable, yet essentially inaccurate, representation. Each of these three methods of treatment entails a certain falsification of values. The chronological method is apt to give an erroneous impression of continuity, and to omit the element of synchronisation as well as the element of fits and starts. The piece-meal treatment, though valuable for purposes of lucidity, ignores the interrelation of subjects and gives no account of the effect of obstruction in one area upon concession in another. The ' conflict of wills ' system errs on the side of over-simplification, and attributes to Wilson, Lloyd George and Clemenceau antagonistic as well as protagonistic positions which are often exaggerated.

There is, however, one quite central problem of the Peace Conference which lends itself readily enough to all three methods. That problem is the problem of the Adriatic, or, in its wider sense, the position of Italy at the Peace Conference. Here is a subject which is fairly continuous in time, which is comparatively self-contained within its own limits, and which certainly does reflect, in its crudest form, the opposition between the hopes of the New World, and the desires of the Old. I propose in this chapter to take the Italian question as an isolated whole, and to indicate the corrosive influence of that problem upon the moral and diplomatic basis of the Conference of Paris. It furnishes a convenient, and comparatively simple illustration of the type of complexity in which the Conference became involved. The same sort of difficulty (the conflict, that is, between the intensive egoism of one member of a coalition and the extensive egoism of other members) is certain to occur again at future Congresses.

The essential factors, precedent to the Italian controversy in Paris, can be stated in summary form.

Italy, on the outbreak of the European War, was the ally of Germany and Austria. She refused from the first moment to fulfil her obligations under the

Triple Alliance, contending, and rightly, that with her exposed seaboard she would be at the mercy of the British Fleet. She went further. Early in January 1915 she made overtures at Vienna to ascertain what price Austria would pay her for maintaining her 'neutrality.' She asked for Trieste and the Trentino. The Austrian Government refused this concession. Baron Sonnino, the Italian Foreign Minister, then enquired in London and Paris what price the enemies of Austria would offer to induce Italy to desert her allies. He at the same time continued his negotiations at Vienna and obtained a grudging offer of some territory in the region of Trent. On May 3, 1915, he informed the Austrian Government that 'Italy must renounce the hope of coming to an agreement and proclaim from this moment her complete liberty of action.' The expression 'from this moment' was an euphemism : for five weeks already had Italy been engaged in negotiation with Austria's enemies : and the Treaty of London, which was the price which France, Great Britain and Russia had agreed to pay Italy, had actually been signed on April 26, a week before Baron Sonnino discontinued his overtures at Vienna.

The sentimentalists of the British Foreign Office had not entered upon this negotiation with any exuberance of heart. In the first place they had a feeling that Italy, as an ally, might be even more trouble than she was worth. In the second place they did not relish promising so huge a price for Italy's act of betrayal and at the expense of the very people whom she was about to betray. These old-world emotions had, however, to be suppressed in favour of 'war necessity.' Yet the

Foreign Office took unkindly to the task. Sir Edward Grey was so disconcerted by Italy's conduct and demands that he retired to the country on a plea of illness. The Permanent Under-Secretary, in his first conversation with the Italian Ambassador, allowed himself an expression which savoured of somewhat contemptuous realism. 'You speak,' said the Ambassador, 'as if you were purchasing our support.' 'Well,' said the Under-Secretary, 'and so we are.' Marchese Imperiali was much offended by this remark and sought sympathy elsewhere. The details of the Treaty were negotiated by minor officials under the vaguely penitent supervision of Mr. Asquith.

The main provisions of the Secret Treaty of London can be tabulated as follows :

(1) Italy was promised, not only the Trentino, but the whole southern Tyrol as far as the Brenner Pass. This entailed placing 229,261 pure Austrians under Italian rule.

(2) Italy was promised further territories and islands such as Trieste, Goricia, Gradisca, Lussin, Istria, Cherso, and portions of Carniola and Carinthia which would place under her rule 477,387 Jugoslavs.

(3) Italy was promised Northern Dalmatia and most of the Dalmatian Islands which entailed placing under her rule a further 751,571 Jugoslavs.

(4) She was promised full sovereignty over the Albanian town and naval base of Valona, plus a protectorate over the future State of Albania. The northern and southern portions of that State were to be annexed by Serbia and Greece respectively.

(5) She was promised complete sovereignty over Rhodes and the other eleven Islands of the Dodecanese which contained a purely Greek population, and which she had 'provisionally' occupied at the time of the Tripoli war.

(6) In the event of the partition of Turkey, she was promised ' a just share ' in the region of Adalia.

(7) In the event of Great Britain or France increasing their colonial possessions in Africa at the expense of Germany she was promised ' equitable compensation.'

In other words, Italy was by the Treaty of London promised territories which would place under her domination some 1,300,000 Jugoslavs, some 230,000 Germans, the whole Greek population of the Dodecanese, the Turks and Greeks of Adalia, all that was left of the Albanians, and vague areas in Africa. It was not, therefore, a Treaty which was in any consonance with the principle of self-determination or the doctrine of the Fourteen Points.

In return for these vast and wholly indefensible concessions Italy, on her part, undertook two obligations only. The first was to accord the port of Fiume to the Jugoslavs. The second was to declare war upon all our enemies. She evaded both these obligations. The former obligation will be considered later, the latter obligation was also not fulfilled. Italy did, it is true, declare war upon Austria in May 1915, upon Turkey in August of that year, and upon Bulgaria a few weeks later. She did not, however, declare war upon Germany until August 27, 1916. Signor Salandra actually boasted of this evasion as ' an important service rendered to my country.' An attempt was made, in Paris, to get Mr. Balfour to adduce this act of sacred egoism as an omission sufficiently serious to invalidate the whole Treaty of London. He lolled patrician and dissentient. ' That,' he said, ' is a lawyer's argument.' It was only half-heartedly, and at a much later stage of the negotiations, that Mr. Lloyd George raised this point. The Italians, with their wonted irreverence, their unfailing irrelevance, muttered something about a ' scrap of paper.'

So much for the Treaty of London in its pre-armistice stage. Between its conclusion and the collapse of Austria-Hungary certain other events occurred which must be briefly mentioned. The Bolsheviks, in the first place, published the Treaty of London. It was at once assailed, not only in Great Britain, America and France, but also in the Italian Chamber. It was described as a document of shameless imperialism. Upon the Jugoslav portions of the Austrian army it had a galvanic effect. They became more hostile to Italy than ever before. Caporetto taught the Italians that something must be done to conciliate these Jugoslav belligerents. Signor Orlando, who had by then become Prime Minister, encouraged certain deputies to form a committee of conciliation. Under the calm Scotch aegis of Dr. Seton Watson, under the persistent Europeanism of Mr. Wickham Steed, contact was established in London between Signor Torre of the Italian Chamber, and M. Trumbic, the spokesman of the Jugoslav Committee. On April 10, 1918, the ' Pact of Rome ' was concluded between these two authorised although unofficial representatives. Under this pact Italo-Jugoslav differences were to be solved on the principle of nationality. The Italian Government, on September 8, 1918, issued a pronouncement expressing deep sympathy with the desires of the Jugoslavs to form an independent and united kingdom. This, as Vittorio Veneto proved, was a remunerative pronouncement. It was universally felt, at that date, that the Treaty of London had been superseded by these unofficial and yet approved pronouncements and accords. This feeling was increased when Italy enthusiastically accepted the Fourteen Points of President Wilson. Point Nine provided that the Italian frontiers should be defined ' upon clearly recognisable lines of nationality.' It is true that on November 1 Signor Orlando mumbled something about a reservation. When asked to repeat himself he merely mumbled further. It was then suggested to him that Point Nine of the Fourteen Points had no bearing upon the armistice with Germany which was then under discussion. He gladly accepted that suggestion. He did not publish the fact that he had made any reservation until May 1, 1919. This is a classic instance of the dangers of affable imprecision in international negotiation. Signor Orlando was left under the impression that he had accepted the Fourteen Points subject to a reservation upon Point Nine. President Wilson and the rest of the world were left under the impression that he had accepted the Fourteen Points without any reservation. It was this misunderstanding which added a further complication to the ensuing controversy.

2

It must be admitted that the Italian Representatives, on reaching Paris, were in a position of great difficulty. Italy had been brought into the war against her allies, and on the side of their enemies, on the principle of ' sacred selfishness ' : that principle implied that she would receive material, rather than moral, satisfaction in return. Great Britain and France had pledged themselves to deliver this material satisfaction in the currency of the old imperialism, in the form, that is, of annexations and protectorates. By no human ingenuity, by no statistical or other juggling, could it be made to appear that this debt could ever be liquidated in the new currency of the Fourteen Points. Nothing could disguise the central fact that the fulfilment of the pledges of the Secret Treaty would violate the principle of self-determination to the extent of placing some two million unwilling and very self-determined people under Italian rule. The battle was thus unescapably joined between a Secret Treaty and the Fourteen Points, between imperialism and self-determination, between the old order and the new, between diplomatic convention and the Sermon on the Mount. France and Great Britain were bound by the letter of their bond : the hands of President Wilson were fettered only by his own principles. Here, if ever, was an opportunity for the Prophet of the New World to enforce his message upon the old. The Italian problem thus became, for them that knew, the test case of the whole Conference. It was on Woodrow Wilson's handling of the Treaty of London that we decided to judge his essential value. He was tested : and he compromised. We may have taken an unfair issue on which to test him : yet there was the issue that we chose. He failed us. We were shocked by this failure. We ceased, from that moment, to believe that President Wilson was the Prophet whom we had followed. From that moment we saw in him no more than a presbyterian dominie.

I relate these emotions as they arose at the time. I quite see that it was easy for us to choose so vicarious an operation wherewith to test Mr. Wilson's surgical skill. I do not say that we were right, unselfish, clear-headed, or even honest in so doing. I say only that that is what we did.

The claims of Italy were weakened by other considerations. SS. Orlando and Sonnino might have surmised that the principle of self-determination would not be applied with any academic rigour in favour of Germany or even Hungary. It was awkward for the Italians that their claims extended over just those sections of enemy territory which aroused warm feelings in the hearts of both associates and allies. Everybody liked the Tyrolese. Mr. Lloyd George was reported even to have a deep veneration, a fellow-feeling, for the memory of Andreas Hofer. And then there were the Jugoslavs. In Italian eyes, the Croats and the Slovenes were the most pestilential of all our late enemies. It was distressing for Baron Sonnino to discover on reaching Paris that the Americans, the British and the French, regarded these liberated Slavs as the lost sheep over whom there was much rejoicing. The Greeks, again, could claim with justice that the Dodecanese were wholly Greek in population and desire. Moreover, the state of public opinion at home was not very healthy : there were murmurs of socialism, or even worse : these murmurs could only be stilled by large slices of successful imperialism. Yet how, with Woodrow Wilson smiling his evangelical Princeton smile, could those slices be produced ?

One is forced, in common humanity, to have a certain sympathy for the Italians. Behind all these perplexities, were preoccupations of a more compelling character. The complete collapse of Austria had taken Italy by surprise. What they would have

preferred was some 'combinazione' which would have
left a chain of weak and separated states upon their
northern and eastern borders. Instead of this they
saw themselves faced with the Germans as their neighbours in the north, and on the east a strong new
nation of over thirteen million Jugoslavs. I shall
refer later to this important aspect. For the moment
it is necessary to record how inevitable it was that
their thought should have concentrated on the
Brenner and the Monte Nevoso.

It diverts me to find in my diary so much naïve and
confident indignation with the diplomatic tactics of
SS. Orlando and Sonnino. Now that I realise their
immense difficulties, the abysmal futility of those to
whom they were opposed, I am not certain that they
were wholly incompetent. Externally and internally
they were in a very weak position ; they knew that
their political, military and naval strength entitled them
to scant esteem in allied quarters : they knew that
everything they desired was in opposition to the principles of President Wilson : they knew that those
principles would in other areas be strained beyond
bearing under the pressure of France, Belgium, the
New States, and other elements stronger than themselves : they knew that their own public opinion, still
fervent with war propaganda, expected glories which
they could not possibly produce : and they thus
manœuvred for both time and position with a subtlety
and a consistency which to-day compels both my indignation and my unwilling respect for technique. I
should like to feel that Italy would have done better
by throwing herself, virginal and sobbing, upon the
neck of President Wilson and espousing in one rap-

turous gesture the good, the beautiful and the true. I question, however, whether any such gesture would have given birth to the Treaty of Rapallo of November 12, 1920. It would have given birth to communism in Italy and at a stage when Mussolini was no more than a journalist of Milan. To a certain extent Italy was an anachronism in our counsels : yet she was an injured and ill-treated anachronism. I do not, to-day, consider that Sonnino and Orlando were absolutely unjustified in their conduct. I regret merely that this inevitable combination of evils should in effect have destroyed Wilsonism at the Conference of Paris. The attempt to combine the fifteenth with the thirtieth century would, in the best of circumstances, be liable to lead to some misconception of motive. And Paris of 1919 was not the best of circumstances.

The stages by which President Wilson surrendered to Italy, the spasmodic gestures which he made to recover his original position, have not been clearly divulged. It is evident, I think, that Orlando and Sonnino, who did not in everything see eye to eye, divided their functions. Orlando, who was a liberal at heart, concentrated on winning the approval of Colonel House. In this he amply succeeded. He knew that there were two points of weakness in the American armour, two points which they ardently desired. The first was to obtain a moral victory over Europe such as would, once and for all, satisfy their passion for rescue-work and allay their own illusions of cultural and historic inferiority. The second was to obtain that victory without the slightest effort of personal abnegation. These two purposes were admirably combined in a Covenant of the League of Nations

which would include the Monroe doctrine. Signor
Orlando, being a clever if slightly unbelieving man,
was the first to realise that President Wilson would
shut one eye to countless inconsistencies if only a
Covenant, thus emasculated, could be inextricably en-
twined within the fabric of the Treaties. He was quick
to see, when the President returned from his interim
visit to Washington, that the opposition of the American Senate had placed their delegation in Paris in a
highly illogical situation.

Readily did he offer Colonel House the support of
Italy in the League Committee : readily did he assure
the President that there could be nothing easier, or
more just, than to exclude the American continent both
from the sanctions and the responsibilities of the
League Machinery ; to accord it the pleasures of
uplift, with none of the pain of action or interference.
Signor Orlando, with the utmost affability, backed the
clause under which the Monroe Doctrine should remain unaffected by the Covenant of the League. Yet
he made one mistake. He failed to observe that since
the President's return from Washington—since that
ghastly dinner-party at which Senator Lodge had been
so silent—Colonel House was no longer in favour.
Colonel House had taken Clemenceau aside. There
were henceforward two parties in the Hotel Crillon.
The first, which might be called the party of conciliation, was represented by Colonel House and Mr. Henry
White. The second was the party of Wilsonism, represented by the American experts. Nobody, least of
all Mr. Wilson himself, had any consistent idea to
which of these two parties the President belonged. It
was Signor Orlando's assumption that the President

and Colonel House were still at one which led him to assume an attitude which, without American backing, was a very silly attitude to assume.

The Italian Foreign Minister, Baron Sonnino, stood for, and was detached for, other purposes. He represented ' rugged honesty '—a reputation which he had acquired owing to one chance (and one deliberate) circumstance. His mother was of Scottish nationality. That made us all feel that Signor Sonnino was clean of heart. Upon his mantelpiece at home he had inscribed the motto : ' *aliis licet, tibi non licet* ' : the knowledge of this inscription filled us with the certainty that Baron Sonnino possessed independence, high-mindedness, a nimble wit and the humanities. These are immortal assets. They enabled Baron Sonnino to be protractedly unreliable before we found him out.

In spite, however, of these initial advantages of a dual personality and a dual approach, it remains a complete mystery how the Italian Delegation managed to induce President Wilson to consent to Italy being accorded the Brenner frontier and the South Tyrol. It seems that this vitally damaging concession was accorded by Mr. Wilson as early as January of 1919. It has been suggested that the President was still under the emotional excitement of his Roman triumph. It has been suggested that the Italians threatened, unless he consented, to oppose the inclusion of the Covenant in the Treaty of Peace. It has been suggested that they promised, were this concession granted, to be Wilsonian and amenable in all other matters such as those which affected the Jugoslavs, the Albanians, the Greeks and the Turks. Not one of these suggestions is based on any wholly convincing authority. There is nothing

to explain how the President could, at the very outset of the Conference, have agreed to place 230,000
Tyrolese under Italian rule in flagrant violation of the
most central of all his principles. I prefer to accept the
simple explanation that Woodrow Wilson was quite
unaware at the time what his concession really implied.
He confessed subsequently to Dr. Charles Seymour
that his surrender on this point had been due to
'insufficient study.' Professor Coolidge has left the
following record : 'The well founded belief among
our people was that he gave his consent without due
consideration and frankly regretted it afterwards, but
felt bound by his word.'

Whatever may have been the motives which led the
President to hand the Tyrolese over to Italy, the conse-
quences of this concession were disastrous. They
worked out as follows. From the very first days of
the Conference it was widely realised that the President
had already sacrificed the principle of nationality in a
case where no arguments existed for such abandon-
ment beyond the argument of strategic necessity. He
had apparently made this concession gratuitously, and
without demanding any assurances in return. By so
doing, he had, at the same time, implied approval of
the Treaty of London. He had thus compromised his
own moral position and the authority of his delegation
from the very outset. If Wilson could swallow the
Brenner, he would swallow anything. The moral
effect of this discovery can scarcely be exaggerated.
Even on practical, as distinct from moral, grounds, his
concession was an appalling blunder. When he came
to deal with the ensuing Adriatic question he found
that he had already discarded his ace of trumps. In his

desire to rectify this ill-considered gesture he became obstinate and professorial in matters of far less vital importance. He played his hand with a pernickety gesture and provocatively. And as a result the Adriatic problem emerged from the lower regions of a difference of opinion into the nervous peaks of a world crisis.

3

It may be observed that in this vital matter also Mr. Wilson suffered much from his prim and thoughtless rejection of the Jusserand programme of November 29. Had that programme been accepted and imposed, not only would the Treaty of London have been automatically cancelled, but it would have been possible to avoid the dislocation of time and energy by all these Italian impositions. Even had the Conference, at its first sitting, laid down that the first objective was the conclusion of peace with our main enemy, then these Adriatic differences would not with such inevitable insistence have arisen until a later and less crucial stage. Here again it was their lack of scientific planning which landed the Supreme Council in all these complexities from the outset. In their desire to placate the smaller Powers they had gratuitously invited those Powers to state their claims. It was these statements of claim which, in the case of Jugoslavia, Greece and Albania, imposed upon the Supreme Council the necessity of considering as early as February how far these claims were in conflict with the claims of Italy. It is true, of course, that the Italians would, in any case, have striven hard to postpone the signature of the Covenant and of the Treaty with Germany until their own claims against

Austria, Jugoslavia, Greece and even Turkey had, at least in principle, been accepted. Yet the lack of any rigid programme enabled them to achieve this object with a minimum of effort. What should have been an arduous and costly manœuvre was rendered, owing to the amateurishness of the Supreme Council, an easy walk-over.

The main issue of the Italian question, once the Brenner had been disposed of, was what is known generally as the ' Adriatic Problem.' In other words it centred around the dispute between Italy and Jugoslavia as to their joint frontier, and more particularly as to the ownership of Fiume, Dalmatia, and the Islands. The Adriatic problem is too congested with detail to lend itself readily to any practical examination : I shall consider it later in terms of the principles and methods involved. Yet it is impossible to convey any impression of the effect upon the Peace Conference of this incessant controversy with Italy, unless some indication be given of the constant flux and reflux between fact and principle, principle and fact. I shall therefore choose as my ' exhinits ' of these difficulties of detail, not the central problem of Fiume and the Adriatic, but two secondary and far more manageable products of the Secret Treaty of London. I shall choose the problems of Albania and the Dodecanese.

Until the Balkan wars of 1912-1913 Albania, although possessing a distinct Illyrian nationality of her own, had been a province of the Turkish Empire. With the collapse of Turkish rule in Macedonia and Thrace Albania found herself independent but somewhat in the air. Her future status and frontiers were considered by the Conference of Ambassadors then sit-

ting in London under the chairmanship of Sir Edward
Grey. On July 29, 1913, the Ambassadors agreed,
after much benevolence and some wrangling, upon the
northern frontiers of the future Albanian Principality.
These frontiers placed Scutari within Albanian territory, but allocated the Albanian towns of Ipek and
Djakova to Montenegro. The delimitation of the
southern frontier between Albania and Greece was to
be decided after it had been examined by a Commission
on the spot. The recommendations of that Commission had not fully been approved at the outbreak of
the European War. Meanwhile the crown of Albania
had been offered to Prince William of Wied who
landed at Durazzo on May 7, 1914, and who was turned
out of the country on September 4 following by
Essad Pasha, his own Minister of War. On November 25 Italy, although a neutral at the time, seized the
naval base of Valona, while Austrian troops garrisoned
the north and centre. The Treaty of London in the
following April promised to Italy Valona and the
protectorate of a small central Albanian State, whereas
the rest of Albania was to be partitioned between
Serbia and Greece. On June 3, 1917, Italy, without
consulting her Allies, proclaimed the independence of
Albania under Italian protection. The French replied
to this by establishing an Independent Republic at
Koritza in Southern Albania, thus commanding the
important strategic road from Santi Quaranta into
Greece. They obstinately, and to my mind nobly,
maintained forces in that remote district until May
1920. The Serbians for their part crossed the northern
frontier and occupied Scutari and the line of the Drin.
They were subsequently obliged to surrender Scutari

to an interallied force, but still remained in occupation
of the rest of Northern Albania. The position of
Albania at the opening of the Conference of Paris was
thus anomalous and confused.

The situation was further deteriorated by the fact
that each of Albania's neighbours and protectors
cherished designs upon her integrity and frontiers, and
that, in the south at least, the populations were closely
intermingled and the statistics involved. The Greeks
claimed the whole of Southern Albania including
Koritza, on the grounds that it constituted ' Northern
Epirus ' and was mainly inhabited by Greeks. The
Serbs claimed the whole of Northern Albania partly
on strategic and partly on ethnical grounds. Their
main argument, however, was that the Grand Trunk
Railway which was to connect Jugoslavia with the
lower Adriatic could only find its outlet at Scutari and
along the Drin Valley.

The attitude of the Great Powers towards this intricate problem was illustrative and diverse. The
Americans and the British were pro-Albanian in sympathy, although in the south our own enthusiasm was
clouded by a doubt whether it was wise, if Italy were
to obtain a foothold in Albania, to give her the
strategic advantage of Koritza and the Santi Quaranta
road, which was in fact the only line of communication
between Janina and Salonika. The French tended to
adopt our attitude, and it was they who finally persuaded us that Koritza should be given to Greece. The
attitude of Italy towards this problem was illogical,
irritating, and strange.

The Italians, since April 1915, had come to dislike
the Albanian section of the Treaty of London. They

still wanted their naval base at Valona in full sovereignty : they still wanted a protectorate over the
future Albanian State. They still, as always, wanted
the Treaty of London. They were no longer prepared,
however, to fulfil the remaining conditions of that
section of the Treaty, and to hand over to Serbia and
Greece the northern and southern portions of Albania.
The former cession would represent an accession of
territory to Jugoslavia. The latter cession would place
Greece in strategic command of the Corfu channel.
And in any case, if Italy were to be given a protectorate
over Albania, it seemed fitting to her that Albania
should be as large, both north and south, as possible.

The result was that, although on all other matters
(except Fiume) the Italians clamoured, on the basis of
the ' Sanctity of Treaties,' for the integral fulfilment of
the Treaty of London, they argued that in respect of
Albania this Treaty was not fully in accord with the
principle of self-determination. When it was pointed
out to them that the retention of Valona might also be
regarded as a violation of that principle, they contended that in such retention ' the honour of Italy '
was involved.

Day after day were we obliged to listen patiently to
this exegesis of our Italian colleagues upon the doctrine
of Wilsonism, without being permitted to express the
distaste, and indeed the blind fury, which such sophistry evoked. Upon myself the tolerance displayed by
the Americans and the Conference generally in face of
such distortion of doctrine had a most demoralising
effect. The courtesy of international conduct forbade
us to express our righteous indignation by anything
but a pained silence. Yet at any moment it would have

been open to the United States Representatives to explode as follows : ' You have just appealed in this matter to the doctrine of self-determination as overriding the Treaty of London. May I inform my President that Italy will apply this principle to every question in which Italian interests are involved ? ' There would have been no answer to such a question. Yet it was never asked. We endured in silence. And day by day our confidence in Wilsonism as an applicable and self-assertive doctrine was destroyed.

It is necessary to add that the Albanian question was never finally settled by the Paris Conference. The Italians remained in militaty occupation of that country until August of 1920 when the Albanians rose against them and drove them into the sea. An armistice was hurriedly negotiated and the Italians, with small appearance of dignity, withdrew. A policy of financial penetration was thereafter adopted. It was extremely successful. Long after the Paris Conference, the frontiers of Albania and the position of Italy in that country were regularised by diplomatic agreement.

The question of Rhodes and the eleven other Greek Islands of the Dodecanese can be dealt with shortly. The Italians possessed no moral, and small juridical, right to these Islands. Baron Sonnino kept on trying to negotiate with M. Venizelos a direct agreement for the settlement of Graeco-Italian difficulties. The Americans and British were constantly put off by assurances that a settlement agreeable to both parties was about to be arranged. Such a settlement was, in fact, concluded between M. Venizelos and Signor Tittoni, the successor of Baron Sonnino. But when the Greeks fell upon evil days, this arrangement was repudiated by a subsequent Government, and to this day the Italian flag flaunts unrighteously (but I admit hygienically) above the Dodecanese.

I have cited these two problems, not merely as an illustration of the shifts, hypocrisies and pretences which we were obliged to endure in courtly silence, but as an example of the unfortunate extent to which President Wilson and his assistants fluctuated between principle and detail. To that extent, I admit, their professorial training was a misfortune. Our own hands were tied by the Treaty of London and we could say nothing. We longed for the Americans to call down fire from heaven and to proclaim their principles against any array of detail. They hesitated, partly from an exaggerated fear of ' breaking up the Peace Conference ' and partly from a too scrupulous diffidence. Yet once they had abandoned the unassailable fortress of their own principles for the surrounding marshes of detail, they were immediately surrounded, outnumbered and disarmed. The tragedy of the Peace Conference was that the New World consented to meet the Old World on ground of the latter's choosing.

4

It is easy, and not very historical, to depict the Italians as the villains of the whole drama. Objectively, I now realise that there was much, that there is much, to be said in their defence. I admit (I have already admitted) their difficulties. The emotions of the Italian Chamber were even more disordered than those of the House of Commons. It drove them mad to feel that the Fourteen Points were being relaxed in favour of France and Great Britain, while being rigidly enforced as against Italy. The temper of the country was even more hysterical than that of the *Daily Mail.* The labour situation was even more menacing than that at Glasgow. The appetite of Italy was greater, her digestive capacity far less, than that of any other country. She was determined to become a Great Power without the internal force to justify such an ambition. Italy, in January 1919, was obviously at her very worst.

There were other considerations which rendered the issues facing Orlando and Sonnino peculiarly baffling. I have already stated that the complete collapse of Austria-Hungary took the Italians by surprise. It is only fair to elaborate that statement in terms of Italian necessity. The Treaty of London had been devised on the assumption that something, at least, would remain of the old Austro-Hungarian Empire, that some balance of power, as between the Teuton and the Slav, would persist upon Italy's northern and eastern frontiers. This assumption had been falsified by events. Against the German menace they were, it is true, protected by the Brenner line. Yet on the east they were exposed, not (as they had anticipated) to a purely naval or polynesian danger, but to the military menace of a land frontier to be defended against thirteen million Jugoslavs. In other words, the Treaty of London had been devised in terms of Austria-Hungary. Those terms no longer applied. It was essential for a weak country such as Italy, to obtain strategic and economic safeguards against this new menace. These safeguards expressed themselves in terms of two objectives. (1) The Monte Nevoso as a strategical defence against the Jugoslav army. (2) Fiume, as a guarantee of, and a victim to, the economic prosperity of Trieste. Neither of these two objectives had been promised to Italy by the Treaty of London. Both of them violated the principle of President Wilson.

It is only in terms of essential Italian necessity that we can hope to comprehend the apparent mistake of Signor Orlando (once he had obtained the Brenner) in thus selecting as his main objectives the only two points (Fiume and the Monte Nevoso) on which the signatories of the Treaty of London were free to unite with President Wilson. It is frequently stated (by Mr. Lansing among others) that Signor Orlando unloosed upon the Fiume question a public opinion which he was unable subsequently to control. There is a certain truth in this thesis. I question, however, whether the Italian Delegation were to any serious extent the victims of their own propaganda. They knew of course that the Treaty of London promised them Dalmatia and denied them Fiume. They also knew that under the Fourteen Points, Dalmatia was unattainable and that Fiume might, with a little statistical juggling, be obtained. They may have felt that if the Great Voice of the Italian People were incited to yell for Fiume, then the great heart of the Italian people would accept the ensuing surrender of Dalmatia. To a certain extent this may have been their intention and their misfortune. Yet, essentially, they felt that circumstances had changed ; and that the possession of Fiume and the Monte Nevoso was an Italian necessity far more compelling than any flourishes in Dalmatia or the Islands.

I deal in this summary way with the central core of

the Adriatic problem. I make no mention of the
Armistice of the Villa Giusti of November 3, 1918, of
the Italian refusal in Paris to sit at the same table as the
Croats and the Slovenes, of the Jugoslav attempt to
secure the arbitral decision of President Wilson, of all
the notes and negotiations which took place between
April 13 and April 23, of the dissensions between the
House-group and the Bowman-group within the
American delegation, of the ensuing ' Wilson line,'
of our own ' pound of flesh ' attitude towards the
Treaty of London, or of Mr. Lloyd George's wholly
disinterested flitting between the Hotel Crillon and the
Hotel Edouard VII. The main issue can be boiled
down to the following formula :

(1) The Treaty of London promised Italy Dalmatia and
some Adriatic Islands. It did *not* assign to them either
Fiume or the Monte Nevoso.

(2) France and Great Britain were bound by the Treaty
of London. President Wilson refused even to take it into
consideration.

(3) The collapse of Austria-Hungary and the unexpected emergence of a compact and powerful Jugoslav
State rendered it essential that Italy should obtain Fiume
for economic reasons ; the Monte Nevoso for strategical
reasons.

(4) If they abandoned the Treaty of London they
would release Great Britain and France from any contractual obligation at all. If they insisted upon the application of the Treaty of London, they would be frustrated
by the veto of President Wilson.

(5) Their policy was, therefore, with one hand to hold
Great Britain and France down to the Treaty of London,
while negotiating with President Wilson regarding Fiume
and the Monte Nevoso. Once these had been obtained,
a new Treaty could be negotiated with France and Great

Britain which, while releasing them from the European clauses of the Treaty of London, would bind them to the execution of the Asiatic and African clauses.

It is not surprising that the Italian Delegation should have endeavoured in this manner to hunt with the hounds and run with the hare. What is so disheartening is that President Wilson (who held every card except the Brenner ace within his hand) should have adopted a precisely similar method of chase and scurry. He first (on April 14) indicated to Signor Orlando that he was prepared to compromise on Fiume. And he then (on April 23) issued to the Press a statement in which he appealed to the Italian People over the head of their elected Representative. He thus combined the secrecy of the old diplomacy with the most flagrant indiscretions of the new.

It may be surmised that this duality of action on the part of the President was due to the conflicting influences of Colonel House and the group of American experts who ranged themselves behind Mr. Isaiah Bowman. The former was rightly obsessed by the terror of delay and believed that any Treaty, if rapidly concluded, would be better than any Treaty postponed. Colonel House, let it be remembered, was a very wise, though somewhat inarticulate man. The experts felt that the President must, in this last resounding ditch, make a stand for his own principles. They thus addressed to him the sort of appeal which would be most likely to awake afresh his theocratic feelings. ' Never,' they wrote, ' did the President have such an opportunity to strike a death-blow to the discredited methods of the old diplomacy. . . . To the President is given the rare privilege of going down in history as the statesman who destroyed, by a clean-cut decision against an infamous arrangement, the last vestige of the old order.'

It was not, as a matter of fact, the last vestige. Shantung remained as a final humiliation. It was certainly not a clean-cut decision. Yet by these revivalist words the President was revived. On April 23 he issued to the Press a statement of his own views on the Fiume problem, in which he appealed, not without his old eloquence, to the heart of Italy against the brain of the Italian Delegation in Paris. The next day Signor Orlando left Paris in dramatic, although somewhat prearranged, indignation. And the emotions of the Italian people founted in passionate abuse of President Wilson. ' Either Fiume,' they yelled, ' or death.' The President had appealed both to his principles and to The People. And the latter gnashed their teeth at him in rage. He was much discouraged. From that moment he seems to have abandoned all hope of imposing his doctrines on the false democracies of Europe.

The details of the ensuing imbroglio are less important than this defeat of principle. On May 5 the Italians returned to Paris. Mr. Lloyd George thereafter endeavoured (and as I now feel, rightly) to effect a settlement on the basis of vast compensations in Asia Minor. M. Tardieu on May 30 produced his own compromise. In June and July there were troubles in Fiume and some French soldiers were killed. On September 12 D'Annunzio occupied the city. In December Signor Nitti evolved an attempt at compromise. In January of 1920 that compromise was succeeded by another. Both Trumbic and President Wilson (by that time ailing in aloof Washington) refused that compromise. The latter suggested direct negotiations between the two disputants. The problem was thus further negotiated at San Remo in May of 1920, as between Trumbic and Nitti. An agreement was almost reached, when Nitti fell. By November of 1920 the Jugoslavs had lost heart. President Wilson was by then a stricken man : there was no hope of his assistance : the Allied Powers were wearied of the controversy : the Jugoslavs were obliged to surrender to Count Sforza at Rapallo and to accord to Italy what in effect meant Fiume and the Monte Nevoso. It was in this manner, eighteen months after the Conference of Paris, that, while Wilson was dying in Washington, Italy obtained her desires.

I am not concerned with the ultimate solution of the Adriatic problem. I am concerned only with what happened in Paris between January 18, 1919 and June 28. How came it that President Wilson, having surrendered on the Brenner frontier, was unable to impose upon Italy an equitable solution of the Adriatic and Dodecanese questions ? It might be contended that the President, until the day of his death, never actually consented to any concessions on these points, and that his attitude was, in regard to this controversy at least, less illogical than was his attitude regarding Shantung, Poland, the Mandates or the inclusion of War Pensions in Reparation. In the cold light of history it may seem even that, in his dealings with Italy, Woodrow Wilson, except for that error about South Tyrol, did in truth maintain his principles intact. Such was not, however, the impression which spread through the hot saloons of Paris. We recognised, in the methods rather than in the purposes of the Italian

Delegation, all that was most odious in the old
diplomacy. We trusted that the President would also
recognise the danger and confront the Italians with the
strong weapons which he held. The spectacle of
Woodrow Wilson billing and cooing with Orlando
filled us with a blank despair. It was not that he
negotiated unskilfully ; it was that he consented to
negotiate at all. Had he taken a strong line from the
very start as against Italian claims he might have
triumphed later against Great Britain, France and
Japan. It was his early shambling over the Italian
question that convinced us that Woodrow Wilson
was not a great or potent man. That conviction was
a profound disappointment : on its heels demoralisation spread through Paris like a disease.

Chapter VIII

FAILURE

Loss of idealism—Its nature—The hypocrisy of the Conference—How far was it conscious hypocrisy?—The effect of a false position—Examination of this false position and of its causes—Wilsonism versus Balance of Power—The Anglo-Saxon and the Latin—Fear that America would not endorse Wilson's policy—Wilson's personal defects—His loneliness and rejection of advice—His spiritual arrogance—His intellectual narrowness—His resultant blindness—Instances of this—His final surrender—How far did he believe that America would support him?—Did he delude his colleagues on this point?—The tragedy of Wilson—The dangers of vague diplomacy as of diplomacy by conference—What I myself learnt at Paris—Balfour—Smuts—Venizelos—Benes—Eyre Crowe.

I

THE purpose of this book is, I must repeat, not so much to formulate a record of events, as to catch, before it evaporates, the unhealthy and unhappy atmosphere of the Peace Conference ; to convey some impression of that gradual drift, away from our early peaks of aspiration towards the low countries where figures laboured hurriedly together in a gathering fog. I apprehend that unless the pressure (the actual inevitability) of this atmosphere is realised as a determining factor in itself, the historian may approach the Conference with wisdom after the event, and may concentrate, in critical tranquillity, upon apportioning praise and blame. I do not think, however, that any useful description of the Paris Conference can be conveyed in terms of ethical, as distinct from technical, values.

The Conference may, as Mr. Winston Churchill has said, have been ' a turbulent collision of embarrassed demagogues.' I have already indicated some of the causes which led to turbulence, to collision and to demagogic methods. Yet in spite of this, many durable, and some useful things were accomplished. Many evil things were avoided. None the less, there were few of us who were not disappointed : and in some of us the Conference inculcated a mood of durable disbelief—a conviction that human nature can, like a glacier, move but an inch or two in every thousand years.

I wish in this concluding chapter to summarise some, at least, of what might be called the psychological factors (or were they symptoms ?) of failure ; to comment upon the gradual deterioration of our state of mind ; to indicate our ' change of heart ' ; and to ascribe, if possible, this decline of thought and feeling to some tangible causes. The historian, with every justification, will come to the conclusion that we were very stupid men. I think we were. Yet I also think that the factor of stupidity is inseparable from all human affairs. It is too often disregarded as an inevitable concomitant of human behaviour ; it is too often employed merely as a term of personal affront.

What, in the first place, was the nature of this moral and intellectual deterioration ? I can speak with assurance only of my own change of heart, yet I believe that the mutations through which I passed were shared by many others, and that my own loss of idealism coincided with a similar loss of idealism on the part of those (and they were many) who had come to the Conference fired by the same certitudes as myself. Our change of

heart can be stated as follows. We came to Paris confident that the new order was about to be established ;
we left it convinced that the new order had merely
fouled the old. We arrived as fervent apprentices in
the school of President Wilson : we left as renegades.
I wish to suggest, in this chapter (and without bitterness), that this unhappy diminution of standard was
very largely the fault (or one might say with greater
fairness ' the misfortune ') of democratic diplomacy.

We arrived determined that a Peace of justice and
wisdom should be negotiated : we left it, conscious
that the Treaties imposed upon our enemies were
neither just nor wise. To those who desire to measure
for themselves the width of the gulf which sundered
intention from practice I should recommend a perusal
of the several Notes addressed to the Supreme Council
by the German Delegation at Versailles. An excellent
summary and confrontation of these Notes is furnished
by Professor Hazeltine in Volume II of Temperley's
History of the Peace Conference. It is impossible to read
the German criticism without deriving the impression
that the Paris Peace Conference was guilty of disguising an Imperialistic peace under the surplice of Wilsonism, that seldom in the history of man has such
vindictiveness cloaked itself in such unctuous sophistry.
Hypocrisy was the predominant and unescapable
result. Yet was this hypocrisy wholly conscious,
wholly deliberate ? I do not think so. I certainly agree
that the sanctimonious pharisaism of the Treaties is
their gravest fault. Yet was there any conscious dissimulation ? In some cases (such as the article forbidding Austria to join with Germany) a deliberately
evasive form of words was consciously employed.

Yet in most cases, hypocrisy *just happened*. How did it happen ? The fact that, as the Conference progressed, we were scarcely conscious of our own falsity, may indicate that some deterioration of moral awareness had taken place. We did not realise what we were doing. We did not realise how far we were drifting from our original basis. We were exhausted and over-worked. We kept on mumbling our old formulas in the hope that they still bore some relation to our actions. There were few moments when we said to ourselves ' This is unjust ' : there were many moments when we said to ourselves ' Better a bad treaty to-day, than a good treaty four months hence.' In the dust of con-troversy, in the rattle of time-pressure, we lost all contact with our guiding stars. In interludes the dust would settle, the machine would stop, and we would observe, with tired regret, that these stars were them-selves fading pale against the sky. ' *Il faut aboutir* ' they shouted at us : and we returned to the din and dimness of our compromises. We still desired ardently to maintain our principles intact : it was only in the after-vacancy that we realised that they remained for us only in the form of empty words : it was then, and then only, that we faced the fact that the falsity of our position had led us into being false. It was by then far too late.

The above is not written in any desire to defend our state of mind. I am examining only : I am not de-fending. My contention is that this dimming of our moral awareness constituted the most regrettable and perhaps the only interesting element in our deteriora-tion. I wish to explain how it occurred that in the dust of incessant argument, amid the by-paths of unceasing detail, we strayed away from the main avenues of our intention : and how it was unconsciously, rather than consciously, that we boasted, on arrival, to have come the way we meant.

The point is, I think, of some importance. If future generations come to believe that the Paris Conference was, in every single point, deliberately and exceptionally hypocritical, they will (when they also come to attend Congresses) be less on their guard against the tired falsity which is inseparable from any attempt to adjust high general principles to low practical detail. In every discussion between sovereign States claiming equality with each other, decisions can only be taken by a unanimous and not by a majority vote. This inevitable curse of unanimity leads to the no less inevitable curse of compromise. All compromises have an element of falsity, but when they have to be referred back to governing principles or generalisations a double falsity is introduced. I do not deny the ghastly hypocrisy of the Paris Treaties : I contend only that this hypocrisy was not, in every case, conscious or deliberate ; that it was not, in every case, humanly avoidable ; and that similar hypocrisy may not, in every case, be humanly avoidable in the future.

It will be contended by any intelligent reader that the above analysis of the nature of our hypocrisy is not, after all, an explanation, but is merely a lame and empty excuse. Yet the explanation is none the less implicit in my argument. It is this. The Paris negotiators were from the very first in a false position. This falsity increased during the whole time that the German Treaty was being discussed. It was the root-cause of the whole failure, of the rapid deterioration in moral awareness. It requires to be analysed into its component parts.

2

I have already indicated in preceding chapters many of the elements of falsity which afflicted the Paris Peace Conference from the start. I have drawn attention to the contradiction between conditions offered at a moment when victory was still uncertain, and the interpretation of those conditions at a moment when triumph, overwhelming and insatiable, was in our hands. I have suggested that an idealism evolved to mitigate the pangs of possible defeat is apt to shift materially when applied to the appetites aroused by actual conquest. I have also indicated the acute difficulty experienced by the negotiators in Paris in reconciling the excited expectations of their own democracies with the calmer considerations of durable peace-making. Such contrasts can be grouped together under what will forever be the main problem of democratic diplomacy ; the problem, that is, of adjusting the emotions of the masses to the thoughts of the rulers. The new diplomacy may be immune to some of the virus of deception which afflicted the old : yet it is acutely sensitive to its own peculiar virus—to the virus of imprecision. What the statesman thinks to-day, the masses may well feel to-morrow. Yet in conditions such as those of the Peace Conference, requiring extreme rapidity of solution, the time-lag between the emotions of the masses and the thoughts of the statesmen is a most disadvantageous factor. The attempt rapidly to bridge the gulf between mass-emotion and expert reason leads, at its worst, to actual falsity, and at its best to grave imprecision. The Paris Peace Conference was not a sample of democratic diplomacy at its best. It was thus by actual falsity that the gulf was bridged.

This general type of falsity, inseparable from all attempts at democratic diplomacy, was in Paris complicated and enhanced by special circumstances which require in their turn to be stated and analysed. The contrast between mass-emotion and expert reason was stated for us in acute and difficult terms. It took the form—the unnecessary and perplexing form—of a contrast not only between the new diplomacy and the old, but between the new world and the old, between Europe and America. I do not say that this contrast was, in all its implications, fully realised at the time. I contend only that it was determinant throughout the whole Conference : that it was, in fact, an unreal and not a real contrast : and that the attempt to reconcile these two unrealities was the essential misconception of the Conference, and the root cause of all resultant falsity. Let me state the contrast in quite simple terms.

On the one hand you had Wilsonism—a doctrine which was very easy to state and very difficult to apply. Mr. Wilson had not invented any new political philosophy, or discovered any doctrine which had not been dreamed of, and appreciated, for many hundred years. The one thing which rendered Wilsonism so passionately interesting at the moment was the fact that this centennial dream was suddenly backed by the overwhelming resources of the strongest Power in the world. Here was a man who represented the greatest physical force which had ever existed and who had pledged himself openly to the most ambitious moral theory which any statesman had ever pronounced. It was not that the ideas of Woodrow Wilson were so apocalyptic : it was that for the first time in history you had a man who possessed, not the desire merely, not the power alone, but the unquestioned opportunity to enforce these ideas upon the whole world. We should have been insensitive indeed had we not been inspired by the magnitude of such an occasion.

On the other hand you had Europe, the product of a wholly different civilisation, the inheritor of unalterable circumstances, the possessor of longer and more practical experience. Through centuries of conflict the Europeans had come to learn that war is in almost every case contrived with the expectation of victory, and that such an expectation is diminished under a system of balanced forces which renders victory difficult if not uncertain. The defensive value of armaments, strategic frontiers, alliances, and neutralization, could be computed with approximate accuracy : the defensive value of ' virtue all round ' could not be thus computed. If in fact Wilsonism could be integrally and universally applied, and if in fact Europe could rely upon America for its execution and enforcement, then indeed an alternative was offered infinitely preferable to the dangerous and provocative balances of the European system. Backed by the assurance of America's immediate and unquestioned support, the statesmen of Europe might possibly have jettisoned their old security for the wider security offered them by the theories of Woodrow Wilson. But were they certain that America would be so unselfish, so almost quixotic, as to make Wilsonism safe for Europe ? Were they certain, even, that the European Powers would, when it came to the point, apply Wilsonism to themselves ? The Fourteen Points were hailed as an admirable method of extracting motes from the eyes of others : would any great and victorious Power apply them for the purposes of extracting beams from their own body politic ? The most ardent British advocate of the principle of self-determination found himself, sooner or later, in a false position. However fervid might be our indignation regarding Italian claims to Dalmatia and the Dodecanese it could be cooled by a reference, not to Cyprus only, but to Ireland, Egypt and India. We had accepted a system for others which, when it came to practice, we should refuse to apply to ourselves.

Nor was this the only element of falsity by which the gospel of Woodrow Wilson was discredited from the start. The Anglo-Saxon is gifted with a limitless capacity for excluding his own practical requirements from the application of the idealistic theories which he seeks to impose on others. Not so the Latin. The logical precision of the French, and to a less extent the Italian, genius does not permit such obscurantism. The Anglo-Saxon is apt to accuse the Latin of ' cynicism ' because he hesitates to adhere to a religion which he would not be prepared to apply to his own conduct as distinct from the conduct of others. The Latin accuses the Anglo-Saxon of ' cant ' because he desires to enforce upon others a standard of behaviour which he would refuse to adopt himself. The contrast between the two is not, in fact, one between cynicism and hypocrisy, it is one between two divergent habits of mind. The Anglo-Saxon is apt to feel before he thinks, and the Latin is apt to think before he feels.

It was this divergence of habit, this gap between reason and emotion, which induced the Latins to examine the Revelation of Woodrow Wilson in a manner more scientific, and therefore more critical, than we did ourselves. From this examination they reached certain deductions which destroyed their faith.

They observed, for instance, that the United States in the course of their short but highly imperialistic history, had constantly proclaimed the highest virtue while as constantly violating their professions and resorting to the grossest materialism. They observed that all Americans liked to feel in terms of Thomas Jefferson but to act in terms of Alexander Hamilton. They observed that such principles as the equality of man were not applied either to the yellow man or to the black. They observed that the doctrine of self-determination had not been extended either to the Red Indians or even to the Southern States. They were apt to examine 'American principles and American tendencies' not in terms of the Philadelphia declaration, but in terms of the Mexican War, of Louisiana, of those innumerable treaties with the Indians which had been violated shamelessly before the ink was dry. They observed that, almost within living memory, the great American Empire had been won by ruthless force. Can we blame them if they doubted, not so much the sincerity as the actual applicability of the gospel of Woodrow Wilson? Can we blame them if they feared lest American realism would, when it came to the point, reject the responsibility of making American idealism safe for Europe? Can we wonder that they preferred the precisions of their own old system to the vague idealism of a new system which America might refuse to apply even to her own continent ?

It is only fair to record that on the American Delegation themselves this unfortunate disparity produced a sense of impotence. The President himself was able to dismiss from his consciousness all considerations which might disturb the foundations of his mystic faith. Colonel House, being a man of robust intelligence, might have been able, had he possessed supreme control, to bridge the gulf in a wholly scientific manner, to evolve an honest triumph of engineering. Yet upon the other members of the delegation, who were ardent and sincere, the suspicion that America was asking Europe to make sacrifices to righteousness which America would never make, and had never made, herself, produced a mood of diffidence, uncertainty and increasing despair. Had President Wilson been a man of exceptional breadth of vision, of superhuman determination, he might have triumphed over all these difficulties. Unfortunately neither the will-power nor the brain-power of President Wilson were in any sense superhuman.

3

The collapse of President Wilson at the Paris Peace Conference is one of the major tragedies of modern history. To a very large extent that collapse can be attributed to the defects of his own intelligence and character. It is necessary to examine these defects and to relate them to the errors both of strategy and tactics which he committed.

' He possessed,' writes Colonel House, ' one of the

most difficult and complex characters I have ever known.' The bewilderment with which, in Paris, his blindness and irresolution filled those who were closest to him, is reflected in the extravagant explanations which they seek to devise. Mr. Stannard Baker, for instance, goes to all lengths to prove that Woodrow Wilson was the victim of a conspiracy on the part of the old diplomacy. Mr. Lansing, more equable in his judgment, implies that the apotheosis conferred upon the President after he landed in Europe upset the poise of his mind. Others have gone so far as to suggest that the constant twitching of the left side of his face, the illness which, under the guise of influenza attacked him in April, were early symptoms of that paralysis which was to strike him down in October. Be that as it may, the fact remains that the defects of President Wilson's character, his rigidity and spiritual arrogance, became pathologically enhanced after his arrival in Europe. They loomed as almost physical phenomena above the Conference of Paris.

It cannot be said that Woodrow Wilson under-estimated the importance of his mission to Europe or the determinant role which he personally would be expected to play. He may, as Colonel House suggests, have looked forward to the Conference as to ' an intellectual treat.' Yet he was fully conscious of the immense responsibility devolving on him, fully aware of the appalling difficulties with which he would have to cope. He visualised himself (and in this, at that date, was no illusion) as the prophet of humanity, as an ambassador accredited to righteousness by all the world. ' If,' he proclaimed on landing, ' we do not heed the mandates of mankind, we shall make ourselves the most conspicuous and deserved failures in the history of the world.'

It would be inaccurate, in spite of such emotionalism, to regard Woodrow Wilson solely as a demagogic mystic who believed that a few sentences of English prose would at a breath demolish the ancient parapets of Europe. I have already emphasised his mystic, even his superstitious, side. His childish belief in the personal relation between himself and the number 13 is as trivial as his conception of the voice of the ' plain people ' as being identical with the judgment of God, is an important manifestation of this mysticism. Yet he had his practical aspects. He warned the members of the delegation when addressing them in the saloon of the *George Washington* that the battle before them would not be easy. He warned them in the words of Josiah Quincy that they must fight for the new order, ' agreeably if we can, disagreeably if we must.' Mr. Lansing, it is true, condemns the President for his unbusinesslike methods, for his lack of programme or co-ordination. ' From first to last,' he writes, ' there was no team work, no common counsel, and no concerted action.' Such a criticism, if I may venture the remark, might have applied to others among the plenipotentiaries. As compared with his colleagues at the Council table, Mr. Wilson was fully practical, admirably informed, perfectly precise. Mr. Balfour used frequently to assure us that there was no fault to be found with the President's technique. In conference he was invariably patient, conciliatory, calm. He was a trifle slow-minded at moments, but then he was dealing with the swift arrows of Clemenceau's latin intellect, with the kingfisher dartings of Mr. Lloyd George's intuition. The collapse of Woodrow Wilson must be ascribed to causes far deeper than any lack of diplomatic technique or conference equipment.

The President, it must be remembered, was the descendant of Covenanters, the inheritor of a more immediate presbyterian tradition. That spiritual arrogance which seems inseparable from the harder forms of religion had eaten deep into his soul. It had been confirmed in the course of many battles with the Faculty of Princeton. His vision had been narrowed by the intensive ethical nurture which he had received : he possessed, as he himself admitted, ' a one-track mind.' This intellectual disability rendered him blindly impervious, not merely to human character, but also shades of difference. He possessed no gift for differentiation, no capacity for adjustment to circumstances. It was his spiritual and mental rigidity which proved his undoing. It rendered him as incapable of withstanding criticism as of absorbing advice. It rendered him blind to all realities which did not accord with his preconceived theory, even to the realities of his own decisions. He and his conscience were on terms of such incessant intimacy that any little disagreement between them could easily be arranged. The profound, rigid, and quite justified conviction of his own spiritual rectitude ; the active belief that God, Wilson and the People would triumph in the end ; led him to look upon his own inconsistencies as mere transient details in the one great impulse towards right and justice. He identified the Covenant of the League of Nations with this his central impulse, and before the Ark of the Covenant he sacrificed his Fourteen Points one by one. Let it be hoped that the final clouding of his brain spared him the horror of understanding either what he had done to Europe, or what the American politicians had done to him.

His spiritual arrogance, the hard but narrow texture of his mind, is well illustrated by his apparent unawareness of political reality coupled with his distressing awareness of party reality. On the one hand he refused, for party reasons, to associate with himself any outstanding figure among his political opponents. Mr. Henry White, though a Republican, was not the representative which the Republican Party would themselves have chosen. The extreme bitterness with which Woodrow Wilson regarded all political opponents is one of the least agreeable, or prudent, traits in his character. On the other hand, although a violent party enthusiast, he seems to have been strangely blind to his own position in politics. He informed the members of his delegation in a solemn address delivered on board the *George Washington* that not only would America be the only disinterested nation at the Conference, but that he himself was the only plenipotentiary possessed of a full mandate from the people. ' The men,' he said, ' whom we are about to deal with, do not represent their own people.' Yet at that very moment elections were in progress in England which were to send Lloyd George to Paris with a popular mandate more overwhelming than any recorded. M. Clemenceau, a few days later, obtained in the French Chamber a vote of Confidence of four to one. Whereas Mr. Wilson himself, as the result of the elections of a month before, was faced with an actual majority against him in both Houses of Congress. His refusal to confront these facts indicates a mind narrowing down to the exclusion of all outside light. It indicates (and there can be few better exhibits) that his mind was illumined only by the incense of his own self-worship ; God-worship ; People-worship.

As happens to most theocrats, Woodrow Wilson was a solitary and exclusive man. As is the case with many people possessed of active presbyterian consciences, he was secretive, even towards himself. ' He never,' so records his most ardent supporter, ' seemed to appreciate the value of mere human contact.' ' He appeared,' says Mr. Lansing, ' to consider opposition a personal affront.' He was very willing to apply to his own admirable experts for information : he was seldom prepared to listen to them when they ventured to tender advice. In this predilection for the information of his experts in preference to their ideas, President Wilson was not unique among the plenipotentiaries of the Conference. Nor can we blame them ; there were so many ideas : there was so much information : inevitably the plenipotentiaries, overwhelmed as they were, preferred to select from the latter those elements which accorded best with their own conception of the former. This common tendency among the plenipotentiaries accounts for the divergence of opinion expressed by the United States experts when cross-examined by their own Senate upon this very point. Mr. Lamont, one of the most unassailable figures at the Peace Conference, stated that the President consulted freely. Yet Mr. Lamont was a financial and economic expert and the President did not, in such matters, aspire to personal knowledge. Mr. Lansing, on the other hand, who was juridically and politically minded, contends that he took no counsel at all. ' It was,' he writes, ' an entirely personal matter with him.' In this, at least, President Wilson was on a par with his colleagues. The insistence of his critics upon his inability to consult his experts is not, I think, a very valuable insistence. What is interesting is not the area of mentality where President Wilson was like his colleagues on the Council ; it is the area where he differed from them ; it is that area which I desire to explore.

A side-light on the President's character to which I have already drawn attention, is furnished by his sensitiveness to press-criticisms, and especially to ridicule. The point, though I have mentioned it before, is worth examining. Mr. Lloyd George and M. Clemenceau were, in this respect, gloriously pachydermatous. Mr. Wilson retained his school-girl skin. On February 10, M. Capus wrote an article in the *Figaro* which ran as follows : ' President Wilson has lightly assumed a responsibility such as few men have ever borne. Success in his idealistic efforts will undoubtedly place him among the greatest characters of history. *Mais il faut dire hardiment, que s'il échouait il plongerait le monde dans un chaos dont le bolschévisme russe ne nous offre qu'une faible image : et sa responsabilité devant la conscience humaine dépasserait ce que peut supporter un simple mortel.*' President Wilson countered this abhorrent lucidity on the part of M. Capus by threatening to transfer the Conference to Geneva. Yet he suffered much. And in the days of the April crisis his position was weakened by this strange form of suffering. The French Press, by that date, had discovered that President Wilson was not merely theological and inconvenient, but actually funny. They indulged themselves in frivolous antics

at his expense. M. Clemenceau was able to extract
many concessions from the President in return for a
promise to put an end to these witticisms. A sense of
humour is not therefore, in every circumstance, a cause
of weakness : his immunity to that failing proved a
positive disadvantage to Woodrow Wilson in Paris.
Mr. Lansing comments upon the little reserved laugh
with which the President would cover up the slowness of
his mental movements. ' It sounded,' he said, ' almost
apologetic.' Hour after hour would Mr. Lansing
sit beside the President in that extravagant saloon
which was the centre of the Supreme Council, listen-
ing silently to the arid cachinnations with which his
President would seek to evade the tragedy of his own
incomprehension. Mr. Lansing would spend his subservient time scribbling portraits of hobgoblins upon
his letter-pad. Much must be forgiven to Mr. Lansing
for his silent endurance throughout those endless hours
when he observed the sands of resolution slipping
aridly through the President's fingers.

' The world,' thus had the President addressed his
future coadjutors in the expectant smoking-room of
the *George Washington*, ' The world will be intoler-
able if only arrangements ensue ; this is a Peace Conference in which arrangements cannot be made in the
old style.' Having delivered this pronouncement,
Woodrow Wilson wallowed in arrangements as a
tourist agent wallows in cross-country connections.
Within a few days he had accepted an arrangement
regarding the Brenner frontier. He allowed himself to
be persuaded that war pensions could be classed as
' damage to the civilian population.' He allowed himself to believe that the mandatory system was in fact

something different from annexation. He swallowed the war-guilt clause, and the grotesque clauses which arraigned perfectly innocent people among the war-criminals. He allowed the whole disarmament question to be ' shunted off' into the realm of the one-sided disarmament of Germany. He surrendered in Shantung, even as he surrendered on Poland. He surrendered over the Rhineland, even as he surrendered in the Saar. On the reparation, financial and economic clauses he exercised no healthy influence at all, being, as he confessed, ' not much interested in the economic subjects.' He allowed the self-determination of Austria to be prohibited by one of the most specious phrases ever drafted by jurists. He permitted the frontiers of Germany, Austria and Hungary to be drawn in a manner which was a flagrant violation of his own doctrine. He said to his opponents, ' I must stick by my principles, I ask you only to show me how your desires can be made to accord with my professions.' And at the end of these tergiversations he continued to maintain that his original intentions had not, in fact, been infringed—that in the Covenant of the League could be found the whole cornucopia of blessings which he had undertaken to furnish to the world.

It never dawned upon him that in signing the Treaty of Guarantee with France he had dealt a blow to the prestige of his own Covenant from which that messianic doctrine was never to recover. Piteously he grasped at excuses for his own weakness. The Shantung settlement had been accepted to save the world from a new form of militarism. The Rhineland settlement had been agreed to in order to save the world from dislocation. ' The great problem,' he said

on that occasion, ' is the problem of agreement, because the most fatal thing that could happen, I should
say, in the world would be that sharp lines of division
should be drawn between the Allied and Associated
Powers.'   ' Personally,' he added, ' I think the thing
will solve itself upon the admission of Germany to the
League of Nations.'

The Covenant, in fact, became for him the boxroom
in which he stored all inconvenient articles of furniture.
' There is,' said Mr. Lansing, ' in his mentality a strange
mixture of positiveness and indecision. . . . Sudden-
ness, rather than promptness, has always marked his
decisions.'   These, surely, are manifestations of an
essentially weak character.   His transference of faith,
away from the Fourteen Points and towards the
Covenant, is another symptom of that inner insecurity.
The League, however valuable it has been, and will be,
as the clearing-house of international disagreements,
could never have become, even had America adhered
to it, a super-state directing all international activity.
Mr. Wilson, having surrendered so much in the realm
of fact, tried to recoup himself for these defeats in the
realm of theory.   Here again he was lacking in realism.
' He gave them,' writes Dr. Dillon, ' credit for virtues
which would have rendered the League unnecessary,
and displayed indulgence for passions which made its
speedy realisation hopeless.'   There must have been
moments, towards the end of April, when President
Wilson, despite his obscurantism, must have realised
with anguish that he had made a muddle of his own
doctrine.   Yet with what torture of soul can he have
reflected upon the increasing probability that the
American People, that divinity in whom he trusted so

blindly, would be the first to repudiate the only reputable work which he had accomplished ?

4

It is frequently alleged that the least pardonable among President Wilson's errors was his failure to warn his Associates that the United States might perhaps be unwilling to assume the obligation of supporting a system for the furtherance of which these same Associates were being asked to make such heavy sacrifices of personal acquisition and security. Such an allegation is neither wholly accurate, nor wholly fair.

On the one hand the European Powers were perfectly aware that President Wilson was not really representative of American opinion as it stood at the time. Early in January Mr. Lloyd George explained at a secret meeting of the British Empire Delegation the predicament in which he found himself. The Congressional elections of the previous November, the pronouncements of ex-President Roosevelt, the present attitude of the Senate, all indicated that America would not honour the blank cheque which Mr. Wilson desired Europe to accept in place of the older currency. Yet what was to be done ? Constitutionally the President was still the spokesman and the chief executive officer of his country. Was it possible to inform him to his face that we distrusted his credentials ? Obviously such a course was wholly impossible. The only thing which Europe could do was to save the face of the President ; the only thing that Wilson would do was to save the face of Europe. Here, again, was a falsity of position which, although vital, has never been sufficiently stressed. Like most false

positions it seemed too delicate for scientific or immediate probing. This particular abscess was never
lanced.

On the other hand, President Wilson was not himself quite certain to what extent he would be repudiated
by his own people. M. Clemenceau has recorded that
when questioned regarding a possible change in
American opinion the President 'invariably replied
with imperturbable confidence.' ' America,' he said,
' has taken much from me. She will take this also.'
' I admit,' he informed the Supreme Council on
March 20, ' that the United States must assume the
responsibilities, as well as take the benefits, of the
League of Nations. Nevertheless there is great antipathy in the United States to the assumption of these
responsibilities.' His optimism, as when he contended
in perfect seriousness that the United States would
accept a mandate for Armenia or even Constantinople,
filled us with alarm. Yet it was not wholly due to personal self-confidence. It must be recollected that, in
March of 1919, 34 of the 36 State legislatures and 33
Governors had endorsed the League. Even so hostile
a critic as Mr. Lansing admits that, so late as June 1919,
' it was a common belief that the President would compose his differences with a sufficient number of
Republican Senators.' It could not then be foreseen
that Mr. Lodge would be able to twist a world responsibility into a partisan issue. The fact remains, none
the less, that after his visit to Washington in February,
Mr. Wilson must have known that, even if the Monroe
doctrine were inserted in the Covenant and thereby.
released America from all responsibility to Europe, it
was questionable whether the Senate would ratify what

he had done. It might be contended, even, that it was
the realisation of this appalling fact which induced him
to surrender his principles to the desires of Europe.
If this be so, there is as yet no evidence to prove it.
Nor did the methods and manner of President Wilson
before, and after, his February visit differ from each
other to an extent which would justify any such assumption. The fact, such as it was, seemed too terrible to
face. The whole Treaty had been constructed on the
assumption that the United States would be not
merely a contracting but an actively executant party.
France had been persuaded to abandon her claim to a
buffer state between herself and Germany in return for
a guarantee of armed support from the United States.
The whole Reparation settlement was dependent for
its execution on the presence on the Reparation Commission of a representative of the main creditor of
Europe. The whole Treaty had been deliberately, and
ingeniously, framed by Mr. Wilson himself to render
American co-operation essential. Clearly, as M. Capus
had remarked in January, the assumption and subsequent betrayal of such responsibilities was a burden
that no human being could survive. Mr. Wilson did
not survive it.

5

Some experience and much study of international
negotiation have left me with one abiding conviction.
I have attended many Conferences and from each of
them I have derived a definite residue of certainty. It
is this. The essential to good diplomacy is precision.
The main enemy of good diplomacy is imprecision.
It is for this reason that I have endeavoured in

this book to convey an impression of the horrors of vagueness. The old diplomacy may have possessed grave faults. Yet they were venial in comparison to the menaces which confront the new diplomacy. These menaces can be defined under two separate headings. The first is open versus secret diplomacy. In other words a democratic versus an expert conduct of international affairs. Amateurishness, in all such matters, leads to improvisation. Openness, in all such matters, leads to imprecision. No statesman is prepared in advance and in the open to bind himself to a precise policy. An imprecise policy means no policy at all. It means aspiration only. We all have our expectations.

The second menace is that implicit in the expression ' Diplomacy by Conference.' Nothing could be more fatal than the habit (the at present persistent and pernicious habit) of personal contact between the Statesmen of the World. It is argued, in defence of this pastime, that the Foreign Secretaries of the Nations ' get to know each other.' This is an extremely dangerous cognisance. Personal contact breeds, inevitably, personal acquaintance and that, in its turn, leads in many cases to friendliness : there is nothing more damaging to precision in international relations than friendliness between the Contracting Parties. Locarno, not to mention Thoiry, should have convinced us of the desirability of keeping our statesmen segregated, immune and mutually detached. This is no mere paradox. Diplomacy is the art of negotiating *documents* in a ratifiable and therefore dependable form. It is by no means the art of conversation. The affability inseparable from any conversation between

Foreign Ministers produces allusiveness, compromises, and high intentions. Diplomacy, if it is ever to be effective, should be a disagreeable business. And one recorded in hard print.

I can trace in my own development the stages by which I attained 'to this, assuredly incontrovertible, thesis. I can trace my journey to Damascus in terms of my journey to the Paris Peace Conference. I travelled inspired only by the doctrines of Woodrow Wilson. I had, myself, no victorious triumph in my heart, no desire for punishment or vindication. I thought only in terms of the New Europe : and I interpreted these terms through the revelation of the Prophet of the White House. I discovered that this prophet was a dry and uncertain man. I was disconcerted by this discovery. I subsequently acquired the pained realisation that my prophet was not in the least prepared to enforce his own prophecy. I deserted to other teachers. They were there at my elbow. There was Mr. Balfour, and Mr. Lloyd George and General Smuts, and Robert Cecil and Venizelos, and Benes, and Eyre Crowe. It was from them that I learnt my lesson.

Mr. Balfour taught me that emotionalism in politics was always wrong : that there was something between emotionalism and cynicism which was difficult of attainment but which, with intelligence, could partially, and only temporarily, be attained. Mr. Lloyd George taught me that apparent opportunism was not always irreconcilable with vision, that volatility of method is not always indicative of volatility of intention. In his memorandum of March 25, in his great fight of May 4, he showed that a politician is better, when it comes to reasonableness, than a theocrat. The extinction of my worship for Wilson occurred when a member of his delegation informed me how the President had reacted to the endeavours of Lloyd George to render the Treaty more just and reasonable. Mr. Wilson informed his staff that these endeavours had ' left him tired.' I was appalled by this revelation.

General Smuts taught me that, whatever mistakes we may have made in Paris, the only defeat that really mattered was the admission of a durable defeat. It was Smuts—armed, gentle, and aware of present and future horizons beyond my ken—who taught me to disapprove, never to forget to disapprove, and yet not to let my disapproval creep into my soul.

Robert Cecil—with whom I had little contact—taught me one thing. He made a speech at a banquet at which was inaugurated that invaluable creation—the Royal Institute of International Affairs. He said that the test of our value was the extent of our dissatisfaction. That remark was a revelation to me and an encouragement.

Apart from these practical idealists came the idealistic practitioners. Undoubtedly Venizelos was an imperialist, and I suppose that, in his confidence in his own country, he was wrong. Yet here was a man humane above all others, an intelligence always ready for the assault, a gentleness almost virulent in its applicability. Benes taught me that the Balance of Power was not necessarily a shameful, but possibly a scientific, thing. He showed me that only upon the firm basis of such a balance could the fluids of European amity pass and repass without interruption.

And then there was Eyre Crowe. Immediate to me, and incessantly controlling, this man of extreme violence and extreme gentleness became almost an obsession. He was so human. He was so super-human. At one moment we would observe with alarm his outrageous insolence in face of M. Clemenceau or some other bully. 'Crowe,' said Clemenceau (who had an eye for value), 'c'est un homme à part.' At the next moment one would observe his immense solicitude towards a typist who had a cold in her head. It is difficult to speak of Crowe without lapsing into the soft ground of sentimentality. Yet here, if ever, was a man of truth and vigour. I should wish to think that upon myself Eyre Crowe had exercised a determining influence. I feel, however, that I am too small a glass to have received the abundance of such a vintage. Yet one thing at least I did absorb, and it was this : Emotional dishonesty can be forgiven, since it knows not what it does. Intellectual dishonesty can never be forgiven.

It is for this reason, because of this lesson, that I dedicate this book to the memory of Eyre Crowe.

BOOK II

AS IT SEEMED THEN

AUTHOR'S NOTE TO BOOK II

THE extracts from my 1919 diary which are here printed require some explanation. I give this explanation as shortly as possible.

I wish it clearly to be understood that the diary as here printed is not an exact transcript of the diary as written. In the first place, I considered it fitting to leave out such passages as might wound or embarrass people who are still actively interested in public life. In the second place I felt it essential to insert words and passages in all places where the original text was defective or purely telegraphic. The omissions will distress nobody : the insertions may, I fear, induce a suspension of belief. I must therefore justify and explain my insertions.

The diary was not written for publication. It was written merely as an annotation to reinforce my own memory. Above all, it was written under great pressure and, at moments, in verbal shorthand. I have therefore filled in the missing conjunctions and articles. I have gone further. I have at moments reconstructed whole passages. That admission may, I apprehend, discredit the whole diary. Yet I should not wish my readers to imagine that the diary is in any sense a fake.

Let me illustrate the sort of ' editing ' which I have allowed myself. I shall choose a short comparative passage. On Saturday, May 10, I dined with Count Potocki. The event in my diary is recorded as follows : ' Dine Joseph P. : Ritz : anachronism : tell him about P. ; His answer absurd : Chepetowka :

" as an equal ".' That entry, all too clearly, would not convey anything to the common reader. Yet my aural, as distinct from my visual, memory is good. This same passage, as it occurs in the printed version, is as follows : ' Dine with Joseph Potocki at the Ritz. A fine anachronism. I tell him how deeply impressed I had been by hearing Paderewsky make his speech at the Supreme Council. He answers : ' Yes, a remarkable man, a very remarkable man. Do you realise that he was born in one of my own villages ? Actually at Chepetowka. And yet, when I speak to him, I have absolutely the impression of conversing with an equal.'

Now that is a completely accurate rendering of the shorthand notes which actually figure in the diary. I am convinced that all my other expansions are equally justified and equally legitimate. At moments—as in the records of political conversations or interviews with leading statesmen—I recorded at the time and in my diary the exact dialogue which occurred. It is only in such incidental passages as the above that there is often a gap between the written and the printed word. My account of the signature of the Versailles Treaty has, for instance, required but little editing. As also my references to the Councils of X and IV, or my discussions with Mr. Lloyd George and Mr. Balfour.

Nor have I, at any place, attributed to myself ideas or previsions which do not occur in my actual text. To those who specialise in new vices I recommend the fierce temptation of publishing a diary which one has written fourteen years before. The desire to suppress a word here and there, to alter a word here and there, to add a word here and there, is more potent and in-sidious than any of the odd temptations which I have encountered, and to which generally I have lavishly succumbed. Yet on this point I proclaim my virginity. The reader need not believe me. Yet I think he will. I think that he will see on reading this diary, how tempted, how torturingly tempted, I must have been, to suppress certain expressions and opinions which in the cold print of 1933 are shaming to a degree. I think that the intelligent reader will, on the whole, take the diary on trust. And of one thing at least I am absolutely certain. I am certain that the diary, as printed, does in fact reproduce the ignorance, the vanity, the depression, the hope, the essentially good intentions which animated many of those who struggled blindly through the turmoil of the Conference of Paris. The letter of the diary may have been a trifle ' arranged ' : yet even if that, far less so than might be supposed. But the spirit of the thing, to the very core, is accurate in its uttermost essence. And all those who were with me in Paris will confirm that the accuracy of impression is as limpid as could be.

There is a second explanation which I wish to make. This diary is in no sense a historical document. Nor is it a connected narrative of what happened in Paris in 1919. I should wish it to be read as people read the reminiscences of a subaltern in the trenches. There is the same distrust of headquarters ; the same irritation against the staff-officer who interrupts ; the same belief that one's own sector is the centre of the battle-front ; the same conviction that one is, with great nobility of soul, winning the war quite single-handed. It is easy to smile at such things. I was a young man and, as such, vain. Yet had I, on leaving for the Paris Conference, been able to read a diary such as this dealing with similar experiences at the Congress of Vienna, then I might have been more modest at Paris, more determined about essentials, more stable, and less apt to blame the rulers. I repeat that this diary is published only for the use of the young Foreign Office official who finds himself appointed to the staff of the next World Congress. I trust that this young man will read this diary with attention. And that he will not assume too readily that as the whole rush and flurry of the thing develops he will himself be able to avoid the vanities, the prejudices, the utter exhaustion, the decay of moral fibre, into which I trundled myself. He may think that I come out very badly from this diary. He is abundantly right. But let him at least prepare himself to face similar intricate and subconscious temptations. For they will certainly re-occur.

I should ask the ordinary and less specialised reader not to take this diary too seriously. It is an attempt to convey atmosphere only : it is not an attempt to convey information, and even less an endeavour to record history. It is because I do not wish to exaggerate the factual importance of this record that I have studiously omitted all footnotes and indexes. The subjects by which I was perplexed were often wholly unimportant. It is thus wholly immaterial that the reader should be able to understand what my problems were about. What matters it whether he knows who Bratianu was, or what the Banat, or where Miskolcz ? It matters not a whit. All that I wish to convey is the mixture, the interlocking, the constant shifting of principle and detail and detail and principle. I should wish the ordinary reader to skim through this diary with great speed and without any attempt to understand what was happening. I should wish him to read it in the spirit with which he watches a modern film—thinking only of the aggregate, the cumulative, effect ; not of the details. A close-up of a factory siren is succeeded by a picture of an empty street with a newspaper blowing along it in the wind of dawn. A fierce face, talking wildly, flashes on to the screen, and is succeeded by a wide expanse of downland with windmills whirling symmetrical. It is not the continuity of this record which is of any representative value : it is its discontinuity : it is not my views or knowledge which are of any interest : it is my foolishness and ignorance. From that point of view I claim in all seriousness that my picture is exact.

A last observation. I have in general replaced the initials of my narrative by the full name. I have retained only three initials. ' Ll. G.' signifies Mr. Lloyd George—whose great work at the Peace Conference I did not wholly appreciate at the time. ' P. W.' stands for President Wilson. One of the most curious things about my diary is that I hardly ever record our incessant suspicion that the Americans would not be able to deliver the goods. Yet, if my memory serves me aright, that was the most constant of our many worries : and it has been the most constant of my many temptations to put it in.

' A. J. B.' stands for Mr. Balfour, at that time Secretary of State for Foreign Affairs. I am grateful to my diary for its passages on Mr. Balfour. I think that, in this at least, I was right at the time. ' Crowe ' stands for Sir Eyre Crowe—my beloved chief. There are, I think, no other abbreviations of importance.

I. *January* 1 – *January* 12, 1919

CONTACTS

January 1, 1919, *Wednesday*
Busy all day at Foreign Office putting my papers and maps into tin boxes. In evening dine with Gerald Tyrwhitt and on to a show. From there to Henry Churchill's rooms. Holmesdale, Pratt Barlow, Ronnie Griffin, and Gorsky—a Polish officer in a sky blue uniform. Also an unknown and inarticulate American.

January 2, *Thursday*
Clear up at the Foreign Office and leave it after four and a half crowded years in the War Department. Some Abschiedsstimmung. Lunch at the Marlborough. Dine on guard at St. James' with Sam St. Aubyn.

January 3, *Friday*
Leave London for Paris at 11.0 a.m., Charing Cross. Find Eustace Percy and his bride at the station. On the boat meet Taliani—a little Italian friend of Constantinople days. The train after Boulogne is delayed by some accident on the line. Much devastation still around Amiens. Dine in the train with Taliani, Casati (the husband of Marchesa Casati) and de Martino, head of the Italian Foreign Office : a querulous, precise little man. He is to be part of their delegation at the Conference. He insists on paying for my

dinner, stating that my first post-war meal in France shall be at the expense of Italy. He talks of the Treaty of London of 1915, stating that it provides for ' the equilibrium of the Mediterranean.' I say that it does indeed. He tells me that the Italian Plenipotentiaries will probably be Orlando, Sonnino, Diaz and perhaps Bosdari. Reach the Gare du Nord about 11.0 p.m. and drive straight to the Majestic. On arrival find Rex and Allen Leeper in the hall. Take them up to my room—No. 89. Paris very well lit.

January 4, Saturday

Arrange for my registered luggage and tin boxes being fetched from the Gare du Nord. At present there are no regular members of the delegation here except Eustace Percy, the two Leepers and myself. Eustace, being newly married, has established himself in a flat in the Avenue d'Iena (No. 72, Ground floor— left). Go down to Eddie Knoblock's flat in the Palais Royal. Find him packing up. Lunch with him—and then on to see Walter Berry. A bomb from a Gotha had fallen in his courtyard and demolished the house opposite. All his windows broken but no serious damage done. Dine with the two Leepers who pro- duce an American friend, Rhys Carpenter—who had been with them at Balliol. He is serving in some capacity on the United States delegation. He is scholarly and shy.

January 5, Sunday

Spend the day with Eddie Knoblock and in the evening go through my papers and maps. Everything in order.

January 6, *Monday*

Crowe and Vansittart arrive. Have a long conseil de guerre with Allen Leeper. Lunch at Majestic and on with him to visit the American delegation at 4 Place de la Concorde. They have a ramshackle office stretching out over Maxims. The place full of marines of the U.S. Navy unpacking cases. In the furthest room, which must certainly have been a cabinet particulier at Maxims, find the three members of the American Delegation, whom Rhys Carpenter tells us will be our opposite numbers. They are all members of Colonel House's ' Enquiry ' and university men. There is Professor Clive Day of Yale—middle-aged, pale, slim, arid, decent. There is Professor Charles Seymour also of Yale—young, dark, might be a major in the Sappers. Third is Professor Lybyer—silent, somewhat remote. They show us their maps. There is a vast relief map in sections depicting the Adriatic, very beautiful. They evidently know their subject backwards. Nice people —but we enter into no details. A feeling, however, that our general views are identical.

From there on to see Také Jonescu at the Meurice. A hot stuffy bedroom and in the passage outside the dim fustanellas of King Nikita's Montenegrin bodyguard. Lounging exotic on the Turkey carpet of the corridor.

Také is rubicund, dapper, continental. Tries to speak English and then relapses into French. He is extremely bitter about his treatment by Bratianu. Latter had offered him five seats in the coalition Cabinet, *i.e.* Finance (already compromised by promises to the French), Commerce, Agriculture and two other portfolios. On these terms he might be one of

the Rumanian plenipotentiaries. He had indignantly
refused, and stated his intention of going to Cannes.
Why Cannes ? The Rumanian delegates will thus be
Misu, Antonescu (their Minister in Paris whom Také
hates), and possibly Bratianu himself. Také says that
the Bratianu Cabinet is very unpopular in the country :
the inclusion of Constantinescu (' Porco ') has alien-
ated the upper classes : lower classes affected by bolshevism and general economic conditions : Tran-
sylvanians anti-Bratianu though bound to him by his
promise that he will get the whole of the Banat under
the 1916 Treaty. Také had come to some arrangement
with Trumbic under which the Banat would be amic-
ably divided between Rumania and the S.C.S.,[1] and
the Succession States would present a united bloc in
Paris as against the Great Powers. Bratianu had used
his knowledge of this arrangement to discredit Také
in patriotic circles at Bucharest.

He spoke at length on the position of the King : his
impulsiveness : his subordination to the Queen : his,
and her, treatment of Averescu, the agrarian leader.
He told us that the Queen had publicly insulted
Averescu and had subsequently owned to Také that
she had made a mistake. ' J'ai eu tort.' He was also
critical about the cancellation of Prince Carol's mar-
riage and indicated that the latter had done himself
much harm.

Také evidently embittered and revengeful. This
rather affects his moderation and judgment. In the
last resort he looks at things from a parliamentary
point of view. This is a pity, since he is the only man

[1] In the early stages of the Conference the Jugo-Slavs were referred to as
the ' S.C.S.' or ' S.H.S.'

who realises (1) that it is a mistake for the Rumanians
to insist upon the 1916 Treaty, (2) that the Transyl-
vanians will only come in on a ' free union ' basis, and
not on a basis of annexation. (3) That a dispute with
the S.C.S. over the Banat would weaken the whole
position, the whole bloc, of Succession States as
against the Great Powers. His elimination from the
scene will seriously prejudice this bloc, and Italy will
be the one to draw profit.

Dine at the Majestic. Eric Maclagan there. He is
doing some sort of Press work and has an office near
the Embassy. On to Eustace Percy's flat afterwards.
He tells me about the League of Nations—the various
schemes that are at present on the carpet.

January 7, *Tuesday*
Down to Eric Maclagan's office, and obtain particulars as to the treatment in regard to schools, language,
etc., of French Canadians in Canada. This may be of
use in respect of the cultural autonomy of minorities
in the New States.

Lunch with the American Delegation at the Crillon.
The whole place is like an American battleship and
smells odd. Day, Seymour and Lybyer at luncheon.
Also Beer the organising secretary. I gather the
following : (1) Albania. Not so pro-Albanian as I
expected. Rather opposed to Italian mandate but will
accept it in the end. In favour of Ipek and Djakova
going to Albania in the north, and a limited concession
to the Greeks in Northern Epirus. Not Koritsa.
Really the same view as our own. (2) Greece. Cession
of Doiran and Ghevgueli. Some idea of giving Kavalla
to the Bulgars. They throw a fly over us about

Cyprus. The fish does not rise. (3) Serbia. They are
pro-Jugo-Slav of course, but not wildly so. Unim-
pressed by Serbian claims to Pirot and Widin. (4)
Bulgaria. Appear to have same ideas as us as to giving
Ishtib and Kochana—but they rely more on watershed
than on river frontiers—for the sensible reason that
former are less populated than latter. Very opposed
to Greece taking Western Thrace—where I am with
them. Rather want to give Enos-Midia line in Eastern
Thrace to Bulgaria, but pushing Enos to the south
(Maritza marshes) and Midia to the north (Dercos
water supply). (5) Turkey. Want Turks out of Constantinople. Evidently have some idea of entrusting
resultant zone of the Straits to the smaller Powers—
Denmark and Belgium. But not clear at all as to what
that zone should be (? Gallipoli). Would be quite prepared to see us at Constantinople as Mandatory—but
less prepared to act in that capacity themselves. U.S.
opinion not ready for this responsibility, but they
' might ' be ready to assume responsibility for Armenia.
They are very keen on a Greek zone at Smyrna. I
shall know more on Thursday.

Dine with Eddie Knoblock again at Pruniers. Walk
back. Have a long talk with Crowe. He is realistic :
wants facts, not ideas, however beautiful. Talks about
disarmament : about the League : is it to have an
armed force ? if so, what ? and who commands ?
What about its permanent staff ? What about the
Smaller Powers ? Do they enter on a basis of
equality ? That would be ' most unreal.' Yet if
not equal, how are they to be protected ? Compulsory arbitration ? What about ' national honour and
interests ? '

He tells me that Lloyd George does not want the
United States to have Constantinople.   President
Wilson is back from Rome.

January 8, Wednesday
Round to the Astoria where our office is established
high up on the fifth floor.   View of Arc de Triomphe,
smell of lysol and iodoform, bare boards.   It has just
been evacuated by the Japanese, who used it as a
hospital.   Talk to Mance the War Office railway expert
about transit and communications in our part of the
new map of Europe.   He is very intelligent and helpful.
The maps show clearly that the ethnic frontier and the
common sense of railway communication never coin-
cide, but leave wide gaps.   In Transylvania, especially,
the veins and arteries all run in connexion with the
Austrian trunk lines and have no relation to the
Rumanian lines.   This will constitute a very difficult
problem.

After luncheon go with Allen to see Goga—a Transylvanian poet and politician.   A young Transylvanian
Virgil Tilea is there.   They say they are ' too ashamed
to speak of internal questions.'   On external questions,
however, they show no shame at all, demanding most
of Hungary.   They will send us a memorandum about
the Bukowina.   Meanwhile the Rumanian armies have
occupied Arad and Nagyvarad, but have not advanced
further.

While we are there a young Bukovinan comes in
who has been serving in the French foreign legion.
Not very informative or informed.

Dine at the Hotel.   Hardinge, Mallet, Hurst,
Ronnie Campbell and Armitage Smith arrive.

January 9, Thursday

Lybyer and Day come to see us at the Astoria. We
go into details. (1) Bulgaria. Stern justice. Macedonia, Ishtib and Kochana, with alternative railway.
Difficulty of Gostivar-Monastir line. Serbo-Bulgarian
frontier, little change. They do not believe in that
Pirot and Widin nonsense. Much opposed to cession
of Western Thrace to Greece and incline even to give
Struma frontier to Bulgaria, compensating (*sic*) Greece
in Asia Minor. Dobrudja—1913 line without Silistria
and with certain minor rectifications. (2) Albania.
Evidently not very sure. Ought northern railway to
go to Serbia? What about Ipek and Djakova? Incline to their inclusion in Albania. Eastern frontier
same sort of idea. Southern frontier, here they are
divided. Some want to give Greece Koritsa, others to
give Voiussa line. These contend that the Koritsa
road not really essential to Greece, since an alternative
can be constructed. Would give Italy the mandate if
she abandons her claim to direct possession of Valona.
Internal administration to be on cantonal basis. (3)
Greece. Firm on Italy surrendering Dodecanese.
Firm on Smyrna. Anti-Thrace. (4) Turkey. Evidently firm about turning Turks out of Europe, but
vague as to who is to be her successor in the Constantinople zone. As regards limits of that zone
suggest two alternatives, (*a*) Restricted zone, *i.e.*—
Chataldja lines—Gallipoli-Marmora Islands—and, in
Asia, Shile to Gebze. (*b*) Extended zone. East of
Enos to north of Midia. In Asia, line from Edremid
to Sakharia. First zone would establish three different
sovereignties upon the shores of the Marmora and
second zone therefore preferable. I gather that Presi-

dent Wilson wants some small Power, or some group
of small Powers, to administer this Constantinople or
Straits Zone.   His experts object to this (dangers of
condominium, etc.) and want either U.S.A. or Great
Britain to assume the mandate.   They doubt, however,
whether American opinion would allow of them taking
the mandate themselves.

As regards Turkey in Asia they evidently expect to
have to take over Armenia, but are vague about the
rest.

Altogether a most satisfactory discussion.   They are
intelligent, not too distrustful, alert.

Conversation in evening with Crowe and Valentine
Chirol on following problem : ' If, under self-determination a nationality opts for the U.S.A. as mandatory, and latter is unwilling to accept the responsibility,
is it a violation of self-determination to impose another
mandatory upon them, such as Italy ? '   There is no
answer to this problem.   Any solution would seem to
lead to camouflaged partition and humbug.

We hear that the Russians are constituting a committee or ' conference ' of Ambassadors under Prince
Lvoff — Sazonoff — Giers — Maklakoff — Bakhmetieff
and, I suppose, Nabokoff.   This will be highly
awkward for those who wish to ignore Russia.   I am
delighted.   After all, we are dealing with Russian
interests behind their backs, and the above Committee
have only to formulate a protest in writing for the
Conference to be branded in the history of a future
Russia as having deserted her in her trouble.   I hope
the Committee will be given some sort of watching
brief.   Yet our rulers seem to see in Russia only the
welter of bolshevism.

January 10, *Friday*

Have a long discussion with Crowe on general policy. It is a joy to be working under someone so acute and precise. My mind is, with him, always at ease. Crowe was, I hope, impressed by Allen Leeper's arguments—which, as always, were admirable.

He and I lunched afterwards with Tilea at the Griffon. I pressed him on the subject of cultural autonomy for the minorities which will have to be included within the new Rumanian frontier. He contemplates some scheme by which the village communities should elect three representatives (Magyars), who in agreement with three representatives of the central government should nominate the schoolteachers and settle such questions as language and curriculum. All very simple—if it works.

A Council of Relief is instituted. Hoover at the head.

Dine with Lord Hardinge alone. He talks about the reform of diplomacy. As it was he who reformed the Foreign Office he should also reform the sister service. I point out that after ten years' service my actual salary, minus income tax, is £86 a year. How can we get the best people under such a system? He is inclined to agree. He is never unprogressive if taken the right way. Yet he dislikes people having grievances. ' I,' he says, ' *made* my opportunities—why do these young men now ask that opportunities should be made for them ? ' He quite overlooks the fact that at my age he had for long been a second secretary, and was not hampered by this deadly queue which now blocks promotion. Yet I agree with him in a way. We may not rise very quickly in actual rank or salary,

but any energetic person is given important work from
the start.

January 11, *Saturday*

They tried yesterday to assassinate Kramarsh the
Czech Prime Minister. Seton Watson comes to see us
in the morning. He talks about Fiume, saying (1) that
it cannot be detached from the suburb of Susak and
that the two together give a Slav majority, (2) That it
is dominated by the hills behind and that whoever
holds Fiume simply must have a hinterland at the back.
This hinterland is wholly Slav. While he is still there,
Pangal, the editor of the ' Rumanie,' arrives. A long
discussion about the Szeklers, the Banat, the Ruthenes,
etc. No Rumanian statesman, except Také, would dare
to suggest a reasonable solution of all these problems.
We shall have to impose one.

The Americans come to luncheon. We discuss the
difficulty of finding a territorial frontier which, while
giving a sense of finality (and therefore of security of
tenure) will also leave the door open for future revision. He (*sic*) agreed with me that as regards the
Balkans the thing to do was to get it into their thick
heads that the settlement was final in so far as internal
propaganda was concerned : no more massacres, no
more comitadjis : but that some power of subsequent
revision should rest with the League of Nations.

After luncheon Crowe tells me of the objections
raised by the Colonial and other Offices to our ceding
Cyprus to Greece. These objections seem to me to
be both material and immaterial. He himself is
impressed by them.

Lloyd George and the Colonial Premiers arrive.

January 12, *Sunday*

Work all morning at Albanian railways. It is clear that the Nish-Prishtina-Prisrend-Scutari-San Giovanni line is the only one which offers any real advantage over the Salonica outlet (400 kilom. versus 450 kilom.).

There is a preliminary, though unofficial, meeting of the plenipotentiaries to discuss procedure. This is their first meeting.

Lunch with Rhys Carpenter of the American Delegation. A witty man : a philologist and archaeologist : a cultured mind. Talk with Edwin Montagu. Go and see Pierre de Lacretelle : he is away. To Eustace Percy's flat afterwards.

II. *January 13 – January 20*

OPENING MEETINGS

January 13, Monday

First official meeting of the Conference although they do not call themselves that : they meet as the Supreme War Council. The first avowed meeting is not to be till Saturday next.

Work all morning at our own case. Lunch with Seton Watson at Castiglione, Marianu, Pangal and Walter Lippman there. Little of interest.

The British Empire Delegation meet as a body.

Have a talk with Edwin Montagu about future of Constantinople. I gather that if the Americans take it over he will not object to the Turks being turned out.

We get the French programme of procedure, which has been drafted by Berthelot : not very enlightening.

Dine with Eddie Knoblock at the Griffon. Sir William Wiseman there. He is the ' friend of House ' even as House is the ' friend of Wilson.' *Arcades ambo.* We have Pouilly 1906—excellent. Wiseman tells me that after President Wilson and House had had a long talk with Sonnino upon Italian claims in the Adriatic, House said, ' That man is convinced : there *may* be something in it.' To which P. W. : ' Then let him plant his case in the full sun of publicity. If there is anything in it, then it will grow into a great cause. If there is nothing in it, then it will wither away.' I fail to see Sidney Sonnino doing anything of the sort.

January 14, *Tuesday*

Crowe tells me that it has been decided that each
Power must produce their views on all questions in
writing. This seems both to Crowe and me an impossible arrangement, since it will give no scope for
negotiation, and commit everyone to maximum claims
from the start. Anyhow we have still to hear what the
decision actually entails.

Lybyer comes round and we introduce him to
Arnold Toynbee. We discuss the limits of the Constantinople zone and he shows us the American line on
a map. It is a far better line than ours.

Lunch with Eustace Percy and his wife. Go off
from there to the Crillon with Esme Howard and
E. H. Carr. I take with me the papers about the
Italian Treaty (the Secret Treaty of April 1915) as we
had been given to understand that Lloyd George and
Balfour were to discuss it with the Americans. We
find some difficulty on reaching the Crillon, nobody
being aware of any such meeting, nobody being sure
where we ought to go or where we ought to wait.
Uncertainty existing among the marine department of
the United States delegation as to whether we should
be allowed to wait at all. In the middle of this embarrassment Balfour and Eric Drummond arrive. We
rise in the lift to Colonel House's apartments on the
fourth floor. We then learn that the meeting is to take
place at President Wilson's house near the Parc Mon-
ceau. We bundle back into our car and follow Balfour
through the streets. On arrival—pickets of police,
troops, much saluting. Wilson is much guarded. We
are taken up to an upper gallery which contains a glass
roof and a statue of Napoleon in Egypt. The house

is the Villa Murat and is Napoleonic in effect. Balfour is ushered into a room on the right. We others wait outside for two and a half hours, while the drone of voices comes from the next room. Mrs. Wilson passes, her high heels tocking on the parquet, a mass of mimosa in her arms. The old butler enters and puts on the lights one by one. I read the 'Irish Times.'

Suddenly, about 4.45, the door opens and out come Lloyd George, followed by Bonar Law, Balfour and P. W.

'Oh!' exclaims A. J. B., 'dear me! Have you been waiting all this time? I never realised! There were several things I wanted to ask you. For instance . . .'

Then turning to the President: 'This is a young friend of mine who could have told us all we wanted. Now let me see, what was it that we wanted? Oah yes,—Fiume. . . .'

P. W. 'No, not Fiume. We had all that. What we wanted was the exact figure of the Germans who would be annexed by Italy if they got the Brunner (*sic*) frontier. Now can you tell us that?'

H. N. 'Well, not accurately. Mr. President, I have not the exact figures. It should be about 240,000. . . .'

P. W. 'Or was it not 250,000?'

H. N. 'Well, Mr. President, I was going to say 245,000.'

P. W. 'Well, a matter of thousands, anyway.'

H. N. 'Certainly, and anti-Italian thousands.'

P. W. 'You mean they are pro-German, pro-Austrian?'

H. N. 'Well pro-Tyrol, at Bozen above all.'

P. W. 'Then there is another point. Oh yes—about Fiume. Can you give me the figures?'

H. N. hopefully 'Oh yes—do you mean with or without the suburbs ? '

P. W. ' Yes, there is a suburb called Ashak or something.'

H. N. ' Susak. Well, the figures are, the figures are . . .' pause . . . ' I have got them here ' (Scrubble in my pouch : quite rapid production of statistics : read them out impressively).

P. W. ' So I thought—and the line between Fiume and Ashak is a small one.'

H. N. ' A mere rivulet, Mr. President, one cannot possibly separate the two.'

P. W. ' So I gather. But the Italians tell me that if one tries to pass from Fiume to Ashak one is certain to be murdered.'

H. N. " Oh, but Mr. President . . .'

P. W. ' Waal ! I guessed he was talking through his hat. Well, goodnight to you gentlemen. Goodnight, Mr. Balfour.'

We withdraw. This is called ' giving expert advice.'

P. W. is younger than his photographs : glabre : one does not see the teeth except when he smiles, which is an awful gesture : broad shoulders and a narrow waist : his shoulders are out of proportion to his height ; so is his face (not the head itself, but the surface from ear to chin). His clothes are those of a tailor's block : very neat and black and tidy : striped trousers : high collar : pink pin. A southern drawl.

Going downstairs A. J. B. is as courteous as ever. ' I cannot apologise enough for keeping you so long. To tell the truth, the last half-hour we have only been discussing whether Napoleon and Frederic the Great

could be called disinterested patriots.' 'And what
was the conclusion ? ' 'Oh,—I forget the conclusion.'
And so back to the Majestic.

Dine with Armitage Smith and Louis Mallet. Latter
tells me that P. W. read to Balfour a letter which he had
addressed to Sonnino refusing for his part to be bound
by the Treaty of London. All to the good. He had
also had a visit from Weizmann the Zionist. Weizmann had prepared a long series of arguments as to
why the mandate for Palestine should be given to
Great Britain. The President interrupted him with the
words : 'Yes, I know all that. I only wish the British
were prepared to take over all we want them to.'
Weizmann then said how difficult it was to find
a common ground with the French. P. W. : 'I
am with you there. We have no community of
thought.'

January 15, Wednesday

Dr. Madge, the English Doctor to the Rumanian
Court, a clever little man, comes to see us. He is inter-
ested in politics. He says that Také Jonescu is really
delighted not to be a delegate since he sees whither
Rumanian chauvinism is leading, and he is glad to stay
outside and criticize the mistakes of others. An Englishman just back from Kolosvar in Transylvania comes.
He said that Buda Pest was heading rapidly towards
Bolshevism with Karolyi at the helm. He thinks that
Bolshevism when it comes will be short-lived and that
a white reaction will follow. Hungary was very pro-
English and wanted Prince Henry as King. The
peasants have sown nothing this autumn.

Lunch at Griffon with Tilea and Pangal. The Banat

again.   A reference to the Dobrudja being restored to
Bulgaria produces shrill Transylvanian screams.

Back to office.   Write memorandum for Mr. Balfour showing why Italy should not be given Fiume—
even if she declares it a free port.

At 5.0 go round to Mercedes to see the Greeks.
T . . . . . . talks to me about Koritsa as a centre of
Greek culture, adding that the first Greek work ever
printed was printed at Moschopolis.   The Italians in
his view should not be given a mandate over Albania :
they would not succeed : the Albanians would rise
against them : it would be very expensive.   He also
explains the arrangement come to with Serbia regarding access to the Aegean at Salonica.   The Serbs have
their own quays, officials, rolling stock, police and
labour.   He is convinced that a similar arrangement
would work at Kavalla in favour of the Bulgars and
at Smyrna in favour of the Turks.

I then go in and see Venizelos.   In spite of the heat
in the room he wears his black silk cap.   Two evzones
stand in the passage outside.   Venizelos shows me his
ethnical statistics.   ' Je me suis fait un point d'honneur
de préparer une statistique exacte.'   He quotes Die-
trich as confirming his own figures, and as stating that
the whole coast of Asia Minor west of the meridian of
Constantinople is Greek in physical and climatic
elements.

As regards Western and Eastern Thrace I put it to
him that if Greece obtains what she asks she will be
left with a frontier impossible to defend.   He replies,
' Mais de nos jours on ne fait pas de guerres géo-
graphiques.   L'Allemagne en a fait, et vous en voyez
bien le résultat.'   I put to him the danger of irreden-

tism and agitation as between the Constantinople Greeks and the Greeks in Eastern Thrace. He replies : ' What matter ? Do you think we should attack the League of Nations ? Is it not better that you should have at Constantinople a friendly neighbour and not an alien ? '

I put it to him that Bulgaria must have economic outlets to the Aegean. He says what about Varna and Bourgas, which will be far more valuable now that the Straits will be permanently open ? Rumania has only the Black Sea outlet, why should Bulgaria have more ? Consider also the danger of submarines at Porto Lagos. I consider this danger, but it leaves me cold.

He has evidently had assurances from P. W. about the Dodecanese : our hands in this matter are tied by the 1915 Treaty. He sees that. Not a word about Cyprus.

Dine at hotel. Lloyd George there. Work long after dinner.

January 16, Thursday

Work all morning. Benes, the Czech Foreign Minister and Delegate, lunches. His points are : (1) Bohemia wants to reconstruct Mittel Europa on a new basis which is neither German nor Russian. She therefore bases her claims ' not so much on national as on international justifications.' For her, although national unity comes first, and national prosperity second, the ultimate aim is the stability of Central Europe. For this she must have a territorial connection both with Jugo-Slavia and Rumania. The latter connection to be established in Ruthenia : the Galician Ruthenes being mostly Jews do not want to go to Russia, still less to Rumania. (2) Friendly relations with Hungary

will eventually impose themselves by economic necessity. Hungary has always been pro-German even if
anti-Austrian. We westerners have been misled by
assuming that her anti-Vienna policy implied an anti-
Berlin policy also. (3) He found a great gulf between
himself and those of his colleagues, such as Kramarsh,
who had remained in Prague during the whole war.
They thought only in terms of extreme Czech nationalism, and this rendered his own position difficult. His
aim was to maintain in Paris the moral prestige which
the Czechs had won during the war. I say ' Parfaite-
ment, Excellence.'

Altogether an intelligent, young, plausible, little
man with broad views.

After luncheon Crowe, Howard and myself have a
long and difficult talk with William Beveridge, who
has returned from a relief mission to Prague, Vienna
and Buda Pest. He is very pro-Magyar and ignorant
of actualities, which is a pity as he is going to see Lloyd
George.

For some foolish reason the Supreme Council have
allowed Brazil three seats : this will infuriate the
others and in particular Portugal. It will make for bad
blood. Our Dominions get separate representation as
independent countries : this has been taken more
calmly than we expected : people think that it takes us
down a peg. French furious at English being accepted
as an official diplomatic language.

January 17, *Friday*

Venizelos sends his commercial expert to see me to
explain the working of the Serbo-Greek arrangement
regarding a Serb zone of outlet at Salonica. Go into

it very thoroughly as it may serve as a useful analogy for Fiume and Smyrna.

The Press are raging at the lack of facilities given them and wish to attend all meetings. They have gone to great expense in sending their best people here, and they are given no information. We ought to have the most complete publicity, at any rate as regards results. The actual stages of negotiation are more difficult. Yet if the Press get their way and are admitted to all plenary sessions, then the latter will become a farce, at which set speeches will be made by each delegate with an eye to his own public opinion at home. All the real work will be done by private lobbying, which will entail muddle and delay.

Walter Lippman comes to dinner. He is returning to America. What a pity, and why?

Have a talk with Wickham Steed. He tells me that he heard from House that P. W. was about to tell Sonnino that he must give up the Treaty of 1915, but that Mr. Balfour prevented him doing so. I do not believe this. A. J. B. made it quite clear to P. W. on Tuesday that we had no love for the Treaty, but were bound by it.

Madge tells me that Misu, the Rumanian second delegate, is most indignant at my being in charge of the Balkan section. ' Un fort gentil garçon—mais enfin il n'est qu'un troisième secrétaire ! ' I urge Madge to assure Misu that I am not in charge of anything at all, being always under Crowe.

January 18, *Saturday*

The Conference opened officially by Poincaré. Plenary session at Quai d'Orsay at 3.15. Clemenceau rather high handed with the smaller Powers. 'Y a-t-il d'objections? Non?... Adopté.' Like a machine gun.

Jules Cambon said to Ian Malcolm as they were going out, ' Mon cher, savez-vous ce qui va résulter de cette conférence? Une *improvisation*.' Cynical old man.

January 19, *Sunday*

Work more or less in the morning going through stuff that has come over from the F.O. and has accumulated. Motor out to lunch with Charles Sackville West at Versailles. The Derbys and Bob Cecil there. Also General Spears. Latter tells me that Clemenceau said to him the other day, ' Les anglais me grimpent sur le dos.' Not very cheering at this stage. Spears is afraid of French high finance. He told me that Berthelot found himself in a difficult position as he could only work through Pichon, who was obstinate. He is an advocate of leaving the Germans with something in Africa, so as not to render them the sole irresponsible Power when the eventual negro risings mature. I agree with him. But that is looking far ahead. And what is the good of thinking or urging things like that when the whole congress is to be an ' improvisation.'

God! How true and how disheartening that is!

I am distressed about Cyprus. The British Empire Delegation have decided to retain it on strategical and other grounds. They are wrong entirely : its retention compromises our whole moral position in regard to the Italians.

To see Jeanne de Hénaut in the evening. She is much changed.

January 20, *Monday*

Allen Leeper has a long talk with Misu. The latter is moderate and western, but he cannot hope to educate Bratianu.

Lucien Wolf of the League of British Jews comes to see me. He has a scheme by which the Jews of all Europe should have international protection while retaining all national rights of exploitation. A. F. Whyte comes and remains to luncheon. Foster Fraser there. Work all afternoon. In the evening to a cinema with Marie Murat.

The Supreme Council discuss Russia and hear what Noulens has got to say about it all. The Food Council is formally appointed. Hankey is to be head of our Secretariat.

III. January 21 – February 5

THE COUNCIL OF X

January 21, *Tuesday*

With Crowe to a meeting in Lord Reading's room regarding the relief and feeding of Austria. (Present : Reading, Tyrrell, Crowe, Beveridge, Llewellyn Smith, Sir J. Beale.) Lord Reading is excellent as chairman : he insists on exclusion of all political activity from the scope of the proposed relief mission. He urges that their terms of reference should be confined to the provision of food and the transport of that food. The mission should not touch even such cognate questions as unemployment, and commercial arrangements between Austria and the Succession States : once they start doing that sort of thing they will be accused of interfering in politics and there will be the devil of a row. The seat of the relief mission is to be at Trieste with branches elsewhere.

Lunch with Madge and Goga at Fouquets. More about the ' terms ' on which Transylvania will ' consent ' to join Rumania. All rather in the air.

Dine with A. J. B. He is as charming as usual. He says that ever since his visit to America he had had a deep regard for President Wilson as a man and as a scholar, but he had never seen him actually at work. He is astonished therefore to find him as good round a table as he was on paper. His attitude at the meetings of the Big Five is firm, modest, restrained, eloquent, well-informed and convincing.

I raise the question of the Italian Treaty. A. J. B. said that he had spoken to P. W. as follows : ' When, during the war, we were in a bad way we asked Italy to come in with us at a certain price. She delivered the goods, and, if she asks us, we are bound to foot the bill. On the other hand both we and the Italians have since pledged ourselves to the Wilsonian principles : these principles place our price in a new currency. If the Italians are willing to be paid in this new currency, well and good. If they insist upon being paid in the old currency, then we shall have to fulfil the letter of our bond.'

I ask him whether there is not a danger of the French, in that they control the machinery of the Conference, rushing things through before the Plenipotentiaries quite realise what is happening. His view is that this danger can only be averted by the early appointment of committees of experts to thrash out the details.

He is worried by the fact that P. W. has got to return to the United States in order to dissolve Congress. He has a great feeling for House, but fears that his health may not stand the strain. If House collapses we should be left with only Lansing, Tasker Bliss, and Harry White—who are no good at all.

He told me that after Saturday's official opening of the Conference he walked down the stairs with Clemenceau. A. J. B. wore a top hat : Clemenceau wore a bowler. A. J. B. apologised for his top hat : ' I was told,' he said, ' that it was obligatory to wear one.' ' So,' Clemenceau answered, ' was I.'

January 22, Wednesday

Work all morning. Crowe is cantankerous about Cyprus and will not allow me even to mention the subject. I explain (1) That we acquired it by a trick as disreputable as that by which the Italians collared the Dodecanese. (2) That it is wholly Greek and under any interpretation of Self-Determination would opt for union with Greece. (3) That it is no use to us strategically or economically. (4) That we are left in a false moral position if we ask everyone else to surrender possessions in terms of Self-Determination and surrender nothing ourselves. How can we keep Cyprus and express moral indignation at the Italians retaining Rhodes ? He says, 'Nonsense, my dear Nicolson. You are not being clear-headed. You think that you are being logical and sincere. You are not. Would you apply self-determination to India, Egypt, Malta and Gibraltar ? If you are *not* prepared to go as far as this, then you have not right to claim that you are logical. If you *are* prepared to go as far as this, then you had better return at once to London.' Dear Crowe—he has the most truthful brain of any man I know.

Gerald Talbot, the 'friend of Venizelos,' comes to tell me in strict secrecy that Sonnino has offered the Greeks a deal under which the Italians would support Greek claims to the Dodecanese and Smyrna, provided the Greeks will give up all claim to northern Epirus and thus give to Albania (*i.e.* to Italy) the coast opposite Corfu. Greece to retain the Koritsa enclave. I suggest that Sonnino by now realises that P. W. is determined that the Greeks shall have both Smyrna and Rhodes, and that he wishes to get 'compensation' for a surrender which he may have to make in any case. Would it not be best for Venizelos to reply ' taking grateful note ' of Sonnino's agreement with Greek claims at Smyrna and in the Dodecanese, and adding that he will willingly submit the question of Northern Epirus to the decision of the Council of Ten.

January 23, Thursday

A. F. Whyte in the morning. The Press are getting restless at the apparent inability of the Conference to settle down to the task of making peace. They blame Lloyd George for not at once delegating work to expert committees. The Prinkipo decision is regarded as impulsive and badly staged. They suspect the French of wishing to mark time until P. W. has left Paris : so long as he is here he constitutes an over-whelming moral force, and once he has gone the French may be able to rush the others into decisions. As a matter of fact Ll. G. these days has been jogging the Supreme Council along pretty quickly. They have discussed Russia, the Kaiser, and the German Colonies.

Venizelos lunches. I ask Day, Carpenter and Lybyer to meet him, as he is not yet in personal touch with the American experts. He has a fierce argument about Bulgarian Thrace with Lybyer, who is a Bulgarophil. He is moderate, charming, gentle, and apt. A most successful luncheon.

In the evening dine with the American Delegation at the Crillon and meet Victor Bérard. ' Ich bin kein kolonial,' he says, and then proceeds to explain a scheme for the partition of Turkey into five bits, one for each of the great Powers.

(Letter of January 23 to my father) :

' There is a great deal of rather desultory work and I wonder how much of it is any good. One feels that the questions will be decided by the Big People in a hurry, and that our own schemes and plans will not even be looked at.'

January 24, Friday

A useless day. In the morning Voshniak, a Slovene. Very imperialistic. Asks for Istria, Klagenfurt, Temesvar. No good at all. Talbot tells me the Venizelos-Sonnino deal has broken down. Meet Winston Churchill in the passage. ' Halloa ! ' I say to him, ' have you come over to hurry us up ? ' ' No,' he answers, ' I have come to get myself an army.' Dine with Spears. Supreme Council issue solemn warning to the Small Powers against their practice of staking out claims by military occupations.

January 25, Saturday

Lunch again with Spears to meet Bratianu and Diamandi, who have just arrived to conduct the fortunes of Rumania. Charles Sackville West, Brodrick, Cecil Higgins there. They all speak perfect French which sounds odd from British officers. Bratianu is a bearded woman, a forceful humbug, a Bucharest intellectual, a most unpleasing man. Handsome and exuberant, he flings his fine head sideways, catching his own profile in the glass. He makes elaborate verbal jokes, imagining them to be Parisian. He spends most of luncheon inveighing against the Russians and Sarrail for not having rescued Rumania in 1916. I talk at length to Diamandi who is a quiet dove-like little

man. I tell him that it is a false move to insist on the
1916 Treaty being still operative, since it was cancelled
by Rumania's making a separate peace with Germany.
To insist on the Treaty will irritate the Ten and infuriate the Jugo-Slavs. Diamandi cooes gently.

Supreme Council has been meeting regularly. Five
Expert Committees have been appointed, viz. League
of Nations, Labour, Reparation for damage done,
International Transit, and War Criminals.

January 26, Sunday

Work all morning at a précis and commentary upon
the ' Statement of Greek claims ' which Venizelos has
presented to the Conference. I support it on the whole,
although his line in Asia Minor is excessive.

Feeling in Paris is turning against Wilson and the
Americans. It is at present merely a vague dislike,
and not documenté. They are furious that P. W.
should have waited till to-day before visiting the devastated areas.

In the evening to the Etienne de Beaumonts, where
Jean Cocteau reads aloud his Cap de Bonne Espérance.
Not very convincing. Painlevé, André Gide, Paul
Adam there. Talk to Gide about his reputation in
England. He is very modest. Walk back with Jean
Cocteau in the snow. We pass the Rohan mansion
with its gables outlined in white. ' Bravo, Princesse ! '
says Cocteau, applauding with slim hands.

(Letter to my father, January 26) :

' There is much work to do, but it is largely voluntary,
and to a quite disheartening extent desultory and unconvincing. The Big Ten or the Big Five, as they are alter-
natively called, decide important questions *in camera* and

on what seems a wholly empirical and irresponsible basis.
They seldom take the trouble to notice the facts and arguments prepared for them by their staffs. Sooner or later
this disregard for technical opinion will lead to a smash.
For the present, except for the Prinkipo operette, no harm
has been done—but it is uphill work preparing memoranda
which one feels will not be read, acted on, digested, utilised, or even rejected. We have not really got to grips
as yet and all this delay is merely the reflection of Council
indolence and jealousy. When practical questions *do*
come up for judgment they will be decided in a hurry,
whereas if the technical committees had been at work
these past weeks we could prepare quite easily a case for
the Big Five to consider. Damn! Damn! Damn! The
Prinkipo decision was taken it seems without consulting
the Russians themselves. No wonder they have turned
it down.'

January 27, Monday

Complete my summary and commentary upon Venizelos' statement. I take the line that North Epirus
justified, except for Koritsa. Thrace both East and
West justified. Asia Minor justified, but not with the
whole of the Aidin vilayet and the Meander valley.

A visit from C. B. Thomson, who has apparently
been writing a similar memorandum for Henry Wilson.

Go to a luncheon offered by the French Press at the
Maison Dufayel, 300 guests. Pichon, Tardieu, George
Riddell speak. Not a very interesting luncheon. Yet
I gathered a vivid impression of the growing hatred of
the French for the Americans. The latter have without
doubt annoyed the Parisians. There have been some
rough incidents. The United States authorities are
beginning to get uneasy and are importing their
own military police. Wilson shares this growing

unpopularity.   Lafayette is becoming a hazy bond of union.

January 28, *Tuesday*

Aubrey Herbert comes round in the morning in a groping untidy way.   He represents, he says, the Albanians of America.   He is distressed at my thinking Greece should have Argyrocastro, but pleased that I think Koritsa should remain Albanian. I send him down to see the Americans at the Crillon.   A loveable man.

Work all day.   Otiose work.   Dine with Venizelos. His sitting room overheated—mimosa and roses on the table—Venizelos very much the host.   He is in great form.   He tells us stories of King Constantine, his lies and equivocations. He tells us of the old days of the Cretan insurrection, when he escaped to the mountains and taught himself English by reading the 'Times' with a rifle across his knee.   He talks of Greek culture, of modern Greek and its relation to the classical, and we induce him to recite Homer.   An odd effect, rather moving.   He talks of King Ferdinand and Daneff and the London Conference after the Balkan Wars.   The whole gives us a strange medley of charm, brigandage, welt-politik, patriotism, courage, literature—and above all this large muscular smiling man, with his eyes glinting through spectacles, and on his head a square skull-cap of black silk.

There has been a row in the Supreme Council between Japan and China over Shantung.

January 29, *Wednesday*

To the Quay d'Orsay in the morning.   I have been summoned, as the Czechs are to make their statement to the Council of Ten, and I am supposed, for some odd reason, to be a Czech expert. In the ante-room are Kramarsh and Benes sitting on gilt chairs as if awaiting the dentist. Kramarsh large, bluff, hair en brosse, exuberant, has a nice German smell. Benes small, yellow, silly little imperial, intelligent eyes rather like Keynes', fine forehead. We speak about Teschen, its coal : Oderberg, its railway connections : the Hungarian Ruthenes, the ' Carpatho-Russians.' In the middle Pichon emerges from his room like a fussy owl. Says we needn't stay. Off we go.

Lunch with Toynbee and meet a Major Johnson, the geographical expert of the American delegation. He is crammed with information and I shall go into things thoroughly with him and look at his maps. Work hard afterwards at the Czecho-Slovak ' case ' as presented to the Supreme Council. Conclusions : Bohemia and Moravia, historical frontier justified, in spite of fact that many Germans would be included. Teschen, Silesia, Oderberg, justified : Slovakia, Danube frontier not justified to extent claimed : Hungarian Ruthenes justified and desirable ; the ' Serbs of Lusatia ' mere rubbish : the ' corridor ' to connect with Jugo-Slavia completely unjustified.

The French Press are beginning to sneer at P. W. and the Americans.

January 30, Thursday

Meeting of Delegation at the Astoria to discuss Constantinople. Hardinge takes the chair. Representatives of the War Office, Admiralty, Board of Trade and India Office. The fighting services object to Constantinople being placed in the hands of any first class

Power. They wish it left to Turkey under international control. Crowe argues against any ' mixed decision.' He is always for *des situations nettes*. In the end decided that the Turk must go and that some sort of international regime must take his place.

Trumbic the Jugo-Slav Plenipotentiary lunches. A gloomy man. He says that the capital of the new State will probably be Sarajevo and not either Belgrade or Agram. He suggests that they might call themselves ' Dalmatia ' instead of S.C.S.—which is a silly provocative sort of name.

January 31, *Friday*
Another delegation meeting on future of Asia Minor. Hardinge takes the view that Turkey must retain Smyrna. In this he is supported by the soldiers. Crowe takes opposite view. In the end decided that it should go to Greece with a zone as shown on my map.

Lunch with Jacques Blanche and André Gide. Have to dash off early to Council of Ten. Again that wait in the ante-room. Opposite us sprawls P. W.'s personal detective reading ' A bed of Roses.' Hankey fetches me in. Pichon fetches Bratianu, Misu, Pasic and Trumbic. What a gang !

A high room : domed ceiling : heavy chandelier : dado of modern oak : doric pannelling : electric light : Catherine de Medici tapestries all round the room : fine Aubusson carpet with a magnificent swan border : régence table at which Clemenceau sits : two chairs opposite for the Rumanians : secretaries and experts on little gilt chairs : about twenty-two people in all. The lights are turned on one by one as the day fades behind the green silk curtains. The Big Ten sit in an irregular row to Clemenceau's right. Pichon crouches just beside him. Dutasta behind. Silence—very warm—people walking about with muffled feet—secretaries handing maps gingerly.

Bratianu, with histrionic detachment, opens his case. He is evidently convinced that he is a greater statesman than any present. A smile of irony and self-consciousness recurs from time to time. He flings his fine head in profile. He makes a dreadful impression.

A. J. B. rises, yawns slightly, and steps past his own armchair to ask me for our line of partition in the Banat. Leeper, whose subject it is, produces it at once. A. J. B. shows it, with marked indifference, to Sonnino. Vesnic replies to the Rumanian case. He does it well and modestly. He attacks the Secret Treaty. Then Bratianu again. Then Trumbic and old Pasic. President Wilson gets pins and needles and paces up and down upon the soft carpet kicking black and tidy boots. He then goes and sits himself down for a moment among the Jugo-Slavs. Then we all disappear again through the double doors. General feeling that Bratianu has done badly. Misu dines with us in the evening.

February 1, Saturday
Work at Astoria all morning. In afternoon to Supreme Council again to hear Bratianu continue. He says this is the second time that he has had to face a viva examination in Paris. The first time was when he took his degree in law. ' On that occasion my examiners knew more than I did.' Silly ass. He is on this occasion very verbose and unconvincing and Balkan. Suddenly we are all bustled out of the room

by Clemenceau. I am in terror as I have given A. J. B. all my maps and papers and he has a trick of losing official documents. Hankey however recovers them for me. In the evening a dinner offered by the Rumanian Colony in Paris. A fine speech by Také Jonescu. I hate dinner parties.

February 2, Sunday

Go to meet Ned Lutyens at St. Lazare but he never turns up. Dine with Antoine Bibesco, Jean Cocteau, and Elizabeth Asquith. Antoine and Elizabeth are engaged. Leave them to meet Lutyens at St. Lazare, who this time actually arrives.

February 3, Monday

To the Supreme Council in the morning to hear Venizelos deliver his oral statement on his claims.

This is a different sort of thing from Bratianu's performance. He begins by bringing with him some fine photograph albums showing the sponge fisheries in the Dodecanese. He says that as they have all had his written statement he will not repeat it but merely tell them some stories to illustrate his argument. He talks gaily and simply and they look at his photograph albums which put them in a good temper. He begins by paying a deft compliment to the Italians, which gives a good *stimmung*. He then goes on to Northern Epirus and says that the language test is of little real significance. ' For instance,' he says, ' many prominent Greeks, such as Admiral Condouriottis or my colleagues MM. Danglis and Repoulis, speak Albanian in their homes, even as Mr. Lloyd George would speak Welsh to his own children.' Ll. G. beams at this.

'The better test,' continues Venizelos, 'is that of
school attendance. Here are the figures of those who
attend the Greek schools, and here the figures of those
who attend the Albanian schools. You will see that
the Greek schools have a far higher ratio of attendance.
And this is not in the least because the Greek schools
give a better education than the Albanian Schools.
Not in the least. For the Albanian schools in the
main centres have the benefit of American teachers
. . .' Wilson beams delight.

We are then turned out. I meet Orpen in the ante-
room, followed by an orderly carrying his paint pots
and going towards the Salle de l'Horloge. Ned
Lutyens lunches. Also Augustus John. The latter is
painting an 'allegorical' picture of the Conference.
Oh my !

Dine with Bratianu. A hateful dinner. League of
Nations Committee meets.

February 4, Tuesday

To the supreme Council to hear Venizelos conclude
his statement. He talks of Greek claims in Asia Minor.
He is again extremely good, but not so logical and
effective as he was yesterday. The Italians say a few
nice words when it is all over, which is applauded by
P. W. 'Hear ! Hear ! ' says P. W. clapping silent
palms. Clemenceau as usual wears the half-smile of
an irritated, sceptical and neurasthenic gorilla.

I stay behind a few minutes while they discuss
whether they shall appoint a Committee of Experts to
examine the Greek claims. Lloyd George proposes it,
P. W. seconds it. Clemenceau concludes abruptly—
'Objections ?. . . Adopté.' The Italians gasp, as

they do not want a Committee of Experts in the least.

Outside in the anteroom—as we sidle through the heavy double doors with our books, our maps, our pouches—is the official liaison officer to the press, dictating the communiqué just adopted to a shy little woman at a type-writer. A bowed mouse. Thus it will issue in a few moments to the world, and Vita will see it in an hour upon the green notice board at the Casino. Come back with Hankey. Do not know yet whether I am to be on the Greek Committee. I know Ll. G. suggested me.

The Conference has done good work these days. So have we. We are to keep in close touch with the Americans, and although we are not to present a *joint* front (because of French and Italian susceptibilities), yet it is evident that we are expected to coordinate our points of view. I feel that my constant discussions with the Americans since I arrived will make this easier. We have established mutual trust.

Labour situation at home seems dangerous. There have been grave riots on the Clyde.

February 5, Wednesday

To the Council of Ten to hear the Czechs state their case. Benes does the talking and Kramarsh sits sturdily behind. The latter shares Bratianu's indignation at being treated as of no importance. I must say that Clemenceau is extremely rude to the small Powers : but then he is extremely rude to the Big Powers also.

Benes begins his case at 3.0 and finishes at 6.30. A lengthy and exacting performance. He dwelt too long

on minor points, and after all, these viva voces are a
pure farce. Clemenceau, when it was over, approached
Kramarsh. ' Mais il a été d'une longueur, votre
Benes ! ' The worst of Clemenceau is that he is so
terribly audible. I sit behind Ll. G. and Balfour, who
embarrass me rather by discussing whether or no I
should be put on the Czech Committee. Dine with
Grant and Knox of the ' Morning Post.' Drink too
much burgundy. Hear I am to be attached to the
Greek Committee as technical adviser, whatever on
earth that may mean. Crowe and Sir Robert Borden
are to be our two official representatives.

IV. *February 6–March 9*

COMMITTEES

February 6, Thursday

In the morning go over the Rumanian and Czech claims with Charles Seymour and the American geographer Major Johnson. Our views are really identical. Castoldi of the Italian Delegation lunches : he was a member of the Delimitation Commission which went with Doughty Wylie to South Albania in 1913 : he has thus great local knowledge. He is a nice old, sly old, thing. Afternoon go with Crowe to Sir Robert Borden to coach him upon Greek claims. He is easy and intelligent and will make a good representative.

February 7, Friday

Spend most of day tracing Rumanian and Czech frontiers with Charles Seymour of the U.S. Delegation. A great work and something really done. There are only a few points at which we differ. Our Greek Committee was to have started work to-day, but was put off till Monday, and now, I hear till Thursday. Borden is furious and wishes to make a row. I expect that the Italians are at the root of the delay as they still hanker after a separate arrangement with Greece over Albania.

February 8, Saturday

Again work all day with the Americans. Practically cover all my subjects. The Rumanian Commission

(Crowe and Allen Leeper) have their first meeting. The ground work we have done in conjunction with the Americans is of great value. In evening go to Boni de Castellane's party.

February 9, Sunday

Dispirited and depressed. Walk down to Crillon and go over Greek claims with the Americans. The Italians are really determined to do a separate deal with Greece, by which they will obtain for their Albanian protectorate the Greek districts in the south, thereby covering the Corfu channel. The Americans are determined not to accept this deal which to them savours of the Congress of Vienna. As regards Thrace they are still pro-Bulgar. Dine with Titulescu at the Café de Paris : Helène Vacarescu there : a bright body.

February 10, Monday

Work all day, telephoning three times to London. Dine at Jockey Club with Brodrick. Many French people there. The feeling against Wilson and the Americans is growing. They loathe the League of Nations and say that Wilson's insistence on its being taken first is delaying the Peace. This is nonsense, as it is only being done in Committee after dinner till midnight, and the rest of the day is perfectly free for the Council of X to go ahead with other things.

Ll. G. has left for London to deal with Strike Situation.

February 11, Tuesday

The Supreme Council are becoming alarmed at the attitude of the Weimar Congress and the reconstituted

German nation. They decide, when renewing the armistice, to put such terms as shall, if accepted, constitute a real basis of ' preliminary ' or rather military peace. Then they can demobilise as fast as they like. The French are always cursing Lloyd George for demobilising too rapidly, and our own papers are cursing him for not demobilising quickly enough. Meanwhile the armed force of the Alliance is melting away. There are rumours of great trouble among the French and British troops.

A dreadful attack on Wilson yesterday in the ' Figaro.' I hear he is furious, and threatens to transfer the Conference to Geneva. It would be a good thing if he did.

February 12, *Wednesday*

Lunch at Maturin with Venizelos and Talbot. The former very anxious to hear about the Greek Committee (not ' Commission '—Crowe being a man of verbal exactitude will not allow me to call it ' Commission.' ' My dear Nicolson, a Commission is a body which is despatched to a definite place, a body that sits at the centre is a Committee '). Anyhow our Committee meets in the afternoon in the Grande Salle à Manger at the Quai d'Orsay at 4.0, Jules Cambon chairman. Other members, Laroche, de Martino, Castoldi, Day, Charles Seymour, Borden, Crowe—and myself as ' technical delegate.' We discuss North Epirus. Nobody wishes to show their hand, and Cambon tells us all to go away and come back with something on a map.

The Supreme Council have a heated meeting about renewal of the Armistice.

February 13, Thursday

Have a touch of flu, or anyhow a bad cold. Martino and Castoldi lunch. Spend whole afternoon poring over North Epirus maps. I have also been appointed to the Czech Committee. My No. 1 is Sir Joseph Cook, Premier of New South Wales.

February 14, Friday

Spend the morning coaching Sir Joseph Cook as to his functions. . . . Third plenary session of Conference. Wilson reads out his draft Covenant. He then leaves Paris for Washington for purpose of adjourning Congress. Pours with rain.

February 15, Saturday

Greek Committee adjourned because de Martino is ill. Borden is indignant and writes Jules Cambon a stiff letter. Crowe afterwards meets de Martino out at luncheon. All very Italian. Have a long and distressing interview with old Bourchier of the ' Times.' He feels the defeat of Bulgaria terribly and is old and deaf and inarticulate. Dine with Lutyens at the Meurice and back to the Majestic where they have a dance on. Prince of Wales there—still shy and sad.

February 16, Sunday

Armistice renewed. Walk down to Dufayel Club for luncheon. As I cross Champs Elysées, I see coming towards me a British serjeant who looks very strange. I see that he is blubbering, great tears pouring down his cheek. I then recognize him as Walter Wilson, Mark Sykes' orderly, secretary, companion. He

comes up to me. He is sobbing hard. He tells me
Mark is dying and will I telephone to London or
rather to Sledmere to warn the agent and the family.
Lady Sykes is here.

February 17, Monday

Mark Sykes died last night at Hotel Lotti. I mind
dreadfully. He is a real loss. It was due to his endless
push and perseverance, to his enthusiasm and faith,
that Arab nationalism and Zionism became two of the
most successful of our war causes. To secure recognition of these his beliefs he had to fight ignorance at the
F.O., suspicion at the I.O., parsimony at the Treasury,
obstruction at the W.O., and idiocy at the Adty. Yet
he conquered all this by sheer dynamic force. He made
mistakes, of course, such as the Sykes-Picot Treaty,
but he kept to his ideas with the fervour of genius. I
shall miss him—boisterous, witty, untidy, fat, kindly,
excitable—with a joy in his own jokes and little
pictures (that brown fountain pen scribbling pictures
and Mark giggling as he did so). I feel glum and
saddened. He had a position in the House of Commons and could have done much good at this juncture
when that Assembly seems guided by pure hysteria and
war-nerves.

Dine with Latham of the Australian Delegation. He
is secretary to Hughes. Poor man. Able and in-
quisitive.

February 18, Tuesday

Greek Committee in morning. We discuss North
Epirus. South of Voiussa our line is identical with the

Americans. French want to give Greeks Koritsa.
Crowe is inclined to agree, but I beg him to reserve
decision.

In the afternoon the Jugo-Slavs come before the
Council of Ten. The idiots claim Trieste. There is a
row at the end as to whether the Jugo-Slav claims
should also be referred to a Committee similar to the
other Committees. The Italians refuse to submit the
question of ' frontiers directly and indirectly affecting
Italian interests ' to any Committee at all. Nor will
they allow such questions to be treated by P. W. in
the role of mediator. In the end it is decided that a
Jugo-Slav committee shall be constituted but that
they shall be empowered only to deal with those
portions of the Jugo-Slav frontier in which Italy has
no interest. The Rumanian Committee are to act in
this capacity.

February 19, *Wednesday*
Greek Committee at 10.0. We sit waiting for Jules
Cambon who does not appear. He then pokes his head
round the door and says that Clemenceau has been
assassinated. He asks Borden to carry on while he
himself goes off to the Rue Franklin where old Clemenceau lives to find out the truth. We start a rather
desultory talk on Northern Epirus and eventually
Jules Cambon returns. He says the old man is not
dead, but that he has a bullet in his lung. 'Le médecin,'
he says, ' lui a défendu de parler, mais le vieux gaillard
cause tout le temps.' Expressions of sympathy.
Crowe, in the excitement of the moment says that his
brother-in-law has had a bullet in his lung ever since
the war of 1870. ' Ah,' says Cambon, ' aussi un boulet

boche.' Crowe sniggers assent.   And we then return
to N. Epirus.   On driving back to the Majestic, Crowe
says that the boulet which still lodges in the lung of his
brother-in-law was in fact a French bullet, since his
brother-in-law is German.   We discuss moral courage.
Ought Crowe at that moment to have contradicted
Cambon and said, 'No, it was a French bullet!'
Crowe says he ought and that he feels a worm for not
having done so.   I say he ought not—it would have
shown no sense of occasion.   'Humbug,' says Crowe.
Dear Crowe !

Meanwhile at the Committee we go on with
Northern Epirus.   The Italians produce a comic
Admiral who explains at great length how essential to
the future existence of Italy is the Corfu channel.
Martino then turns on old Castoldi to tell us all about
the delimitation commission of 1913.   Luckily I have
brought with me the Procès Verbaux of that commission.   Castoldi says that they had unanimously decided
that the district of, I think, Argyrocastro should go to
Albania.   I quickly looked up the reference.   It said
that the Italian Delegate (*i.e.* Castoldi himself) had
expressed this view, but that all his other colleagues
had dissented.   Crowe reads this out.   Castoldi turns
purple.   He tries to bluster.   ' *Lascia stare,*' snarls
Martino at him.   It is all very embarrassing.   But
Castoldi, who is a good fellow, took it well : ' vous
êtes un terrible diable,' he said to me afterwards.   We
decide to go no further into it until we have heard the
representatives of the people concerned.

To A. J. B. after.   Explain Albanian question to
him.   Then work hard at Czecho-Slovak case.

February 20, *Thursday*

Greek Committee in morning. We do Thrace. We agree that Greek claim should be admitted in principle and that the three Delegations (*i.e.* ourselves, French and Yanks) should draft a frontier line. The Italians as usual obstructive and sulky.

Old Bourchier comes again. He wants an autonomous Macedonia including Salonika and Uscub, but excluding all Bulgarian territory. I think he is a little unhinged. He is pathetic, and I hate seeing this old friend of Sofia days and my own childhood in such painful circumstances.

Lady Muriel Paget dines. She is off to a relief mission at Prague. Her energy is terrifying. She sends Prime Ministers scuttling on her behests.

February 21, *Friday*

Greek Committee. Asia Minor. The Americans state their views in opposition to Greek claims. We state ours in favour. The Italians, when asked, say, first that the question is not within our terms of reference, and then, when beaten on that point, say they have no instructions and can't say when they will get them. The French produce a line more or less like ours. We decide that we shall wait till the Italians have their ' instructions ' (whatever that may portend) and we meanwhile return to Europe.

I can't understand the Italian attitude. They are behaving like children, and sulky children at that. They obstruct and delay everything—and evidently think that by making themselves disagreeable on every single point they will force the Conference to give them fat plums to keep them quiet.

Lunch with Také Jonescu to meet Vaida the Transylvanian leader : a dignified and sensible man. I wish
they were all like that.

Dash off to Council of Ten. The Albanians have
been convoqués. They are represented by Turkhan
Pasha who was Turkish Ambassador in Petrograd
when father was there. Very, very old and sad. He is
accompanied by Mehmed Bey Konitza, who is young
and gay and witty.

Dine with Norman. A great fuss about the impending bankruptcy of Austria. It keeps me busy till
1.0 a.m.

February 22, *Saturday*
No Committee in morning. Work at Austrian debt
and Thracian frontier. Crowe, who is very busy on
other committees is apt to rely on me for preparing our
statements and lines : Borden relies on Crowe : the
Committee generally accept the views of our delegation. Thus the responsibility is great. Spend the
whole afternoon in the anteroom at the Quai d'Orsay
as the Council of Ten are supposed to be going to take
Albania. But they get stuck arguing about future
procedure and the Albanian question never comes up.
A waste of precious time. We are given orders to the
effect that all the reports of all the Committees must be
sent in not later than March 8.

February 23, *Sunday*
A holiday. With Allen Leeper and Rhys Carpenter
to the Forêt de St. Germain. A sense of spring in the
black twigs.

February 24, Monday

Greek Committee in morning. Venizelos had been summoned to give evidence before the Committee. We arrive to find him already installed in the large Salle à Manger where we have our meetings. Sitting alone on a little gilt chair with his black skull cap. Eventually Jules Cambon arrives and Venizelos is turned out while we discuss among ourselves what questions we are to ask him. We ourselves put up no questions. The Italians put up several. They had evidently gone through Venizelos' statement to the Ten and ticked off all the more awkward points. Some of these questions were disallowed by Cambon, on the ground that they were devised merely to put Venizelos in an uncomfortable position. After this preliminary skirmish Venizelos is sent for from the next room. I almost expect him to begin, ' Animal, vegetable or mineral ? ' He doesn't. He is overwhelmingly frank, genial, and subtle. His charm lights up the room. As always he has the triumph of his personality, but no real ice has been cut. These ' auditions,' even before a so-called body of experts, are a farce. Lunch with Osusky and Muriel Paget. Former is the Czech agent in London with a fine Chicago accent. Appearance of great moderation.

Back to Quai d'Orsay afterwards. The Conseil des Dix confront old Turkhan Pasha with the Albanian case, or rather the other way round. Turkhan has a fid of typewritten pages in front of him and drones into his henna-dyed beard. The Ten chatter and laugh while this is going on. Rather painful. In the end the whole Albanian question is referred to our Greek Committee, which means still more work.

Walk back with Day to the Crillon and study possible Thracian lines. A disheartening job. How fallible one feels here! A map—a pencil—tracing paper. Yet my courage fails at the thought of the people whom our errant lines enclose or exclude, the happiness of several thousands of people. How impossible to combine speed with examination! There is *nothing* more that we can learn from books, statistics, maps, interviews—and yet there is a definite inarticulate human element behind it all somewhere, and somewhere there must be a definite human desire behind all these lies and lies. It is impossible short of five years to find out what a majority is, and what it really wants. Our views and our decisions must of necessity be empirical, guided only by a real honesty of purpose.

Day tells me that the French are trying to get Wilson to let them have the Rhine. *Sie sollen ihn nicht haben.* . . .

February 25, Tuesday
A 'free' day. In morning go round to Venizelos at the Mercedes and talk about Thrace frontiers. Work hard all day.

BRITISH DELEGATION,
PARIS.
25th February, 1919.

MY DEAR FATHER,
        Lady Muriel Paget spoke to me yesterday, hoping that you would lend your name to the Czecho-Slovak Relief Fund which is being organised more or less under Sir Samuel Hoare. I hope that you will do so, not only because I am on the Czecho-Slovak Commission here, but also because I feel that it is our duty to do all we can to diminish the effects of the blockade upon those subject races who have taken risks and action on our behalf.

Conditions in Bohemia are simply appalling, and there is an absolute lack of milk and fats, with the result that something like 20% of the babies are born dead, and something like 40% die within the first month of birth. I sincerely hope that you will get on to the Committee of the fund, and use your influence with the Foreign Office to get something done, as it is the one way in which we can mitigate the moral responsibility of our blockade.

As regards the Conference generally—it is proceeding in a rather irresponsible and intermittent way. They wasted six weeks before appointing the obvious Commissions, and they have now told the wretched Commissions that their reports are to be sent in by March 8th! This will mean, of course, that a great deal of the detailed work will have to be scamped; and although I fully recognise the value of a time limit, yet I think that they are pressing us a little too much for their own political purposes.

The Commissions themselves, which only consist of eight members, are efficient and valuable, and of course all the real work of the Conference is done by them. The Council of Ten should also be valuable and powerful; but, as always happens with such Olympian assemblies, they are so ignorant of what are really vital points that they waste their time and energies over perfectly secondary considerations.

On the whole I find that the Americans are a great help, since they are well-informed, broad-minded and extremely honest. The French are behaving far better than I imagined, and are sufficiently intelligent to see that the only possible line to go on is that of honesty and reason. The great difficulty comes from the side of the Italians, and Sonnino is the evil genius of the piece. He appears to have given a mot d'ordre to his Delegation that they are to adopt the tactics of delay and obstruction, with the result that unanimity of action is frustrated at every point by perfectly wilful obstruction on the part of the Italians.

It is all working up to a real row, and I am extremely anxious lest the Italians will saboter the whole thing rather than give way. The obstinacy and malevolence of Sonnino are quite unrealisable.

As regards our own Delegation, Crowe, as could be foreseen, is the centre of everything. I must say that the Prime Minister has been extremely good to the Foreign Office, and that the whole direction of all but essentially non-political and economic questions is entirely in our hands. The result is that the large military and naval missions here are becoming extremely indignant, and some of them have already left in disgust.

The work is so passionately interesting that one has no time to be exhausted, but I feel that another month or so would wear us all out. Apart from the actual strain of continuous labour, there is the moral exhaustion of realising one's own fallibility and the impossibility of extracting from the lies with which we are surrounded any real impression of what the various countries and nationalities honestly desire. With the time allowed to us we can only come to more or less empirical decisions, and the only justification for such decisions will be the honesty of intention in which they are conceived. Whatever result is arrived at will be attacked by the champions of all the lost causes ; but I must say that this is a matter of complete indifference to me.

I can't tell you the position that Venizelos has here ! He and Lenin are the only two really great men in Europe.

February 26, Wednesday
Greek Committee in morning. We continue our examination of Venizelos. We ask him otiose questions about the protection of Moslem minorities, and the Greek succession to the Ottoman Public Debt charges. Lunch with Castoldi at the Edouard VII.

On to Day at his office. Have a battle with him over
Thrace. He wishes to exclude the Greeks from the
Black Sea and cares little for Medea or the Symple-
gades. But he accepts my Arda line. Come back and
work hard but feel exhausted. The last fortnight has
been terribly trying and I foresee another fortnight as
bad. The strain is appalling.

In the evening Tyrrell joins with me in giving a
dinner at the Majestic. Venizelos—Také Jonescu—.
They tell us Balkan stories. They talk with deep
affection and respect of old Bourchier although he is
pulling every string in favour of their enemy. Go on
afterwards with Venizelos to a party at Boni de Castellane in his little house in the Rue de Lille. The whole
place is lit by wax candles. Very Congress of Vienna.
The French have heard that some Greek anarchists are
out for Venizelos' blood : we are dogged by detectives
and motor cyclists the whole way. Since the attempt
on Clemenceau the whole of Paris bristles with detectives. The party at Boni's is odd. Sazonoff, Giers,
Boris Savinkoff, Berthelot, and the Archbishop of
Spalato. I talk to him about the idiocy of Croat and
Slovene claims to Gorizia and Trieste. He sighs
deeply. ' A qui le dites-vous ? ' he sighs.

February 27, Thursday
First meeting of Czech Committee. I go down with
Sir Joseph Cook. His attitude is one of benevolent
boredom, but from time to time he gives a smile of
contempt indicative of the fact that although he may
be ignorant of geography as of the French language,
yet he represents a young and progressive country,
whereas we others are ' effete.' But he is a nice

sensible man and an angel of obedience. We discuss
Czech frontier in Bohemia and Moravia. Agreement.
Then Silesia. I point out that we cannot get on with
that without knowing what the Polish Committee
decide. The meeting is therefore adjourned. In afternoon Greek Committee. We hear ' evidence '—
Turkhan Pasha, Mehmed Bey Konitza, and Tourtoulis
for Albania : Karapanos and Adamidis for Northern
Epirus. Not an inspiring or pleasing ceremony. It is
sad to see people who have come all the way from
Dedeagatch or Adrianople given only ten minutes in
that large hot room in front of eight bored people.
Turkhan was particularly pitiable. Dine with Benes
and Kramarsh and thereafter discuss Czech frontiers.
Benes has masses of sketch maps designed for the use
of children, or for the Conseil des Dix. Kramarsh
talks about the corridor to connect Czechoslovakia
with Jugoslavs. I am feeling exhausted and unstrung.
I lose my temper. ' Je vous en prie,' I burst out, ' n'en
parlez pas. C'est une bêtise.' He is extremely startled,
and Lady Muriel Paget who is there looks across at me
with deep blue eyes of reproach. Come back dead to
the world. This is all too much.

February 28, *Friday*

Czechs all morning. Council hear Weizmann the
Zionist. Lunch Madame de Jouvenel. Boris Savinkoff
there. He is the man who shot Plehve and exploded
the Grand Duke Serge. He poses as the regenerator
of Russia and says he can do the trick with 150,000
men and six weeks. There is evidently a great deal in
the man.

Again Czechs all afternoon. General Lerond is

there.   An admirable man : intelligent soldiers are the
most efficient people of the lot.   We discuss Slovakian
frontier and agree about the Ruthenian corridor con-
necting Czechs with Rumanians.   We appoint a sub-
committee to trace the actual frontier line.   Go and see
a doctor who gives me a strong tonic.   Dine with old
Jules Cambon at the Union.   It is restful to be with
this witty, disillusioned but honourable old man.   He
tells me that old Clemenceau against all doctors orders
appeared at the Quai d'Orsay to-day.

March 1, *Saturday*

Czechs all morning.   Greek Committee all afternoon.
Asia Minor again.   Americans oppose Greek claim.
We and French support it in modified form.   The
Italians then flare up, saying that they must refuse to
discuss in Committee any questions covered by the
Secret Treaties of 1915 and 1917.   The Yanks, bless
their hearts, then state solemnly that they were not
parties to these secret treaties and cannot recognize
their validity.   The Italians at that threaten to withdraw.   There is a scene.   I give Borden a paper to read
out to the effect that it is impossible to put Greeks
under a European mandate.   This is a good red
herring and the tumult subsides.   I escape to my Czech
Committee which is droning away in the next room.
Not much progress as to frontiers.   All rather hopeless and loose-ended.   Nobody who has not had experience of Committee work in actual practice can
conceive of the difficulty of inducing a Frenchman, an
Italian, an American and an Englishman to agree on
anything.   A majority agreement is easy enough : an
unanimous agreement is an impossibility;   or if

possible, then possible only in the form of some para-
lytic compromise.

March 2, Sunday

Work all morning. Lunch with Alan Dulles and
Major Johnson at the Crillon. In afternoon draw up
draft report of the Greek Committee's work for presentation to the Supreme Council. It will bristle with
reservations and minority reports. I am assisted by a
French rapporteur, Krajewsky. A nice old man. At 5.0
to Quai d'Orsay for sub-committee of Slovak frontiers.
We put Lerond in the chair, which is a great help. We
begin with Pressburg and secure agreement. Then
we get to the Grosse Schütt. French want to give it to
the Czechs. The U.S. want to give it to the Magyars.
I reserve judgment, saying it depends on whether
German Hungary is given to Austria. Then examine
frontier from Komorn to Jung. The very devil. The
Yanks want to go north along the ethnical line, thus
cutting all the railways. We want to go south, keeping
the Kassa-Komorn lateral communications, in spite of
the fact that this will mean putting some 80,000
Magyars under Czech rule. Eventually a compromise.
The Yanks give way as regards Eipel, and we as regards Miskolcz. As for the rest we decide to wait and
hear Benes. Dine with Princess Soutzo at the Ritz—
a swell affair. Painlevé, Klotz, Bratianu there. Also
Marcel Proust and Abel Bonnard. Proust is white,
unshaven, grubby, slip-faced. He puts his fur coat on
afterwards and sits hunched there in white kid gloves.
Two cups of black coffee he has, with chunks of sugar.
Yet in his talk there is no affectation. He asks me
questions. Will I please tell him how the Committees

work? I say, 'Well, we generally meet at 10.0, there are secretaries behind. . . .' 'Mais non, mais non, vous allez trop vite. Recommencez. Vous prenez la voiture de la Délégation. Vous descendez au Quai d'Orsay. Vous montez l'escalier. Vous entrez dans la Salle. Et alors? Précisez, mon cher, précisez.' So I tell him everything. The sham cordiality of it all : the handshakes : the maps : the rustle of papers : the tea in the next room : the macaroons. He listens enthralled, interrupting from time to time—'Mais précisez, mon cher monsieur, n'allez pas trop vite.'

March 3, Monday

Krajewsky comes round early and we fling ourselves into the drafting of our report. The Italians have sent in a minority report covering every single point. I propose to relegate it into an appendix. That will mean a row. Laroche lunches. He almost convinces me that the Greeks ought to have Koritsa because of the vital road connection with Thessaly. He explains that the establishment of Italy across the only line of communication between Monastir and Santi Quaranta will drive a permanent wedge between Serbia and Greece. It is terribly bad luck on Albania, who has Italy imposed upon her as a Mandatory Power, and then gets her frontiers cut down merely because none of us trust Italy in the Balkans. Czech committee in afternoon. Exhausting and indefinite.

March 4, Tuesday

Krajewsky again for the last touches to our report. Czech sub-committee. We summon Benes and ask

him endless questions : never have I known so voluble
a man. At 4.0 we have our penultimate meeting of the
Greek Committee. (1) Frontier with Albania. We
give way to French about Koritsa. Americans insist
on modified line south of Voiussa. Italians want 1913
frontier. (2) With Bulgaria and Turkey. We agree
to give Venizelos what he asks, *i.e.* both Eastern and
Western Thrace. The Conseil des Dix may however
cut him off from the Black Sea by swinging the Enos-
Midia line more to the north. (3) Asia Minor. We
accept the French line with reservations as to the
Meander Valley. The Yanks refuse absolutely. The
Italians refuse even to discuss the matter. (4) Islands.
All agreed.

I feel heart-heavy about Koritsa. I am convinced
that it ought to go to Albania, Italians or no Italians.

March 5, Wednesday
Work hard all morning. Maps, plans, partitions,
watersheds, canalisation—all those intricate processes
of thought which have become a jog-trot in my brain.
The strain moral and mental is great : even the
puddles in the pavements assume for me the shapes of
frontiers, salients, corridors, neutralised channels, demilitarised zones, islands, ' becs de canard.'

At 4.30 full Czech Committee. We decide on what
I trust is quite a good line in Silesia, *i.e.* Teschen,
Karvin, and Oderburg Railway (not town) to the
Czechs : rest to Poles. The whole thing will be fixed
up by my sub-committee on Friday. Still busy at
night with my Greek Committee report.

March 6, Thursday

Ll. G. is back. He is going to make a stand against principle of compulsory military service. All to the good.

Fuss all morning about getting maps drawn out for the Greek report. Our geographical section are superb. Seldom have I seen grace and efficiency so well fused. Lunch alone with Venizelos. I suspect that if Albania were to be really independent he would not think of claiming Northern Epirus, and that his sole reason for claiming it is to prevent Italy setting herself across the Santi Quaranta road. This is the real argument and it is unanswerable, since peace will be better secured by maintaining Graeco-Serbian relations than by satisfying the Korziotes. But it is all wrong really. Venizelos is nice about my distress. ' Mais, mon zer, voyez-vous, mon zer? . . .'

He is distressed at the American opposition to his Smyrna claims. I told him that the best thing to do was to wait patiently till President Wilson gets back and then to tackle him direct. He says that so long as we and the French support him he will not feel really anxious. He read me telegrams from Janina showing that the Italians are busy getting up a ' demonstration ' in Northern Epirus if and when the district is given to Greece.

Go on to Sir Robert Borden and go through my Greek report with him. He approves it in principle. Then down to the Quai d'Orsay. Final sitting of Greek Committee. My report read and adopted in principle although the Americans insist on some important changes. Personally I think it was a good report so far as it was possible to state clearly such

conflicting principles. This view was not shared by
my colleagues on the Committee. In fact there was
rather a ' froid ' about it.

Rush back and send off the Report to the Imprimerie
Nationale. Of course the Italians try to alter it again
when they get back to their Edouard Sept. This
means more fuss, worry, irritation and distress for
me.

Back to Astoria after dinner. Piles of documents in
from the F.O. Boxes full. Work! Work! Work!
Work!

Supreme Council are squabbling over military
clauses of the Treaty. Ll. G. is fighting like a little
lion.

March 7, Friday

Alan Dulles of the American Delegation comes in
early and we work at the Slovak frontier. The position is this. We are all agreed, except on the section
between Pressburg and Satoralja. Crowe and Sir
Joseph Cook insist upon giving the Grosse Schütt to
the Czechs. I cannot persuade them out of it. I am
sure they are wrong and it is heart-breaking to have to
support a claim with which I disagree. I am anxious
about the future political complexion of the Czech
State if they have to digest solid enemy electorates,
plus an Irish Party in Slovakia, plus a Red party in
Ruthenia, to say nothing of their own extreme socialists. However, as I am tied one end by the Grosse
Schütt and the other end by Satoralja, the only concessions I can make are on the Satoralja-Komaron
sector. In the afternoon meeting at the Quai d'Orsay
I and Lerond give way on this sector and accept the

American line. I come back, as so often now, dispirited, saddened, and one mass of nerves jangled and torn.

Dine with Jules Cambon at the Union. The Poles and the Czechs are there. Oh God !

March 8, Saturday

The day ordained by the Supreme Council on which the reports of all Committees are to be ready. My Greek report is ready and I take it round, with a feeling of maternal pride, to Hankey. No other report is ready.

Czech Committee. They approve our Sub-Committee's line. They rule out the corridor with Jugo Slavia. They argue about Bohemia. At last we agree. Sir Joseph Cook who till then had been holding what was more or less a watching brief, blinking Australian eyes, is startled by being asked suddenly by Cambon to record the official view of the British Delegation. ' Well,' he says, ' all I can say is that we *are* a happy family aren't we ? ' An expression of acute agony twitches in the face of the interpreter. ' Le premier Délégué britannique' he translates nobly, 'constate que nous sommes une famille très heureuse.' There is a silence pénible. But old Cook is all right. He has sense. The French the other day started an endless argument about the Delbrück nationality laws. When the whole thing had been translated into English, old Cook was asked to record his views. ' Damn Delbrück ' was what he said. And how right, how true. But to the interpreter Sir Joseph is a thorn in the flesh.

Dine with Jean de Gaigneron. Very tired, dispirited and uneasy. *Are* we making a good peace ?

Are we ? Are we ? There was a very gloomy telegram in from Plumer. He begs us to feed Germany.
Says our troops cannot stand spectacle of starving
children.

March 9, Sunday
(Letter to my father.)

BRITISH DELEGATION,
PARIS.
Sunday, March 9.

" I had hoped that to-day would see me through the
really bad part of the work, and in fact the Greek and
Czecho-Slovak Commissions have their reports ready.
But now comes an edict from the Council of X to say
that we must put these reports in the form of Treaties—
and so again there opens before me a thick week of committees, drafts, articles, proposals, counter proposals,
statistics, compasses, rulers, tracing paper, coloured inks
—and dossier after dossier to read. I feel quite dead with
it all—and so dispirited. It is as though four architects
had each designed an entirely different house, and then
met round a table to arrive at an agreement, which means,
of course, a compromise, in which all the designs are
fused into a conglomeration which has no sense or co-
herence. Even the worst individual design is better than
a fusion of four.

But perhaps I am unduly dispirited.

V. *March* 10–*April* 1

COORDINATION

March 10, *Monday*

A FREE day in so far as the Conference and Committees are concerned. See people—an American from Prague and an Englishman from Fiume. Lunch with Michael Sadler to meet Francis Carco—author of *Jésus la Caille*. A twittering little man.

March 11, *Tuesday*

A full day. Czech sub-committee 9.30-1.0. Details of Bohemian frontier—Glatz, Schmiedberg, Freistadt, Rumberg, Eger, Furth, Feldsberg. Reach agreement in all but Eger and Rumberg. Czechs again in afternoon. Full committee. Approve our morning's work. Dine at Ritz and talk to Dr. Preis, Czech Minister of Finance. He can only talk German, and I find that in the last five years my grasp of that language has become a trifle weak. He talks of gold credits.

March 12, *Wednesday*

An empty day. Osusky comes to see me and we talk of Rumberg and Eger. He tells me nothing. General Phillips comes on his way to Albania. An unpleasant interview, as he tries to get things out of me. I feel ashamed to confess to such people that we are sacrificing Koritsa to the Greeks, and solely upon a strategical argument. Anyhow I have fought hard for it and it was only the soldiers who defeated me. If it weren't for Koritsa and the Grosse Schütt I should feel happy enough about our own frontiers. Both these places will be engraved on my heart. T....... comes to see me and shows me telegrans which show that the Italians are intriguing everywhere, Epirus, Thrace, Turkey, Hungary. They are organising comitadji in these places for 'demonstrative purposes.' They are in close contact with Nouri Bey, the new Vali of Smyrna. I send a note to A. J. B. suggesting that we should send ships to Smyrna and Aivali. The Italians may be contemplating some sort of landing.

Have a talk with Whyte and Gertrude Bell who is back from governing Mesopotamia. She is as alert and delightful as ever. Dine with Carnegie to meet Swope—the star turn in the American journalistic world. On to Boni de Castellane. Margot Asquith there and Elizabeth.

March 13, *Thursday*
Czech sub-committee in the morning. We discuss Rumberg and Eger enclaves. The Yanks want to take both away from the Czechs. The French and ourselves oppose this. In order to secure unanimity I agree to give the Yanks Rumberg, if they will give me Eger. This they refuse to do, so that we shall not have an unanimous report. This means further delay. Damn !

March 14, *Friday*
Czech Committee. We read and approve our report to the Supreme Council. Lunch with Francis Carco at the cantine of the ' Journal.' A young French

subaltern of some nineteen years comes to our table.
He is unshaven, greasy, and covered with spots like an
ethnographical map. He tells us, with great precision,
of his adventures in the brothels of Marseilles, boasting
with arrogance of his own physical prowess. Finally
he leaves us. 'Ah,' exclaims Carco, 'mais tout de
même—c'est une belle chose que la jeunesse française!'
Well. Well. . . .

P. W. returns to Paris. He is not now in the Villa
Murat but in another house somewhere close to
Ll. G.'s flat.

March 15, Saturday

Work all morning. Work all afternoon. In evening
a dinner at the Majestic for the Balliol men forming
part of the Delegation. At least 60 % of the Civil
Staff were at Balliol. We feel proud. There seems
to be great trouble going on between Foch and the
Supreme Council over the Rhine frontier.

March 16, Sunday

Lunch with Margot Asquith. On to see Jean de
Gaigneron's pictures, the Degas at the Louvre, and
Augustus John. Come back to find message from
Venizelos. Would I come across at once ? He reads
me a letter he is sending to President Wilson about
Greek claims at Smyrna. It is admirably written and
quotes the President's own speeches. He is not
opposed to the idea of receiving a very small enclave
with the rest under mandate from the League of
Nations.

A 'Coordination Committee' has been appointed
to coordinate the results of the several territorial com-

mittees. They object to the lack of unanimity in our Greek report. Cannot we meet again and reach an unanimous verdict ? Mezes, the United States representative on the Committee, is particularly keen to coordinate. I suggest a scheme by which the mandate principle might be extended in preference to territorial cessions. I also write a letter to Wiseman to give House.

Dine with the Wedels in the Rue de Suresnes. Marvellous food.

The Press is clamouring over the delay. The French papers accuse Wilson of ' holding up the Treaty for the sake of his Pact of the League of Nations.' This most unfair.

March 17, *Monday*

Czechs in morning. We consider the legal aspect and begin to draft the actual terms of the Treaty. Then attend the Coordination Committee who are discussing our Greek report. The Council of Ten are very insistent that we should ' agree.' It is hopeless. Everybody sticks tight to the reservations made in the report of March 8. The matter is further complicated by our ignorance of what the Supreme Council is going to do with Constantinople itself. Obviously the extent of the Greek zone will be much affected by the extent of the Straits Zone, and by the nature of the administration there to be established.

March 18, *Tuesday*

More drafting of the Treaty. The Legal experts, Hurst and Fromageot are marvellous. Impassive and quick. Like electricians fixing a short-circuit.

March 19, *Wednesday*

Deep in drafting committees. Too rushed to write this diary.

March 20, *Thursday*

Meet Stefanik at luncheon. The young Czech Commander in Chief and Minister of War—slim, anaemic, nervous, energetic, powerful : a yellow face with a granulated nose : eyes wide, staring—Bright's disease or heart : or perhaps a little mad. Yes, his eyes goggle, it may be lunacy or great intelligence. Speaks bad French very quickly. Bored by Conference. He thinks only of the Siberian position, of his army there, of the hopeless way in which the Council of Ten only finger the Russian nettle. He was one of the first to reach Ekaterinburg after the Tsar's murder. He says they cut his throat, buried him, and killed a horse over his grave. The Tsarevitch was so weak and ill that he cannot have realised what was happening. They cut his body into little bits and poured petrol over them. The Empress, Grand Duchesses and women were violated and stabbed. He was full of such atrocity stories. He had seen a peasant in early spring sticking a knife into a young tree, ' because it had no right to blossom.' This too Tchekov to be convincing.

Smodlaka comes to see me. He is deputy for Spalato. Same old talk.

Dinner with T. E. Lawrence. He tells of his adventures in Arabia. All very vivid and exciting. Can't make him out.

Supreme Council to-day rejected the Polish report. Lloyd George attacked it on the basis of the XIV

points. Wilson defended it as against those points.
They also decided to send a Commission of Enquiry
and Research to Asia Minor ' to obtain the wishes of
the peoples themselves.' Very pretty, but what about
a Treaty of Peace with Turkey ? Relations between
French and ourselves becoming strained over Syria.

March 21, *Friday*

Greek Committee in morning to discuss the draft
articles of Peace prepared by the drafting Committee.
A short sitting. Work all afternoon with Alan Dulles
on Czech report. It seems almost impossible to hurry
the thing up.

March 22, *Saturday*

Current work in morning. A long and tiresome
visit from P . . . . . . who claims to represent Montenegro. He talks rubbish. In afternoon news arrives
of a Bolshevik revolution in Hungary. This was foreseen, but is none the less very serious. There is a real
danger that we shall get no peace at all. But what is to
be done ? We have all demobilised so quickly that we
cannot enforce our terms except by the blockade which
is hell.

(Letter to V. S. W.) :

> BRITISH DELEGATION,
> PARIS.
> *March* 22.

' I am worried about the progress of the Conference.
It was all going so well when the Commissions were dealing with it—but now that the Council of X are fiddling
with the reports it is hanging fire. The fact is that the
whole business is too complex for centralisation, and the

Council of X, being men of no real vision, feel jealous of the great expert machine which is turning out the peace, and want to leave their own stamp on it. So they stop the machine and look at the works and try and make it work backwards and then fiddle generally. *All* waste time.'

March 23, Sunday

(Letter to my father) :

' The Conference is deteriorating rapidly and I am depressed. It all seemed to be going well enough so long as the Committees were at work, but now the Council of Ten are atrophied by the mass of detail which pours in upon them. The Hungarian revolution is nasty and may lead to our abandoning Rumania for the second time. We are losing the peace rapidly and all the hard work done is being wasted. The Ten haven't really finished off anything, except the League of Nations, and what does that mean to starving people at Kishineff, Hermannstadt and Prague ? It is despairing.'

March 24, Monday

Hardinge sends for me and asks me to negotiate direct with the Americans an agreement on all outstanding questions affecting South Eastern Europe and Turkey. Go down to see Mezes, who is the titular head of their Delegation. We agree about Asia Minor—a semicircle line from Aivali to the north of Scala Nova. That is something.

The Council of Ten has in practice broken up into two bodies. First the Council of IV (Clemenceau, P. W., Ll. G. and Orlando), and next the Council of V, composed of the Foreign Ministers. This is the only possible way to get a move on. I am delighted.

(Letter to V. S. W.):

'I am so depressed about the way the Conference is going. It all seemed to be humming beautifully when the Committees were doing the work, but now that the Council of X are supposed to be passing the work of the Committees it is all hanging fire. You see, the work is all extremely technical—and our rulers know nothing about it—and rightly or wrongly hesitate to pass it all. It is so disheartening as there is no time to waste. Every day makes it less likely that the Germans will accept our terms. They have always got the trump card, *i.e.* Bolshevism—and they will go Bolshevist the moment they feel it is hopeless to get good terms. The only hope, therefore, would be to give them food and peace *at once*, and if we are going to stop and argue—what *will* be the good or the hope ? It will be too awful, if after winning the war we are to lose the peace, and I must say it all looks as if there was a good chance of our doing so. In fact I am very depressed about it. What we want is a Dictator for Europe and we haven't got one.

And never will have ! '

March 25, *Tuesday*

Coordination Committee in morning. They pass our Czech report. In afternoon continue my discussions with Dr. Mezes. Deal with North Epirus. I suggest autonomy under League of Nations, with mandate for Greece. This frightens him considerably.

Ll. G. is so enraged by leakages to Press that he insists upon the Supreme Council sitting, as four people, *in camera*.

March 26, *Wednesday*

Work out in detail scheme for partition of Turkey. Lunch with Madame de Jouvenel, Briand and A. J. B.

there.   Briand inveighs against French haute finance
and their capitalists.   He has a voice like the great
bassoon.   He and A. J. B. are not the same type in the
least.

March 27, *Thursday*

Work out scheme for an autonomous Epirus.

Venizelos comes to see me.   He says that Colonel
House has hinted to him that the United States will
accept the Franco-British line in Asia Minor.   He was
pleased about it.   He also talked about Northern
Epirus.   He liked my autonomy scheme.

Lunch with Allen Leeper, Popovic, and Vosnyak.
The Jugo-Slavs are not frightened of Bolshevism in
the S.C.S.   They regard the Buda Pesth revolution as a
put-up job.   But it is none the less dangerous for that.
The fact is that our Government for electoral reasons
allowed the country to imagine that the Armistice
meant peace.   This it most assuredly was not, and we
should have strengthened and not weakened ourselves
after its signature.   In any case we cannot attack Bolshevism by force.

Go round afterwards to see A. J. B. at the Rue
Nitot.   Explain to him about Turkey.   Impossible to
extract from him any answer or decision.   He merely
lolled and looked bored.   Anyhow, I got enough out
of him to go on working at my partition scheme.

Dine with Boris Savinkoff.   Nansen there.   They
both agree that we are mad to deal with Russian territory behind her back.   But there is no vision here, no
will, no direction.

March 28, Friday

With Arnold Toynbee to the American Delegation. We discuss the future of Turkey. We agree upon a frontier for the future Armenian State. We also finally agree on a joint line for the Greek Zone in Asia Minor, subject to some alteration if Italy is given a mandate in the same region. As regards the Constantinople zone, we want to bring the Turks down to the Marmora at Panderma, but the Yanks want to exclude them completely.

March 29, Saturday

The work is diminishing. Everything is now concentrated in the two Councils of IV and V. I am glad to get a clear day as the current papers containing questions from the unhappy F.O. at home accumulate horribly.

March 30, Sunday

A lovely walk in the Val de Chevreuse. Lunch at Dampierre. Snow and sunshine.

March 31, Monday

A joint session of the Polish and the Czech Committees. Work all afternoon. In evening dinner at Ritz. Queen of Rumania, Foch, Briand, etc. Hellish. I gather that there has been a great crisis all this week as between Ll. G. and Clemenceau. The French want the Rhine frontier as their bulwark against Germany. We refuse to give it them. There is a marked atmosphere of strain and tension.

VI. *April* 1 – *April* 9

COMMUNIST INTERLUDE

April 1, *Tuesday*

ANOTHER committee meeting in the morning. Short.
Get back at about 12.0. Allen Leeper tells me that we
are both to leave at once for Buda Pesth. It seems that
the Supreme Council have given up the idea of sending
General Mangin to reduce Hungary to order with
the help of the Rumanian Army. They are sending
General Smuts instead and on a peaceful mission. His
terms of reference are very vague : he is to see whether
Bela Kun will accept the peace. Go across to Majestic
and start packing. We are to leave in some sort of
special train this evening. After luncheon Hardinge
comes in and says that A. J. B. won't let me go. This
is a disappointment, as I want to see Bolshevism in
being. Smuts however insists on taking me, bless his
heart. A. J. B. gives way. Leave Gare de l'Est at 7.15
in a long sleeper tacked on to the new Paris Bucharest
train. Our party consists of General Smuts, Allen
Leeper, Colonel Heywood of the Military Intelligence,
Cyril Butler of the Food Control Commission, Lane
(Smut's personal A.D.C.)., one of Foch's aides de
camp whose name I don't know and an Italian aide
de camp. Latter two are merely to ' show the uniform ' and give the mission an international aspect.
We have also Law as cypher clerk, two other clerks for
typing, and four orderlies. We take with us cases of
army rations. Sleep well.

April 2, Wednesday

Wake up at Basel. Snow everywhere. Have a long discussion with Smuts and Allen Leeper. We both gather the impression that although the ostensible purpose of our mission is to fix an armistice line between the Hungarians and the Rumanians, yet the real idea at the back is to see whether Bela Kun is worth using as a vehicle for getting into touch with Moscow. Neither Allen or I like this sort of thing. We don't want another Prinkipo muddle. Smuts is very reserved. I cannot make out what his own view is. I get the impression, and so does Allen, that Smuts wants us to handle this side of the business on our own, and without engaging *his* responsibility. If that is really so, we shall do the stupid, and pretend not to understand what is expected of us.

Coolidge of the American Mission joins our train. A splendid type—with a voice like a child. Also the Archbishop of Spalato, rustling stiff silk in the corridor of the Wagon Lit.

April 3, Thursday

Wake up in Austria. My first sight of an enemy country. The train goes slowly, stopping at stations. The suburban trains are packed with people and nearly all the windows are broken. They only run about four a day owing to fuel shortage. Everybody looks very pinched and yellow : no fats for four years. The other side of the blockade.

Arrive Vienna at about 10.0 a.m. Allen and I walk to the Embassy, where our mission is in residence. The town has an unkempt appearance : paper lying about : the grass plots round the statues are strewn

with litter : many windows broken and repaired by
boards nailed up. The people in the streets are de-
jected and ill-dressed : they stare at us in astonishment. And indeed we are a funny sight, when viewed
in a bunch like that. Smuts in his General's uniform,
the French and Italian A.D.C.'s, Heywood and Lane
in their red tabs, the neat English clothes of the
civilians. I feel that my plump pink face is an insult
to these wretched people.

At the Embassy are Sir Thomas Cuninghame, head
of our Military Mission, and Philpotts of the Consular
Service. From the first instant it is clear that Smuts
does not take a fancy to Sir Thomas Cuninghame. It
is also clear that he takes a great fancy to Philpotts.
They say they have ordered luncheon for us at Sachers
and that arrangements will be made to provide us with
a train on to Buda Pesth. Meanwhile we must warn
Bela Kun somehow that we are about to arrive, and
must have a safe-conduct. I telephone to the Hungarian Bolshevik headquarters and ask to see the head
man. He is out, but will be back at three. Go off to
Sachers to luncheon. We are followed by a staring
shambling crowd. The police walk with us. Smuts
is silent, dignified, reserved. A huge luncheon at
Sachers which costs 1200 kronen. Smuts is furious.
He ticks Cuninghame off sharply. He calls it a ' gross
error in taste.' He decrees that from now on we shall
feed only upon our own army rations and not take
anything from these starving countries. His eyes
when angry are like steel rods. But it was a good
luncheon all the same.

Walk about with Smuts afterwards. He calms down.
We then return to the Embassy and Allen and I explain

the frontiers to Smuts, as also the armistice line. He
turns Cuninghame out of his own room, and the latter
roams about the Chancery nervous and apprehensive.

I go round to the Bolshevik headquarters. It is a
little difficult to get them to understand who I am and
what I want. The place is crowded with men, women
and children scrambling for passports. Nearly all are
Jews, struggling to get to Buda Pesth and the hope of
loot. The whole building reminds me of the refugee
camps in the Balkan wars. At last I am taken upstairs
and shown into the Commissar or whatever he calls
himself. He is a Galician Jew, educated in America
and speaks English perfectly. I explain that General
Smuts has arrived on a special mission from the
Supreme Council at Paris, and that we wish to go on to
Buda Pesth to-night. He gasps. I have seldom seen
upon a man's face such successive waves of astonishment. ' That means,' he said, ' that you recognise the
Government of Bela Kun ? ' I say it means nothing
of the sort. It means only that we are proceeding to
Buda Pesth, and wish to discuss with the authorities
at present in control of the capital the terms by which
an armistice can be arranged between them and the
Rumanians. We are collecting a train at Vienna. We
propose to leave to-night. Will he telephone at once
to Buda Pesth, get hold of Bela Kun personally, tell
him of our impending arrival, and extract from him
an assurance that we shall be given safe conduct and
civilised treatment ? With fingers trembling with excitement he fiddles among his papers, gaining time.
Then he leaves me and I hear telephoning in the next
room. I read the paper. In about half an hour he
returns beaming. It will be all right. Bela Kun will

be delighted to see us. He will give every assurance
as to our courteous reception and full safe-conduct.
I rise to leave. He says—may he come too? Have
we room in the train? He will be useful as an interpreter. I say yes. He beams again. Still beaming,
and with an almost possessive manner, he leads me out
through the congested anterooms to the door.

We dine with the Kapelles, Schenker's agent, and
the right-hand man of the Food Mission. Good
pictures and tapestries, ugly furniture. Nice frightened people. Smuts reserved and courteous. At 10.0
we leave by car for the station, where our train has
been assembled. It consists of two sleeping-cars, a
dining-car, a fourgon for our supplies, a carriage for
the orderlies. Bolgar, meanwhile—that is the name of
the Bolshevik Commissar from Chicago—telephones
during dinner to ask when the train leaves and from
where. He asks also if he may bring his secretary. I
say yes he may, but they will have to share a compartment. On reaching the station we find that the said
secretary is a pretty little woman with flaming hair.

April 4, Friday.

Wake up to find our train already resting in a siding
of the Ostbahnhof at Buda Pesth. There are red
guards all along the platform with fixed bayonets and
scarlet brassards. On the other platforms the crowds
collect, gaping across at our long brown train in
astonishment. From the town comes a dull murmur
and the occasional scream of a factory siren. We have
breakfast and walk up and down the platform afterwards. Bolgar disappears into the town to fetch Bela
Kun.

Our first visitor is Colonel (?) Domorny—the man who had formerly been attached to the Allied Military Mission. He is to be our liaison officer. He is in civilian clothes and is accompanied by two lieutenants. He stands to attention when addressing Smuts as if he were still in uniform. He looks bewildered and unhappy. He is evidently terrified of telling us anything about the situation. Realising this, Smuts ceases asking him questions.

Our next visitor is Professor Brown—one of President Wilson's ' enquirers ' and now in Buda Pesth. He takes a Wilsonian, *i.e.* an unpractical view. He talks of ' natural social evolution,' speaks of the excellent order Bela Kun is maintaining, and says that he is supported by the iron-workers union, 40,000 strong. Yet he is evidently not very sure about it all : idealistic but bewildered, he mumbles something about ' a few foolish excesses ' : says there is no enthusiasm for Kun's red army, which only amounts to some 7000 : says that Hungary is incapable of fighting : speaks of dangers of a foreign and especially a Jewish influx into the city : says that 1500 wild men arrived from Vienna last night to join the Red Guard.

What I gather happened was as follows : (1) On news of the armistice, general feeling one of relief and enthusiasm for the Entente Powers. (2) Delays at Paris, and continued stiffening of the armistice terms, led to general disillusion, uncertainty and unrest. (3) This feeling increased by arrogant and tactless behaviour of Colonel Vyx, head of the French Military Mission, and by reports which reached Buda Pesth of the conduct of the Czechs, Rumanians and Jugo-Slavs in the occupied provinces. (4) Whole position terribly complicated by economic barriers established by the New States and the loss of markets and raw material. (5) Governing class, and particularly Karolyi, discouraged by refusal of Paris people to listen to their appeals. Karolyi was regarded in Hungary as the proved friend of Western democracy : they imagined that a republic under his guidance would be welcomed almost as an ally : instead of this he was snubbed and disregarded, with the inevitable result of disillusion and despair. (5) Then came two incidents, (*a*) Colonel Vyx's letter about the armistice line, (*b*) The incident about the Danube shipping. Karolyi resigned in despair and the communists found the door open.

Some reaction was already setting in. They thought they were going to have a Valmy and all they find is the Commune.

While Brown is still talking Lane comes into the dining-car which we use as an office to say that Bela Kun has arrived. I go to meet him. A little man of about 30 : puffy white face and loose wet lips : shaven head : impression of red hair : shifty suspicious eyes : he has the face of a sulky and uncertain criminal. He has with him a little oily Jew—fur-coat rather moth-eaten—stringy green tie—dirty collar. He is their Foreign Secretary. Bela Kun is shown into Smuts' compartment with Bolgar. I tackle the Foreign Commissar in mine. He takes the high culture line. He speaks of Hume, Mill, Spencer. He quotes, with great irrelevance, ' I stood in Venice on the Bridge of Sighs.' The rain patters on the roof of our carriage and slides down the windows. Our siding is outside the main roof of the station. My Commissar then goes on to talk of Ramsay MacDonald, Henderson, and

Longuet. His German is difficult to follow, being very
Galician and Magyar. He then discourses upon what
Bolshevism will mean to Central Europe. Work and
happiness for all, free education, doctors, Bernard Shaw,
garden suburbs, heaps of music, and the triumph of
the machine. I ask him what machine ? He makes a
vague gesture embracing the whole world of mechanics.
Luckily, before my patience is wholly exhausted, Kun
rises to take leave. I conduct him on to the platform
and to the barrier at the end of the platform which
serves as our front door. The Red Guards do not
salute him. They stand and stare. An engine driver,
however, of a suburban train leaves his engine and
advances towards Kun. He says something I do not
understand. Kun replies with the Magyar equivalent
of ' Of course, Comrade,' and holds out the stump of
the cigarette he has been smoking. The engine driver
enclosing Kun's freckled little podge of a hand in his
own black fingers draws a light from that stump. He
returns to his engine puffing a proud comradely
cigarette. Bela Kun darts little pink eyes at me to see
whether I am impressed by this proletarian scene or
whether I think it ridiculous. I maintain an expression
of noble impassivity.

On my return to our train Smuts tells me what
passed with Kun. The latter would like some settlement with the Powers, but is afraid that having come
in on what is really a nationalist wave he might fall
were he to give way to us completely. It seems that
his Red Army, such as it is, is still officered by the old
regime people, and that they work in with Bela Kun
merely because they think that, Bolshevik though he be,
he is fighting for Hungary. He daren't let these people

down. He suggests that we might arrange a Conference, either at Vienna or Prague, between Hungary
and the Succession States. Smuts wants him to come
to Paris.

We lunch off army rations. Beans and cheese. Bela
Kun had requisitioned the Hungaria for us, which is
the Ritz of Buda Pesth. He has, it seems, hoisted a
huge Union Jack and a huge Tricolour on it, hoping
to parade our presence as an advertisement that Paris
had recognised him and come as suppliants to his
capital. Smuts refuses to budge from the train. Here
we are to stick. He does not want us to enter the
town or to leave the station. So all the air we shall get
is pacing along our own stretch of wet platform
towards the dry platform under the station roof.

At 3.0 Bela Kun returns. I sit with him and Smuts.
Bolgar interprets. A wagon lit is not the ideal place
for a diplomatic conference. One has to turn sideways
all the time, which gives one a funny feeling and a
stiff neck. Kun promises to go off, hold a meeting
of his Cabinet, and return.

Ashmead Bartlett suddenly appears upon the platform. He was out here when the revolution happened
and had the guts to remain when all the other people
bolted. He says that Bela Kun has little influence outside the capital, and that the whole thing would
collapse at the slightest push.

At 3.30 persuade Smuts that Allen and I, at least,
might be allowed out of the station. He agrees. Our
liaison officers provide a car and come with us. I had
not seen Buda Pesth since I stayed here on my way to
Constantinople in 1912. Most of the shops are shut
and it seems even sadder and more unkempt than

Vienna. Everything bedraggled. Rain pouring on
yellow faces and clothes in rags. Groups of Red
Guards going about with hat-stands on which they
drape ' presents.' We met three or four of these little
groups—generally about fifteen or twenty of them
armed with bayonets and one of their number carrying
a wooden hat-stand stolen from some restaurant. If
they find a shop open they go in and take ' presents,'
which they hang on the hat stand. Boots, sausages,
red underclothes. All this in soaking rain. No other
signs of revolution or Bolshevism except a universal
sadness and shabbiness.

At 6.0 Commander Freeman comes to the train. He
has something to do with the Danube flotilla. He
gives me £4500 in English notes to take home.
Afraid it may be bagged. He is calm, uninterested in
politics, and intent only on doing his job here as long
as he can. I am quite vague as to what that job is, but
refrain from asking him. We dine by the light of two
candles as the electric light has given out on the train.
Then Bela Kun comes again. I get him to sign a
paper undertaking to release all British subjects whom
he has imprisoned. The rain still patters on the roof
and glistens in the light of our candles, golden drops
upon the pane. How sad it all is. Bela Kun does not
strike me as a man who enjoys the fruits of office. He
sat there hunched, sulky, suspicious, and frightened.
Smuts talks to him as if he were talking to the Duke
of Abercorn : friendly, courteous but not a touch of
any surrender of his own tremendous dignity.

The Spanish and Swiss Consuls come to our train,
wet umbrellas outside the half-lit sleeping cars. They
say that it is all nonsense to say that Bela Kun has

shown moderation. The prisons are packed with people huddled there in crowds. The Red Guards are getting out of hand. There is fear of a massacre. They confirm what everybody says, namely, that Bela Kun is just an incident and not worth treating seriously.

April 5, Saturday

Bela Kun comes at 10.0. Smuts hands him a draft agreement providing for the occupation by the Great Powers of a neutral zone between him and the Rumanians. If he agrees to this we shall raise the blockade. It is clear that Bela Kun longs to accept it. The signature of such a document would imply official recognition of his regime, which he desires passionately. But he is suspicious and afraid. Clasping the document he leaves us—saying he must consult his Cabinet. That means he must consult Moscow. He promises us a reply by seven. Smuts says we must be prepared to leave at 7.15. Lane makes all arrangements.

More bully beef and beans for luncheon. Smuts presides at our trench-meals as if giving us a banquet at the Savoy.

Our liaison officers suggest a drive to the golf course as the weather has cleared. They produce a car. Smuts gives us leave. Off we go—bumping and rattling through the shoddy town, which looks even more bedraggled in sunlight than it did under the rain. The car breaks down after a bit, but they repair it and we return. The car stops at the Hungaria. Our officers say that Bela Kun wishes to offer us tea. This is awkward as I do not think the General would like us to enter a hotel. But they look so frightened when we refuse that we agree. It is clear from the moment that we enter that it is a put-up job carefully staged to impress us. The foyer of the hotel is full of people having lemonade and coffee at little tables. An orchestra plays Hungarian tunes. It has all been arranged to show us that even under Bolshevism Buda Pesth remains the gayest city in Central Europe. But two serious mistakes have been made. In the first place there are Red Guards at all the doors with fixed bayonets. And in the second place they omitted to tell the people at the tables that they must make conversation with each other. It is a curious effect. It is some time before I realise what is wrong. It all looks very like the tea hour at any continental hotel. But there is something uncanny about it and unreal. Then it suddenly dawns upon me that each single table is absolutely silent. Not a word do they address to each other as they sip their lemonade. If one looks up suddenly one catches countless frightened eyes, and at the back of those eyes a mutely passionate appeal. Then the eyes flick away towards the lemonade, and this ghastly silence continues under the wail of the violins and under the gaze of the sentries guarding every exit. It is quite clear that all these huddled silent people have been let out of prison for the afternoon in order to fill the foyer of the Hungaria. I shudder and feel cold. We leave as soon as possible. Silent eyes search out at us as we go, our voices sounding loudly, to the door. Sheep in a thunderstorm.

We get back at 6.30. At 7.0 Bela Kun, Garbai, Kunfi and Bolgar come, accompanied by the Commander of the Red Guards. There, in the half-lit dining-car, Smuts receives them. They hand him a Note which he reads twice over and then hands to me.

It accepts our terms but adds a clause. That clause is that the Rumanian army should be told to withdraw behind the Maros. I give the paper back to Smuts. He hands it to Bela Kun. ' No, gentlemen,' he says, ' this is not a note which I can accept. There must be no reservations.' They look silent and sullen. Smuts makes a final appeal to them, asking them in their own interests to accept our proposals without reservations. He is very frank. He says that the Conference will not agree to send the Rumanians back to the Maros. They evidently think that he will propose some third line of compromise and fix a meeting for to-morrow. Smuts has come to the conclusion however (and rightly) that Bela Kun is of no importance or seriousness and that he is not capable of giving effect to any treaty. Smuts is determined to break off negotiations that very night. They do not know this. ' Well, gentlemen,' he says, ' I must bid you good-bye.' They do not understand. He conducts them with exquisite courtesy on to the platform. He shakes hands with them. He then stands on the step of the train and nods to his A.D.C. They stand in a row upon the platform, expecting him to fix the time for the next meeting. And as they stand the train gradually begins to move. Smuts brings his hand to the salute. We glide out into the night, re-taining on the retinas of our eyes the picture of four bewildered faces looking up in blank amazement.

We then dine. Smuts is delightful, telling us stories of the Veldt with a ring of deep homesickness in his voice. A lovely man. Our rations are even more Spartan than before, since we gave all our chocolates and condensed milk to our liaison officers. The old Colonel cried when we left. Poor man, he goes back to jail from which he had been released for our benefit.

Ashmead Bartlett comes with us. He is a plucky fellow. But his nerves were about to break.

April 6, Sunday

Wake up in Vienna. Go to Embassy. C. B. Thomson had been sent after us by Henry Wilson but missed us. Smuts is not very polite to him. He doesn't care for Henry Wilson. This is bad luck on C. B.

Smuts has interviews all day and I sit in the Chancery writing a report. It is odd to find the paper in the letter racks which has been there since the place was sealed up in August 1914. Our train leaves for Prague with the electric light mended at 5.0. I continue dictating our report to a shorthand clerk. He is very interested in it. It is seldom that a shorthand writer takes in what one is saying. A clever A.S.C. boy. We reach Prague at about ten at night. Coulson and Gosseling meet us. We have a long talk with them in a half-lit carriage, since the light has again failed. They say that the Czechs are behaving badly in the occupied districts.

April 7, Monday

Still in Prague Station. Wake up at 7.0, and at 8.0 go off with the General to see Masaryk. A lovely morning with a mist over everything and the spires emerging above. We motor up to the old palace. There is a strong smell of beeswax and endless corridors with white settees and portraits of eighteenth century Archduchesses. A Maria-Teresa feel. Masaryk receives us in his study. A slim, sturdy old

man whom I had met before in London.   It is frowsty
in his room with a big stove.   Smuts tells us to leave
him alone with Masaryk.   We retire to a stiff ante-
room and Smuts and Masaryk remain closeted together for an hour.   We then get into our large motor
again and hoot our way across the bridge.   The mist
is lifting.   Prague is superb.   We regain our train and
leave at once for Vienna.

A lovely spring morning.   Dictate the whole time.
Stop the train at Gmünd, as I want to see whether the
station and the town are really separate as Benes insisted before our sub-committee.   There is certainly
some distance between the two.

Reach Vienna at 5.0 p.m.   Walk slowly towards
the Embassy with Allen Leeper.   Buy some books.
The exchange is 4½ kronen to the franc.   The people
are delighted to see us.   They think it means food
somehow and protection against Bolshevism.   A knot
of people follow us about.   ' Gib uns zu essen . . .' an
old man exclaims.   Poor souls !

We dine at a cheap restaurant—Smuts being determined that we are on some sort of campaign.   Leave
by the Hütteldorf station.   A jolly motor drive there
and our train waiting for us.

April 8, *Tuesday*
Wake up near Innsbruck.   Another coach has been
attached to our train containing the Archduke Maxi-
milian, who is fleeing from what he fears will shortly
be a Bolshevik Austria.   Work all day.   Rather exhausting as our wagon restaurant has deserted us and
we live on biscuits.   Arrive Basel 9.15.

April 9, Wednesday

Arrive Paris 8.0 a.m.   On to Majestic, where I have
a much-needed bath.   We are told that a flood of telegrams were sent to us at Vienna, Prague and Buda
Pesth, ordering us to go on to Bucharest, Belgrade and
Constantinople.   They can only have missed us by a
few minutes.

The papers say that the Smuts mission has been a
' fiasco.'   I think it was in a way, but then our whole
purpose was obscure and illogical.   Yet we have gained
the following : (1) A conviction that Bela Kun and
Hungarian Bolshevism is not a serious menace and
cannot last.   (2) A valuable talk between Smuts and
Masaryk.   (3) A conviction that Austria-Hungary *is*
an economic unit and that these trade barriers are
fatal, (4) negatively—Smuts refrained from using Kun
as a liaison with Moscow.   His sense and dignity were
superb.

Revise our report all day.   Dine with Crowe.   He
tells me that during the last week things have been
humming hotly.   The French insisted on the Rhineland.   P. W. and Ll. G. held out.   Both of them retired to their beds.   P. W. ordered the ' George
Washington ' to be sent to Brest.   This has frightened
the French, and Tardieu and Headlam Morley are
working out a compromise scheme on the basis of a
demilitarised Rhine and occupation for a period of
years.   Meanwhile the French have got Northcliffe to
stir up the House of Commons against Ll. G. on the
ground that he is being chicken-livered and pro-
German.   Crowe may dislike the Germans, but his
feeling for them is as nothing compared to his contempt for the present House of Commons.   He calls

them a ' pack of ninnies.' Nor is he a Lloyd Georgite
—anything but. But he is incensed at this torpedoing
of the little man 'by an alliance between scamps,
lunatics and ignorant boobies.' I have seldom seen
him so violent.

Meanwhile everything is being rushed at a feverish
pace. The Sarre, reparations, everything is boiling
over at the same time.

VII. *April* 10–*May* 6

THE DISPUTE WITH ITALY

April 10, *Thursday*

Pick up threads of work interrupted by our mission.

It is extraordinary how little has been agreed to since we left. In fact I see no progress at all, only further oceans of disagreement—and the general depression is terrible. We are getting weaker every day and our enemies know it. ' Peak upon peak, and Alp on Alp arise.'

The French have got a bad attack of nerves. ' Shellshock ' as Smuts says. The result is that Lloyd George (who is indignant at the attacks made upon him in the French Press—which can hardly be made without official encouragement) is becoming irritable and in conjunction with P. W. is beginning to ride a high horse. The whole situation, in fact, is full of menace, uncertainty, tension, sorrow and discontent.

Dine with Allen Leeper and Rhys Carpenter. Work after dinner getting the essence of our report on the Smuts Mission into the form of a Resolution of the Supreme Council. It is no good writing memoranda, however succinct : the only thing that fetches them is something which begins with the words It is Resolved. That makes them sit up and take notice. Resolution, unlike Mesopotamia, is in Paris a most blessed word.

April 11, *Friday*

Telephone home in the morning and arrange that I shall fly over for Easter. I need a holiday. Too much

play and no work makes Jack a dull boy. Fourth
Plenary Session : they discuss Labour Charters.

Lunch at the Meurice with Swope, an American
correspondent. He bursts with boost. He is very
vulgar. He is a nice man. My liking for the Americans is becoming a vice. I like the scholarly sort, such
as Coolidge, Seymour, Day and Allen Dulles, because
they are quiet and scholarly and because they like the
truth. I also have a weakness for the noisy sort such
as Swope, because he is so unlike myself. I feel like a
mouse much impressed by a jaguar.

Jacques Blanche is there. He says ' Mais, mon cher,
nous sommes perdus.' He is a defeatist by temperament. He may paint flashy pictures, but he writes
damned good books.

Bullitt there. He was on House's ' Enquiry.' A
young man with beliefs. He was sent to Russia by the
President and has returned with a pro-Bolshevik report.
He talks about them. I blink politely. He probably
thinks me a lousy official. Better blink therefore. But
in fact I am an agnostic about Bolshevism—I simply
do not know and do not pretend to know. Here we
are told only of the atrocities and the executions : they
are probably true ; but there must be another side,
some reality behind it all whch has produced this firm
and successful government. Bullitt says that the only
danger for Lenin comes from the left extremists, not
from the whites. I said that that was my own impression of Buda Pesth. But he did not like my saying
that Bela Kun was a silly little man.

A lovely spring day, Really hot. In the afternoon
Dulles and Day drop in. I tell them of our mission.

By the way, before breakfast I had a long talk with

Smuts. He is just off to London. I gave him the draft Resolutions, which he approved. What a man ! His sense of values takes one away from Paris and this greedy turmoil.

Dine with Knox and Grant of the ' Morning Post ' at Bougival. We drive back afterwards in the moonlight. It is supremely lovely. Nice people.

April 12, Saturday

Ronnie Campbell is off for a few days leave. I am therefore acting as Private Secretary to Hardinge. It entails little work. And God knows I am busy enough with my own jobs.

A. F. Whyte and Laroche lunch at the Majestic. Allen Leeper is ill with toothache—a face of swollen but suffering patience.

April 13, Sunday

Spanish exhibition at Petit Palais : Goya tapestries : the paintings are dead and faded. Zuloaga is a bad painter.

Talk to George Grahame afterwards about the reform of diplomacy. He agrees with my radical views. Dine with William Goode. Ll. G. goes to London.

April 14, Monday

Ask Day to come up to the Astoria and have a long talk about Northern Epirus. He explains why it is that his delegation do not ' stay put.' I do not follow his explanation, which is involved ; but it is a good thing that he should realise that they have contracted a habit of going back on all agreements. I feel he will not give way about Koritsa and I hope he won't,

though I do not say so.   Yet there is that danger of
the Italian protectorate and of placing Italy at that vital
junction of communications.

Toynbee and I plot together about Constantinople
and the Straits. We agree : (1) That no mandatory
will be able to run Constantinople without a fairly
large zone behind him.   On the other hand a big zone
will include Greek populations, while cutting the
future Turkey off from all communication with the
Marmora. (2) That as we have demobilised so quickly,
and as people at home are bored by the future settlement, we shall be unable to put the Greeks into
Smyrna.   I mean keep them there.   They can't hold it
without allied support or unless the whole of Turkey
behind them is split up among the Allied Powers.   Yet
if they do not get Smyrna Venizelos will fall from
power. (3) We agree, therefore, to propose to cut the
Gordian knot.   Let the Turks have Anatolia as their
own.   Give the Greeks European Turkey only.   And
let the Straits be kept open by a ' Commission Flu-
viale ' with powers analogous to those of the Danube
Commission.

Such a solution would at least have the merit of
finality.   All other solutions would entail trouble in
the future.   We put this down on paper ; we sign it
with our names ; we send it in.   It will not be considered.

The Germans have been invited to send a Delegation
to receive the Peace Terms.

April 15, Tuesday

I put a pistol at the head of the United States regarding Northern Epirus, which is dragging on too

long. Either they must accept our scheme for autonomy or else they must leave the decision to the Four.
I wonder what will be the result.

Eddie Sackville West and David Cecil lunch.

We are all very excited as to what Lloyd George
will say in the House to-morrow.

A visit from P......, who talks more Montenegrin
rubbish. He is a fraud. Telephone to F.O. about
sending de Salis on a mission of enquiry to Montenegro. We simply do not know the real situation and
cannot trust people to tell us the truth.

Valentine Williams of the ' Daily Mail ' comes to see
me. He is far too intelligent to be employed by such a
paper. He is bitterly hostile to Lloyd George. I try
to put him more or less right.

April 16, *Wednesday*

Jim Barnes comes to help in our office. I shall turn
him on to doing Albania, as he is far more Albanophil
even than I am myself.

Lunch with Vesnic the Serb. He tells me that his
people are sending an infantry division and two
brigades of cavalry to occupy Buda Pesth and turn out
my friend Kun Bela. I don't believe it. If true, then
it is a coup de main on the part of Franchet d'Esperey.

Crowe is quite good about Toynbee's scheme for
the solution of the Turkish question. He sends our
memorandum to A. J. B. with his blessing. He is a
wonderful man to work for.

Go to the Opera with Hermitte. A coup de
théâtre provided by the entry of Paderewsky into the
Presidential box : the Polish national anthem : hand-
kerchiefs and cheers amid a risen audience : ' Bravo !

Bravo ! ': I stand up limply : Paderewsky bows and smiles. Not a presidential bow : a concert-platform bow. His wife looks like hell in orchids. His box bristles with A.D.C.'s.

April 17, Thursday

Work all day at Foreign Office work. How they must hate us over there, poor people. We never tell them what is happening and we never answer any of their letters. Dine with the Americans. They refuse to accept my scheme for an autonomous Northern Epirus. I am secretly delighted. I had come to loathe that scheme. Read Ll. G.'s attack on Northcliffe. Bitter but well-deserved. He returns later.

April 18, Friday

Lunch with A. F. Whyte at Dufayel. We talk about the reform of diplomacy. I want to fuse it with the Consular Service. That would mean more jobs for the efficient in either service, and more pigeon-holes for the fools.

April 19, Saturday—April 22, Tuesday

Fly home for Easter.

April 23, Wednesday

Michael Sadler wants to found a literary paper. Vita agrees to contribute. We ask Keynes to contribute the articles on pictures. He says, ' Will it be a good paper ? ' This throws cold water over our enthusiasms.

The Adriatic question has come to a head while I

was over in England. Wilson has issued to the Press
a statement showing up the Italian claims. The
Italians say that they will leave Paris. Good riddance.

The seventeen main Committees have split up into
thirty Sub-Committees. This will hurry the pace.

April 24, Thursday

Orlando goes off. Japanese threaten to leave also.

April 25, Friday

The Grand Fleet sailors are here being entertained
by the City of Paris. Very well behaved.

Orlando's departure has caused a flutter. The
Japanese are also threatening to go. The 'Temps'
heads its leading article, 'Le *voyage* de M. Orlando.'
In effect he will come back. The Italians have made
the mistake of being obstructive and untruthful. They
hoped by opposing everything all along the line to
obtain a snap decision at the end. The snap has come
all right—but not of the sort they wanted. They must
now either climb down and creep back to Paris or else
break with their allies. The whole business in the end
will increase the prestige of the Conference and of
Wilson personally. Of course the Italian feeling against
the latter is now almost hysterical, and I gather that at
the Gare de Lyon when Orlando left there were
cries of ' Abbasso Wilson ! '

Leeper is working out a compromise scheme about
the Adriatic against their return. Fiume to be international as also Dalmatia. The Islands to Italy. Deep
down I have a sneaking sympathy for the Italian case.
They suffered horribly in the war, and it is poor fun
running away. Yet they have behaved at the Confer-

ence with a trickiness which chills all sympathy. I also
have an uneasy feeling that it would be a mistake to
give the Slavs too firm a footing on the Adriatic. What
should we do with a Slav block from Vladivostock
to Fiume, from Danzig to Samarcand ? Les Scythes
ont conquis le monde. This, probably will be one of
the great problems of my middle age. What will the
new Russia care for the League of Nations ? They
will argue that it is a ramp on the part of the victorious
Powers.

Have a visit (1) from two members of the Society of
Friends sent by Smuts from London. They want to
do relief work in Vienna. Help all I can. (2) A depu-
tation of the Syllogue Grec of Constantinople, who
want Lloyd George and A. J. B. to become honorary
members. I am not helpful. I ask them to get
Ramsay MacDonald. They write his name down carefully. A bad joke.

April 27, Saturday
The Americans come to discuss Leeper's compromise scheme for the Adriatic. Seton Watson
attends the meeting. We decide on a ' minimum
scheme.' (1) Treaty of London line in Tyrol, Gorizia,
Gradisca, and Carinthia, plus Tarvis and Sextern
valley. (2) Modified line in Istria wobbling down the
centre. (3) Fiume corpus separatum under the Jugo-
Slavs. (4) Dalmatia Jugo-Slav with nationality rights
for the Sole Mios. (5) Lissa and Lussin to the Italians.
(6) Personal mandate for Duke of Abruzzi for Albania.
This is very bright idea. He is a good man and they
will turn him out in a few months. (7) A mandate in
the Caucasus.

To this we add three categories in order of desirability, and containing further concessions if necessary. Category A. (1) Idria. (2) Fiume corpus separatum under League. (3) Cherso to Italy, (4) Zara a free city. (5) Italian mandate in place of the Abruzzi personality over Albania. Category B. (1) Fiume free city with joint flag. (2) Pelagosa, Cazza, to Italy. (4) Stampalia as naval base in Dodecanese. (5) Concessions in African colonies. Category C. (1) Full sovereignty over Valona. (2) Mandate for Anatolia, excluding the Greek Zone. This at least will give the Four something to work on.

April 27, *Sunday*

Johnson appears and says that the American Delegation cannot support yesterday's compromise scheme, as P. W. insists on a ' non possumus ' attitude. If he sticks to his guns all will be well. We are overjoyed.

April 28, *Monday*

In order to twist the Italian tail the Council of Four or rather of Three decide to recognize the Jugo-Slav State officially. Rather late in the day. Allen is busy preparing a formula of recognition, and bundles off to the Quai d'Orsay to consult Laroche.

Plenary session of the Conference. They adopt the Covenant of the League. Eric Drummond to be Secretary-General. Pours with rain.

Dine with Smuts, who is back. We talk religion, anthropology (pigmies, bushmen, hottentots, golden bough), on which the General knows a good deal in a picturesque way. He is simple and intricate.

April 29, Tuesday

Snow and cold.   Work at our memorandum on the
Adriatic compromise.   Prepare a lovely map.

I go and bother Hermann Norman about the rights
of minorities in the ceded territories.   I draft a resolution.   A. J. B. funks it.   What a bore this indecision
is !   It simply is not fair on us.

A. F. Whyte comes.   He is always to the point.   We
discuss the Italian situation.   The Germans (Brockdorff Rantzau and Co.) reach Versailles in the evening.

April 30, Wednesday

Cold and stormy.   Light a fire as well as hot pipes.

Get our Adriatic scheme into shape for the printer.
I do not think it will come to much as Philip Kerr and
the P.M. have got a scheme of their own, of which, of
course, we know nothing.

Lunch with that ghastly P....... He is a tiresome
and untrustworthy person and represents Montenegro
no more than I do.   I cannot help feeling that there is
some shady business going on down there.

Hear that the Council of Three thought better of
recognising the Jugo-Slav State on the ground that it
would be ' petty ' to do so.

Dine with Jean de Gaigneron at the Ritz, Gladys
Deacon there.   Very Attic.   Also Marcel Proust.
Very Hebrew.   Sit next him.   He asks more questions.
I am amused by this.   I suggest to him that the passion
for detail is a sign of the literary temperament.   This
hurts his feelings.   He says, ' Non pas ! ' quite abruptly
and then blows a sort of adulatory kiss across the
table at Gladys Deacon.   But he soothes down
again later.   We discuss inversion.   Whether it is a

matter of glands or nerves. He says it is a matter of
habit. I say, ' surely not.' He says, ' No—that was
silly of me—what I meant was that it was a matter of
delicacy.' He is not very intelligent on the subject.
Marie Murat is there. She laughs in a way that makes
one giggle. Also Carlo Placci. He talks to me in a
saddened way about the Adriatic. ' My dear Nicolson,
you do not understand my countrymen. . . .' He may
be right. But if feverish conceit is a thing I am expected to admire then I should feel angry even with
Carlo Placci—bless his nice Savonarola face. But all
the same I try to get out of him what is at the bottom
of the Italian point of view. He says that they feel that
we and France have got everything we wanted out of
the war and that Italy has been pushed on one side and
got nothing. That is absurd : but dangerous. There
is, he says, also a feeling that Wilson has strained his
XIV points in favour of France and Great Britain
(that bloody freedom of the seas—those foul mandates)
and is now trying to ' se refaire une virginité ' at the
expense of Italy. He would feel this even more
strongly if he knew what is happening about Shantung.
Thirdly, he says that the Italians regard the Croats even
as I would regard the Germans. I say that I regard the
Germans as a perfectly delightful people of great
culture but having suffered from bad government.
' You are not serious,' he says, sighing deeply. ' That
is the worst of your public school education. You
are never serious.' I fear I have hurt his feelings.
I am terribly polite and receptive for the rest of the
evening.

May 1, Thursday

The French socialists take this occasion to mobilize their proletariat. As a result Paris resembles Edinburgh on Sunday. Socialism has a way, somehow, of becoming glum and sabbatarian. No taxis, tubes, theatres, restaurants or (Thank God in heaven !) newspapers. It pours all day, which adds to the Edinburgh feel. I hear that there has been some trouble near the Opéra. One man being shot.

Send our Adriatic report to the printer.

Jean de Gaigneron blows in in the evening. His attitude towards Wilson and the peace is typical of the whole Paris atmosphere. It combines deep irritation at not being allowed to apply the ' vae victis ' principle with a real congenital fear of Germany. One must *force* oneself to see the French point of view and to visualize in terms of their minds the nightmare of French security. They are a profoundly *defensive* people. And they long to create a ditch between themselves and the outer world. It is *not* militarism in the least.

Wace of the British School at Athens comes to see me. He has just come from Greece. He says they are clamouring for help at the Legation. I expect they will want me to go there when all this is over.

Smuts comes and talks to me after dinner. He deplores the influence of French ' shell-shock ' upon the peace. I say that after all this *has been* a shell, there *is* a shell, and there *will remain* a shell. He says it is jingoism none the less and that it has ruined the fine spirit in which we came to Paris. There is something in what he says. Paris was not a good place for the Conference. Its atmosphere is far too particularised and far too insistent. He contends that the whole delay in our work has been caused by the need of finding some middle path between French realism and American idealism. Obviously. I quite admit that the French cannot see beyond their noses ; but after all they are *their* noses : and, my word, what they *do* see, they see damned clearly.

Hermann Norman tells me he was present to-day at the delivery of the German full powers at the Trianon Palace Hotel. Jules Cambon who conducted the ceremony was polite but icy. Brockdorff Rantzau was pale and nervous—trembling in every limb. Norman did not think that he was trembling with rage.

May 2, Friday

The stream of work which has kept up a general trickle, flowing in spate at moments, dried up to-day. I had little to do. I go to see pictures. Fantin Latour and Sisley. In the evening dine with Venizelos. A long talk. (1) I tell him that I have been appointed to the Legation at Athens. ' En voilà,' he exclaims, ' une bonne nouvelle.' He adds that he had thought of asking for me, but had thought it better not to do so. He says we shall travel together—a ' voyage de Sparte '—and forget all this. (2) We discuss the effect of the Italian crisis upon Greek claims. I express the fear that Italy will be given ' compensations ' in Anatolia for what she is forced to surrender in the Adriatic. He sighs deeply—' But,' he says, ' I have received assurances of comfort and support from Lloyd George and Wilson.' In fact the former, when he heard that the Italians were sending two men-of-war to Smyrna, gave instructions that a British Dreadnought and a

Greek Cruiser should also go there. The Italians, by trying to steal a march on the Asia Minor Coast, have helped the Greeks more than they know.

In general he adheres to his view that if Italy is to be given a Protectorate in Turkey in Asia, Greece should have the Smyrna zone, plus Aivali, and the rest of his own claims under a similar ' mandate.'

(3) I told him that the idea was being mooted that Greece should be given Constantinople as an inducement to make her surrender Smyrna. He was most indignant. He disclaimed all connexion with such pronouncements, abused the ' Eleutheros Typos ' for publishing any such suggestion, and said that he would take the first moment to repudiate the attribution of these intentions to Greece. ' Vous voyez, mon zer, que je suis le seul Grec au monde qui puisse refuser Constantinople.'

(4) I then asked him about the Military League which is being formed in Athens in his support. He did not like it. He said that his intention was to publish his programme after the elections for a Constituent Assembly and to go to the country quite independently of party. He would even resign his leadership of the Liberals. I murmured something about a Dictatorship. He laughed. ' Une Dictature élective,' he chuckled. ' Mais vous savez, mon zer,' he added, ' ze ne suis pas un homme vaniteux. Mais ze me trouve dans une position exceptionnelle. Aucun homme politique n'a le prestige que moi ze possède.'

He explained that King Constantine had been obliged to have recourse to the old party methods : that he had dragged out obscure politicians from the

dustbins of a forgotten and discredited period : and
that the political ' honesty ' which he, Venizelos, has
struggled to introduce, had, of recent months, had a
set-back. It would, therefore, be necessary for him to
cleanse the Augean stable on his return. He might
have to punish his supporters as well as his opponents.
For this he must have an absolutely free hand unhampered by party allegiances.

He said he was opposed to a Republic for fear of
pronunciamentos on the part of the Generals.

(6) As regards Bulgaria, he and Pasic had had a long
talk with old Clemenceau. The latter had not agreed
to their extending the Armistice line. But he had
agreed about sending to Salonica the Bulgarian war
material which General Chrétien has collected at Sofia.
' A precautionary measure.'

May 3, Saturday

Warmer. Lunch with Michael Sadler.

In afternoon go down to the ' Conseil des Cinq,'
i.e. the subsidiary Supreme Council, of the Foreign
Ministers. It is still held in Pichon's office where the
old Ten used to sit. It is a scrubby affair compared to
the old Clemenceau-Ll. G.-Wilson days. There is a
feeling of ' another place.' The emptiness of the room
is emphasised by the absence of the Italians. And in
fact the only people there are Lansing, Pichon, Hardinge
and the Japanese. The secretaries and experts have
become more familiar and take liberties which they
would never have dared in the hot silence of the old
Ten. Even the interpreter is not Mantoux, but a dim
diffident person in pince-nez.

They agree to the recognition of Finland. They

then pass to the Grosse Schütt. When in Prague I had begged Smuts to urge on Masaryk not to claim that wretched Danubian island. He had done so. Masaryk had agreed that if they could obtain a bridgehead across the river at Pressburg they would abandon the Grosse Schütt. I begged Hardinge to bring this offer up before the Council. He did so, in an admirable manner. I had even drafted a specific resolution (I have learnt the value of ' resolutions ') to that effect. To my dismay, however, Pichon put up Laroche to say that he had heard from Benes that Smuts had ' completely misunderstood ' old Masaryk. All the latter had said was ' that *some* people in Czechoslovakia thought this would be a good arrangement, but that the Czech Government thought it would be a very bad arrangement. . . .'

This, I fear, is untrue. It increases my dislike of Kramarsh, who is behind everything nasty that Benes does. They are in the pockets of the French. The French will now tell them that they have ' déjoué ' an anti-Czech intrigue on my part. Yet it wasn't an intrigue. It was an eleventh-hour attempt to right a palpable injustice.

Anyhow it is to be referred to a Committee.

Polovtsoff, Director of the Hermitage Gallery, dines. The Bolsheviki have behaved well in matters of art. They have even saved private collections by having them ' nationalised.'

May 4, Sunday

Bela Kun, it seems, has bolted and a middle government will be created. Some ex-Hungarian officers raided the Hungarian Legation at Vienna, arrested my friend Bolgar and his lovely secretary, and decamped with all the money.

To Jacques Blanche.   Dine with Maggie Greville.

May 5, Monday

Czech Committee in morning. We discuss Smuts' conversation with Masaryk on the Grosse Schütt. I have to admit that I was only in the adjoining room. Laroche backs up his argument by producing a written note from Benes. We are forced to give way. The Czechs will have their Magyars and their Island. I do not feel this to be a wise decision : but I have done my best. Evidently Masaryk committed a gaffe and has been forced to deny it by his Government.

The Italians are returning to Paris ! Discuss next step with Eustace Percy who is now doing Private Secretary to A. J. B.

VIII.　May 6–May 20

'COMPENSATIONS'

May 6, Tuesday

STEFANIK, the Czech Minister of War—a great hero
with only half a stomach and the will of a superman—
is killed in an aeroplane accident at Bratislava. It was
he who organised the Czech army in Siberia and thus
put the Great Powers under so deep an obligation to
the Bohemians. A good death—at the moment of his
final return to a liberated and triumphant country.
Lesser hands can now carry on his work. But he is a
distinct loss, as he gave a champagne feeling to the
heavy beer of the Czech temperament.

Endless telegrams pour in from the two Ambassadors in Rome suggesting various schemes for a compromise on the Adriatic question. Their suggestions
are not helpful, as they all imply eventual Italian
sovereignty over Fiume. This the Jugo-Slavs will
never accept : nor will P. W. It seems that Ll. G. and
P. W. are firmer on this point than ever. This is
the result of Italian diplomatic methods. Had they
adopted western instead of Mediterranean, or even
Neapolitan, processes, we should have been bound in
common fairness to meet them half-way. As it is, their
obstructive behaviour throughout the Conference, the
outrageous conduct of their local officials at Fiume,
Sebenico, Spalato, Albania and Rhodes—to say nothing of Asia Minor—has put everyone against them.
They can rely only on sympathy, not upon their in-

herent force : and they have sacrificed that sympathy by incessant ill-temper, untruthfulness, and cheating.

I hear that Lloyd George and Clemenceau are allowing Venizelos to land a Greek division at Smyrna. This means at least that the Smyrna question is settled. A personal triumph for Venizelos.

Go to the Cirque Medrano with T. E. Lawrence. Cannot understand him. His foreground is so different from his background, and he hops from one to the other.

The Sixth Plenary Session meets to approve the terms of the German Treaty. Foch rises to protest against the military clauses. Willy de Grunne tells me that after it was over he was standing close to Foch when Clemenceau rolled up in a passion. ' And why, Monsieur le Maréchal, did you choose to make such a scene in public ? ' Foch drew himself up and twirled his moustaches. ' C'était pour faire aise,' he answered quietly, ' à ma conscience.'

May 7, Wednesday

A lovely day : great chestnut trees drinking gulps of sunlight.

There is a row about our not having invited the Hungarians to Paris at the same time as the Austrians. The French say that the Conseil des Trois had decided that such an invitation should be sent, and that the British cancelled this decision. It was rather my fault, as we had heard that Bela Kun had fallen. Anyhow, doesn't matter much.

In the evening get a message from Hankey to say that the Conseil des Cinq are going over the Austro-

Hungarian frontiers for a final revise. Kept late at night preparing memorandum and notes thereon for A. J. B. Peace Treaty presented to Germans at Trianon Palace Hotel.

May 8, Thursday

Another cloudless day. At about 11.0 Eric Drummond comes in and asks me to ' step outside.' In the passage he says : ' Look here, would you like to join me on the League ? ' I say that I should love to, provided that the F.O. have no objection and that I do not lose in salary, etc. This means that I do not go to Athens. It also means that I shall work with Drummond in organising the Secretariat of the League—a body which is certain to become of vital importance. I am delighted beyond words. I could not conceive of a cause, a job, a chief which I should prefer to these. In the evening have a further talk with Drummond. For the first months we are to be in London, laying the foundations of the Secretariat. In September and October we are to go to America to get possible candidates for posts and to sound opinion. We shall not establish ourselves in Geneva till the autumn.

During the afternoon there is the final revision of the frontiers of Austria. Go round to the Rue Nitot at luncheon and coach A. J. B. Down with him to the Quai d'Orsay. There (in that heavy tapestried room, under the simper of Marie de Medicis, with the windows open upon the garden and the sound of water sprinkling from a fountain and from a lawn-hose)—the fate of the Austro-Hungarian Empire is finally settled. Hungary is partitioned by these five distinguished gentlemen—indolently, irresponsibly partitioned—while the water sprinkles on the lilac outside—while the experts watch anxiously—while A. J. B., in the intervals of dialectics on secondary points, relapses into somnolence—while Lansing draws hobgoblins upon his writing pad—while Pichon crouching in his large chair blinks owlishly as decision after decision is actually recorded—while Sonnino, returned to Canossa, is ruggedly polite—while Makino, inscrutable and inarticulate, observes, observes, observes.

They begin with Transylvania, and after some insults flung like tennis balls between Tardieu and Lansing, Hungary loses her South. Then Czecho-Slovakia, and while the flies drone in and out of the open windows Hungary loses her North and East. Then the frontier with Austria, which is maintained intact. Then the Jugo-Slav frontier, where the Committee's report is adopted without change. Then tea and macaroons.

Bob Vansittart's play in the evening.

There is a great row going on because Brockdorff Rantzau failed to stand up at yesterday's ceremony when replying to Clemenceau. The ' Daily Mail ' calls his attitude ' impudent and unrepentant.' Hermann Norman, who was standing close to him, says that he was on the verge of a collapse and could not have stood up even if he had wanted to. I ask A. J. B. whether he shares the general horror and indignation. ' What indignation ?' he says. ' Oh, about Brockdorff Rantzau's conduct yesterday.' ' What conduct ? ' ' His not standing up when replying to Clemenceau.' ' Didn't he stand up ? I failed to notice. I make it a rule never to stare at people when they are in obvious distress.' A. J. B. makes the whole of Paris seem vulgar.

May 9, Friday

Spend morning writing a Note to A. J. B. on the Austrian frontiers, what he is to say and do. Down to the Conseil des Cinq again for the Austrian frontiers. They begin with the Czech frontier and within a few seconds adopt the Committee's report without discussion. They then pass on to the frontier with Jugo-Slavia and come up with a bump against Klagenfurt. On this area there is no Committee report as the Italians refused to allow any experts to deal with it. Sonnino (the scalp of his head flaming pink under its white stubble) tries to get them to decide there and then, hoping to rush through a decision which shall deprive Jugo-Slavia of the Assling triangle. Lansing with great virulence opposes this manoeuvre, stating that he cannot decide without expert advice and pressing hard for the appointment of a Committee of technicians. Tardieu, with his splendid sense of the opportune, says, ' Very well, Gentlemen. I see that most of the members of the Jugo-Slav Committee are assembled in this room. We shall withdraw to another room at once and provide you with an immediate opinion.' The scalp under Sonnino's hair becomes purple. He grunts disapproval. But he cannot obstruct any further. The Committee rise from their little gilt chairs and leave us. I remain behind, as Essad Pasha is on the agenda.

Meanwhile they discuss Relief—namely the feeding of the Baltic States. Hoover is summoned. He

makes a perfectly admirable statement. They come
to no decision and adjourn at 6.30.

May 10, Saturday

The Conseil des Cinq again upon the frontier between Austria and Jugo-Slavia. The committee had
sat all the morning and produced a 3-1 report, really
the work of Allen Leeper. The discussion is from the
start very tentative : it then begins to become sticky :
it then culminates in a row between Lansing and
Sonnino over whether the Slovenes should, or should
not, be regarded as ' enemies.' Lansing, there is no
doubt about it, is rude. Sonnino almost bursts with
suppressed fury. A. J. B. then rouses himself. He
launches off upon a really brilliant analysis of our
guiding principles. It is crushing in its logic. When
he *does* consent to intervene he is a whale among
minnows. Sonnino, his hands trembling so that the
little table in front of him shakes like an aspen, replies.
He adopts the *vox humana*. ' I am appalled,' he says,
' by the atmosphere of hostility which Italy encounters
in this room.' Cries of ' Oh, no, surely not,' from
A. J. B. The interpreter translates Sonnino into
French. ' Le Baron Sonnino constate qu'il est effrayé
par l'inimitié . . .' ' Mais non ! *Mais* non ! ' from
Pichon. Finally old Sonnino collapses and the
majority line is adopted amid general satisfaction.

A. J. B. languidly turns round to me. ' I had,' he
says, ' resigned myself to being unable ever to return
to Germany or Austria. It distresses me to feel that
henceforward Italy will also be barred against me.'

Dine with Joseph Potocki at the Ritz. A fine
anachronism. I tell him how deeply impressed I had

been by hearing Paderewsky make his speech at the
Supreme Council. He answers : ' Yes, a remarkable
man, a very remarkable man. Do you realise that he
was born in one of my own villages ? Actually at
Chepetowka ? And yet, when I speak to him, I have
absolutely the impression of conversing with an
equal.'

May 11, *Sunday*
Lunch with Jacques Blanche. René Boylesve there.
Rest the remainder of the day.

May 12, *Monday*
Conseil des Cinq. Or rather des Dix. For the Big
Three join in and emerge from their Olympian retire-
ment. The whole Austro-Hungarian settlement is
approved without contradiction.

May 13, *Tuesday*
Lloyd George is trying his hand at reaching a settle-
ment with the Italians on the Adriatic Treaty. They
have apparently threatened that they will return to
Rome, or will at least refuse to sign the Treaty unless
they are accorded satisfaction over the Fiume business.
As I expected, the idea of ' compensations ' in Asia
Minor is much to the fore.
Go round to the Rue Nitot with Louis Mallet. We
first go up to A. J. B.'s flat and then down to Lloyd
George's flat. Barnes, the Labour Minister attached
to our delegation, is there. He is interested in the
Adriatic for some odd reason. We then move into
the dining-room. I spread out my big map on the
dinner table and they all gather round. Ll. G., A.J.B.

Milner, Henry Wilson, Mallet and myself. Ll. G.
explains that Orlando and Sonnino are due in a few
minutes and he wants to know what he can offer them.
I suggest the Adalia Zone, with the rest of Asia Minor
to France. Milner, Mallet and Henry Wilson oppose
it : A. J. B. neutral.

We are still discussing when the flabby Orlando and
the sturdy Sonnino are shown into the dining-room.
They all sit round the map. The appearance of a pie
about to be distributed is thus enhanced. Ll. G. shows
them what he suggests. They ask for Scala Nova as
well. ' Oh no!' says Ll. G., ' you can't have that—it's
full of Greeks ! ' He goes on to point out that there
are further Greeks at Makri, and a whole wedge of
them along the coast towards Alexandretta. ' Oh, no,'
I whisper to him, ' there are not many Greeks there.'
' But yes,' he answers, ' don't you see it's coloured
green ? ' I then realise that he mistakes my map for
an ethnological map, and thinks the green means
Greeks instead of valleys, and the brown means Turks
instead of mountains. Ll. G. takes this correction
with great good humour. He is as quick as a kingfisher. Meanwhile Orlando and Sonnino chatter to
themselves in Italian. They ask for the coal-mines at
Eregli. Ll. G., who really knows something about his
subject by now, says, 'But it's rotten coal, and not much
of it in any case.' Sonnino translates this remark to
Orlando. ' Si, si,' replies the latter, ' ma, l'effetto
morale, sa ! '

Finally they appear ready to accept a mandate over
the Adalia region, but it is not quite clear whether in
return for this they will abandon Fiume and Rhodes.
We get out the League Covenant regarding Mandates

We observe (I think it was Milner who observed) that
this article provides for ' the consent and wishes of the
people concerned.' They find that phrase very amusing.
How they all laugh! Orlando's white cheeks wobble
with laughter and his puffy eyes fill with tears of mirth.

We agree to put it all down on paper. I leave with
Balfour. Instead of going upstairs to his own flat he
sends for his big black hat. ' I am coming with you,'
he says, ' to your office.' We drive to the Astoria.
A. J. B. is pensive and solemn. I feel that he is profoundly shocked. We got up to my bare office and I
send for Miss Stafford. She appears with her pad and
pencil prepared to take down. A. J. B. treats her as
though she were the Queen of Holland. He then
strides about my little room, looking lanky and
enormous, suddenly galvanised into a quite different
A. J. B., and dictates a memorandum which will undo
all that was provisionally decided in Ll. G.'s dining-
room. He suggests (a) Greek Zone. (b) An Independent Turkey embracing all Anatolia, but put under
International Control in the shape of foreign advisers
in all the key ministries. (c) A zone of commercial and
immigration interest for Italy in the region of Adalia.

Then lunch. Back at 4.0 to the Rue Nitot. Go
across with Ll. G. and A. J. B. to President Wilson's
house opposite. Ll. G. sends Balfour away, and I wait
in the ante-room reading ' The Portrait of Dorian
Grey' in a bound edition fully annotated by Francis
de Croisset. Young Esmond Harmsworth is there.
He is acting as Ll. G.'s A.D.C. He lounges huge
and handsome in a chair.

The door opens and Hankey tells me to come in. A
heavily furnished study with my huge map on the

carpet. Bending over it (bubble, bubble, toil and trouble) are Clemenceau, Ll. G. and P. W. They have pulled up armchairs and crouch low over the map. Ll. G. says—genial always—' Now, Nicolson, listen with all your ears.' He then proceeds to expound the agreement which they have reached. I make certain minor suggestions, plus a caveat that they are putting Konia in the Italian Zone. I also point out that they are cutting the Baghdad Railway. This is brushed aside. P. W. says, ' And what about the Islands ? ' ' They are,' I answer firmly, ' Greek Islands, Mr. President.' ' Then they should go to Greece ? ' H. N. ' Rather ! ' P. W. ' RATHER ! '

Anyhow I am told to go off and draft resolutions at once. Clemenceau says nothing during all this. He sits at the edge of his chair and leans his two blue-gloved hands down upon the map. More than ever does he look like a gorilla of yellow ivory.

I dash back to the Astoria and dictate resolutions. They work out as follows : (1) Turkey to be driven out of Europe and Armenia. (2) Greece to have the Smyrna-Aivali Zone and a mandate over most of the Vilayet of Aidin. (3) Italy to get a mandate over South Asia Minor from Marmarice to Mersina, plus Konia. (4) France to get the rest.

It is immoral and impracticable. But I obey my orders. The Greeks are getting *too* much.

I take this to Hankey, who approves and asks me to draft further resolutions providing for the United States accepting a mandate over Armenia and Constantinople.

This I do after dinner.

Nearly dead with fatigue and indignation.

May 14, *Wednesday*

Austrians arrive at St. Germain.

Get up early and redraft clauses providing for America accepting the mandate over Constantinople and Armenia. It is all terribly unreal. Send them to Hankey.

Dictate a note for A. J. B. about the Czech railways.

Lunch with Smuts. He is very pessimistic. His view is that the world-crisis is one between government (he pronounces it ' gurment ') and anarchy. The former, in his opinion, has shown itself incapable of constructive or directive thought. It has followed the stream of public opinion instead of canalising that stream into intelligent channels. He feels that all we have done here is worse, far worse, than the Congress of Vienna. The statesmen of 1815 at least knew what they were about. These don't.

To Conseil des Cinq about Czech Railways. Before they get to my subject the huissier brings me a telephone message. Would I go to President Wilson's house immediately ? Bag a car and dash up through sun-splashed streets to the Place des Etats-Unis. Hardly have I entered the anteroom when Ll. G. comes out from the inner sanctum and fetches me in. I find P. W. extended flat upon the hearth-rug and Clemenceau on all fours beside him. They are still gazing at my beastly map of Asia Minor. They ask me to make some alterations so as to leave Marmarice outside the Italian Zone—the President has already pencilled a line on the map to that effect. They have accepted both my draft resolutions.

Back to Astoria. Discuss matter with Eustace Percy. Urge him to put A. J. B. up to saving things before it is too late.   Ll. G. goes off to the Rhine armies.

(Letter to V. S. W.):

May 14, 1919.

' I scribbled you a note yesterday in President Wilson's anteroom while a man was watering the lawn outside with a hose, under the eyes of an American sentry.   Just as I had finished Ll. G. burst in in his impetuous way. " Come along, Nicolson, and keep your ears wide open."

So I went in.   There were Wilson and Ll. G. and Clemenceau with their armchairs drawn close over my map on the hearth-rug.   I was there about half an hour— talking and objecting.—The President was extremely nice, and so was Ll. G.   Clemenceau was cantankerous. The, " mais voyons, jeune homme " style.

It is appalling that these ignorant and irresponsible men should be cutting Asia Minor to bits as if they were dividing a cake.   And with no one there except me, who incidentally have nothing whatsoever to do with Asia Minor.   Isn't it terrible, the happiness of millions being decided in that way, while for the last two months we were praying and begging the Council to give us time to work out a scheme ?

Their decisions are immoral and impracticable.   ' Mais voyez-vous, jeune homme, que voulez-vous qu'on fasse ? Il faut aboutir ! ' '

The funny thing is that the only part where I *do* come in is the Greek part, and here they have gone beyond, and dangerously beyond, what I suggested in my wildest moments.

Lloyd George asked me to draft resolutions at once, and here I did a clever thing.   I watered everything down. I tried to introduce at least the elements of sanity into their decisions.   I haven't heard yet whether Ll. G. has accepted my draft.

It is all very awkward as it puts me in a difficult position as regards Louis Mallet, Crowe, Hardinge and A. J. B.,

whom I short circuited. (How Oliphant would have *died*
at the procedure thereof ! !)

I really hate being placed in such impossible positions,
but what is one to do ? I knew that if I refused I should
have been disregarded and that it was better to try and
save them from themselves. There will be a terrible row
when it all comes out.'

May 15, Thursday

A Czech committee in morning to hear Benes upon
Ruthenian autonomy. Not very helpful. A further
talk with Eustace on return when I have read the full
minutes of the Council of Three. They are taking
each ' zone of compensation ' separately, and it looks
as if they would end by giving the Italians all they
want in each. Then Colonel House, who is working
separately upon a Fiume compromise, will give them
all they want in the Adriatic. The result will be that
they will be paid a huge sum in Turkish territory in
order to induce them to abate their Adriatic claims, and
then House will give way to them as regards Fiume.
Thus Italian diplomacy will be justified in the end.

Go round to A. J. B. after luncheon. And talk to
him for a whole hour in this sense. I attack the moral
aspect of partitioning Asia Minor. He is tiresome
about it. ' All that,' he says, ' is quite true. But, my
dear young man, you forget that we are now at the
Paris Conference. All you say is pure aesthetics.'
What is wrong with these experienced statesmen is
that they are so used to justifying expediency on moral
grounds that they are not convinced by immorality
even when it is inexpedient.

Anyhow he promises to do something, and meanwhile Ll. G. has gone to visit the battlefields.

Dine with Mrs. Leeds. A. J. B. and House there. I hope they compare notes. It is pretty hopeless as a mess. My own position is awkward. I never know how much A. J. B. knows of what is going on in the Council of Three. I feel as if I were sneaking to him about what happens there. Yet, officially speaking, I am bound in duty to tell A. J. B. everything. After all he is my only chief. I asked A. J. B. what I ought to do in such a predicament. He is interested in ethical problems. He said, ' Well, I promise to tell the little man that you told me.' He is kind about it, but aloof and amused. I feel that I may be exaggerating my predicament and taking a personal view when I am really only a young man with a map and a faculty for drafting clearly.

May 16, *Friday*
Go round to A. J. B. in the morning. Make a final appeal to him about Asia Minor. I try to be less ' aesthetic ' than yesterday and concentrate on the practical side only. I point out that international control exercised through expert advisers to the Turkish ministries would not mean ' condominium.' Sultan would be *really* independent. Italy could under this scheme get a sort of Nogara agreement in the south. And Turkey's integrity would be maintained.

Hardinge and Crowe are there and he reads them the minutes of Wednesday's meeting of the Council of Three. He is very critical. ' These three ignorant men,' he exclaims, ' with a child to lead them.' The child, I suppose, is me. Anyhow it is an anxious child. And one who does not want to have anything to do with leadership in this matter.

A. J. B. agrees in the end to write a further memorandum. I cannot make him out. Hardinge assures
me that he is as distressed as we all are. But that he
cannot help taking the opposite point of view to people
who seem excited. I suppose I *did* seem excited.

Meanwhile Smodlaka has come round to see Allen
Leeper and tells him that the Jugo-Slav Delegation,
after an all-night sitting, have decided to ask President
Wilson to mediate between them and the Italians. If
the Italians accept (which I doubt) this will simplify
the situation enormously and get us away from this
ghastly system of compensations.

The Cabinet at home are showing signs of life.
They have heard of the proposed partition of Turkey.
Montague, Sinha, Bikanir and even Curzon are
threatening to resign. Poor Ll. G.! It is so easy for
us irresponsible people to criticize him; but he is
trying to tie up a kicking hen in tissue paper. The
marvel is that he has succeeded as well as he has.

In the afternoon the Conseil des Cinq discuss the
Bulgarian frontiers. I do not go, as A. J. B. has seen
more than enough of me these days. They do not
decide either the frontier with Rumania or that with
Greece, but they do decide the Serbo-Bulgarian
frontier, giving the Serbs better defensive positions for
the Vardar Railway, and in the Strumnitza enclave. A
good decision.

The Greeks land at Smyrna. Great jubilation at the
Hotel Mercedes.

May 17, *Saturday*

Ll. G. returns.

Czech Committee in morning to discuss Benes'

scheme for the autonomy of the Ruthenes. We accept
it. I am asked to write the report for the Conseil des
Cinq. Rather a bore.

Come back and write it at once.

In the afternoon a visit from Chryssanthos—Bishop
of Trebizond, whom Venizelos had sent to see me
about the Pontic Greeks. I try to comfort him but
without success. A splendid if turbulent priest, wear-
ing upon his vast chest a reliquary set in amethysts and
topaz.

Dine with Boni de Castellane at 71 Rue de Lille.
A. J. B., Venizelos, Paul Claudel, Berthelot, Jacques
Blanche, Anna de Noailles. She looks like a hawk
from some hieroglyph in a Temple at Luxor. Eve
Francis declaims Claudel's poetry afterwards. He sits
there in front of her, a sturdy man, managing to convey
that his applause is directed at her masterly recitation
and implies no praise of the poetry which she recites.

Drive back with Venizelos. He is pleased by the
Smyrna landing. He says ' Greece can only find her
real future from the moment when she is astride the
Aegean.' He is looking ill and tired, but happy.

Hear that A. J. B. has written a memorandum to
Ll. G. and the Council of Three on the lines of what I
said. So he was influenced by my ' aesthetics ' after all.

Ll. G. returns from the front and succeeds as always
in calming everybody down.

(Letter to V. S. W.) :

Saturday, May 17, 1919.
' There is a thunderstorm brewing here against Lloyd
George. It is all about this Asia Minor business. I feel
it difficult for me to guide my tiny row-boat in and out of
these crashing Dreadnoughts.

Even A. J. B. is angry. " Those three all-powerful, all-ignorant men sitting there and carving continents, with only a child to lead them." I have a most uneasy suspicion that the " child " in this case signified myself. Perhaps he meant Hankey. I hope he meant Hankey. After all, Hankey is younger by 35 years than A. J. B., which in my case would make him minus three. Yes, my dear, let us assume that it was Hankey.

Then the P.M. had sent for the Indian Delegation, and they, as is the way with Rajahs, chartered a special train. Only to find that the question had been decided by the three men plus the child, and that Ll. G. had gone off on a motor tour. So there are threats of resignation— Curzon, Montagu, Bikanir—even A. J. B. But keep this dark.

I had better lie low for a bit. I have, I think got my point. But I do not like playing with other people's gun-powder. Yet I love my own.'

May 18, *Sunday*

Spend the morning at the Quai d'Orsay correcting the proofs and translation of my report on Ruthenian autonomy.

Talk with Jim Butler about the League. He says we must create a ' league Patriotism ' which shall over-ride national patriotism. Of course we must. But what enthusiasm, what tact, will be required for such a task. I believe now that hard, diamond in-telligence is better for the world than all the idealism possible. Americanism, when faced with reality, has not been a success. The League Secretariat must concentrate above all on efficiency. Their ' League Patriotism ' will have to be based upon granite founda-tions of good sense. There must be no hysteria, no aesthetics.

(Letter to V. S. W.) :

May 18, 1919.

' I think the mad Asiatic scheme of the Council of
Three has been scotched. I am glad.

I am terribly busy—have been so ever since you left—
and to-day isn't Sunday at all. I am, in fact, in danger of
having to spend the whole day at the Quai d'Orsay.

Dinner with Boni de Castellane last night. . . . Afterwards there was a *diseuse* who recited Claudel's poems.
He was himself there. The poems were good, really good.
But he wore a rather cynical smile while it was going on—
at least *he* knew how the nib had broken when he got to
that line, and how the passage immediately following had
been cribbed from the ' Journal de Lausanne.' No poet
is a hero to himself.'

May 19, *Monday*

Most of the Cabinet have come over from London
to discuss the future of Turkey. I am summoned to
the Rue Nitot, but not asked to attend the meeting. I
sit outside, but as there is only a glass partition between me and the Cabinet I hear what they say.
Curzon presses for ejection of Turk from Europe, and
accepts Greek zone at Smyrna although with deep
regret. Montagu and Milner are all against disturbing
the Turk still further. Winston wants to leave him as
he is, but to give America the mandate over Constantinople and the Straits, with a zone extending as far
as Trebizond. A. J. B. wants Constantinople under
an American mandate, Smyrna to Greece and the rest
of Turkey as an independent kingdom, supervised by
foreign ' advisers.' Ll. G. is non-committal. No
decision come to in so far as, through the glass darkly,
I can ascertain.

In the evening draft telegrams with Hankey ordering the Greeks not to go outside Sandjak of Smyrna and Caza of Aivali.

(Letter to V. S. W.):

May 19, Monday.

'Look here, when you have *nothing* to do, will you please think sometimes about the League? You see, you have got to get a " League temperament." Ready to help me when I become too national and anti-dago. If the League is to be of any value it must start from a new conception, and involve among its promoters and leaders a new habit of thought. Otherwise it will be no more than the continuation of the Conference—where each delegation subscribes its *own* point of view and where unanimity can be secured only by a mutual surrender of the complete scheme. We, WE must lose all that, and think only of the League point of view, where Right is the ultimate sanction, and where compromise is a crime. So we must become anti-English when necessary, and, when necessary, pro-Italian. Thus when you find me becoming impatient of the Latins you must snub me. It is rather a wrench for me—as I like the sturdy, unenlightened, unintellectual, muzzy British way of looking at things. I fear the " Geneva temperament" will be rather Hampstead Garden Suburb—but the thing may be *immense.* We must work for it.

Seriously, you can do as much as I by gentle proselytising. Think that you are a Salvation Army worker, and when you hear the League abused and scoffed at, put on a gentle patient smile and say, " BUT WHY ? " They will have no *real* reason to condemn it, and you can then confound them by . . . " Obviously it will fail if ignorant people attack it before its birth without giving it a moment's thought."

My feeling about the League is that it is a great experiment, and I want you to feel rather protective about it.'

IX.   *May* 20 – *June* 28

THE TREATY OF VERSAILLES

May 20, *Tuesday*

TATA BERTIE turns up from Germany, where he has been working on the Armistice Commission. He has seen a great deal of Erzberger and Noske. He says they have put down the Spartacists by the employment of the most perfected weapons of modern warfare. He thinks the German Government will consent to sign but make a mental reservation as to execution. Later in the day we get a telegram from General Malcolm in Berlin to the effect that they want to sign, but that public opinion will not allow them to go without appreciable concessions on the part of the allies. Hardinge thinks they will refuse to sign. Berthelot thinks they will sign. Finally Kramarsh, whom I saw just as I was off to bed, says that they are certain to sign. This all shows how little we, or they, know at this stage.

Czech committee in morning. My report adopted with thanks.

May 21, *Wednesday*

We are all feeling stale and unprofitable. I simply long for the moment when I can get away from this disheartening turmoil and start serious work on the League of Nations.

An idle day. Write a reasoned minute for Philip

Kerr upon the Bourchier-Buxton appeals for Bulgaria. Help Eustace in preparing a memorandum for A. J. B. on this unceasing Asia Minor question. The balance appears now to be inclining towards leaving the Turk in Constantinople. I feel sure that this is a mistake except from the Russian point of view. Our India Office people are over-nervous about the Khalifat. I do not believe our Indian Moslems care a hoot for the Khalifat as such. What they like is to be able to exercise pressure upon the British Government on behalf of the soldier of Islam.

Dine with Venizelos, Philip Kerr, Maynard Keynes, Politis, Gerald Talbot.

Venizelos is much disturbed at news which has reached him of the lack of discipline among the Greek division landed at Smyrna. They seem to have behaved pretty badly, and there are rumours of civilians having been killed and much arson and looting. It may be exaggerated. Venizelos hopes that the Cretan Moslems who are established at Smyrna may be able to reassure their coreligionists that the Greeks are not such devils after all. But I can see that he is anxious and depressed.

He tells me that on Monday he was summoned to the Council of IV. Sonnino was the last to arrive, and on entering the room said pointedly, ' But I thought we were to be alone.' Venizelos at once offered to withdraw. P. W. begged him to stay. Finally Venizelos insisted on retiring. After a few moments the President himself came out to urge him to return, and abused Sonnino for his lack of manners.

May 22, Thursday

The Germans ought to have let us know to-day whether they were or were not prepared to sign. They asked for and were granted a delay of one week more.

Eric Drummond wants me to join him on June 18. No chance of that at all. The Greek Committee will have to resume its sittings, and there is no hope of my being released.

May 23, Friday

Conseil des Cinq. Bukowina, Banat, Ruthenia. They pass the Banat line and the Bukowina, but Lansing is sticky about the Dobrudja. He advances the view that the United States, not having been at war with Bulgaria, must more or less represent Bulgarian interests at the Conference. Yet why did not Germany have similar neutral representation? A strange doctrine and one to which the Yanks have hitherto paid scant attention.

They discuss my Ruthenian report and pass it. Thank God for that. Something done anyhow. Altogether I am feeling over-worked, peace-weary, and unhappy about things.

May 24, Saturday

Round to see Venizelos in the morning about British rights in the Smyrna-Aidin Railway. He promises that the Turkish concession will not only be recognised by the Greek Government, but extended. He promises to see Lord Rathmore and Colonel Corbett.

He asks me to let Ll. G. know that he has had a

letter from P. W. agreeing to Greece having a mandate over the whole Vilayet of Aidin plus sovereignty over Sandjak of Smyrna and Caza of Aivali.

Feeling run down. Leave with Allen Leeper for a week-end at Fontainebleau.

(Letter to my father):

Saturday, May 24.

' I hope to be able to go to Fontainebleau to-morrow, so I will write to-day. I am feeling very overworked and dispirited at this hum-bug electioneering sort of peace— and I feel a longing to get away from it all and to be at my new work. Eric Drummond wants me to come by the 18th of June, but I see no chance of it. It is *such* a bore waiting on—without instructions. If I could be given a free hand I could easily settle all my stuff in a week.

I wonder what the Press will say if the Germans refuse to sign ? They won't have the honesty to own that it is a Press peace—and a reproach to England.

Anyhow !

May 25, *Sunday*

At Fontainebleau. Lie under trees. Leave in evening. Absorb air and thrust the Conference from me.

May 26, *Monday*

Talk to Allen Leeper about his Albanian scheme, *i.e.* constitution of Northern Albania, with Ipek and Djakova, into an autonomous zone under the Jugo-Slavs. I hate the idea at first but eventually come round to it.

A comparatively idle day. It is odd that the accumulated exhaustion of these four months comes out the first moment one is at a loose end. Besides I chafe to be rid of all this hopeless work and to be concentrating on my new job—which means real construction, not unreal destruction.   The Austrians at St. Germain are getting impatient.   I don't wonder.

May 27, Tuesday

Write a note to Philip Kerr on the general Middle East situation.   Suggest that negotiations with Italy, especially piece-meal negotiations, can only lead to an unsatisfactory settlement : that the friendship of France and the pacification of the East are more in our direct interest than the gratification of Italian vanity : that we should therefore take our stand plump upon the Treaty of London and adopt the pound of flesh policy : that we should leave it to P. W. to get us out of that impasse and join with him in imposing a settlement on Italy based on the Fourteen Points.   (Dear me!   We had forgotten about them!)   This, once imposed, could leave our hands free to give France Anatolia, Greece a big zone at Smyrna, and get for ourselves a really stable solution in Mespot and Persia, while reserving for Russia a mandate for the Caucasus.

Lunch with Day and discuss with him the scheme for the partition of Albania.   He is not enthusiastic in the least.

May 28, Wednesday

Write memorandum about Albania: (1) Union of N. Albanians into an autonomous State under Jugo-Slavia; (2) Central Albania for Italy; (3) Southern Albania for Greece.   (4) Koritsa to be neutralised as a centre of Albanian culture.   This seems the only way of working for eventual Albanian unity.   Naturally it looks like partition, yet it is the only way of saving Ipek and Djakova.

Lunch with Maynard Keynes. Discuss Reparation chapter of the Austrian Treaty. We are fully agreed on the absurdity of applying to Austria the German reparation and indemnity clauses. I hope that the financial sections will be cut out of the Treaty which is to be given to the Austrians to-morrow at St. Germain.

Keynes is very pessimistic about the German Treaty. He considers it not only immoral but incompetent. The Germans can gain nothing by signing and lose nothing more by refusing to sign.

(Letter to V. S. W.) :

BRITISH DELEGATION,
PARIS.
Wednesday, May 28, 1919.

' I have been working like a little beaver to prevent the Austrian treaty from being as rotten as the German. The more I read the latter, the sicker it makes me. The great crime is in the reparation clauses, which were drawn up solely to please the House of Commons, and which are quite impossible to execute. If I were the Germans I shouldn't sign for a moment. You see it gives them *no* hope whatsoever, either now or in the future. I want the Austrians to be given *some* vision of sunlight at the end of the tunnel. The fault is that there is an old man called Lord Sumner and an old man called Lord Cunliffe —and they have worked away without consulting anyone —with the result that the Treaty is only worth the ' Daily Mail ' which it will be printed in. How sad it makes me : you see if the Germans refuse—what *can* we do ? Occupy Germany ? But there is nothing they would like better ! Continue the Blockade ? But they will starve anyhow if they accept our terms. It is sheer lunacy—and the worst thing is that the Hun would have accepted anything within reason. Only this is *not* within reason.

Keynes has been too splendid about the Austrian Treaty. He is going to fight. He says he will resign.

May 29, Thursday
Round to President Wilson's house. We find all the experts there. Tardieu, Laroche, Seymour, Day, Dulles, Johnson, Martino and Vannutelli. We all assemble in the upstairs drawing-room while the IV meet below. After about half an hour they enter the room. Clemenceau and Ll. G. sit side by side on a sofa. P. W. takes a map, spreads it on the carpet in an alcove-room, and kneels down. We all squat in a circle round him. It is like hunt the slipper. He explains what has been decided downstairs about the Jugo-Slav frontier. He does this with perfect lucidity : Princeton returns to him. Towards the end Orlando and Vannutelli, upon their knees, make a pathetic attempt to rescue the Rosenbach tunnel. They say it will be ' inconvenient ' to leave one end in one country and the other end in another country. The President, still kneeling on the floor, throws back his great face and looks upwards to heaven and the paintings upon Madame Bischoffheim's ceiling. ' Why,' he exclaims, ' I have not come to Purris to discuss convenience : in my judgment the test is what the people themselves waant.'

There is no question of his sincerity. Yet he must know somewhere inside himself that our minds long ago have slid away from all such altitudes.

After these heartening words the experts are sent away to draw up articles to be inserted in the Austrian

Treaty in time for its presentation to-morrow. They all go down to the Quai d'Orsay. Crowe and I leave Allen Leeper to do the job, since it is really his concern. He comes back at luncheon in despair. The Italians once again have wriggled out. Nobody in the expert Committee is agreed what President Wilson *did* say. The Italians contend that he said that the Assling triangle must be reserved for a plebiscite. While he is telling us this a message comes from Johnson asking him to come with him to the President. They prepare a list of written questions which the President, who is quite genial, answers categorically. Triumphantly they then drive to the Quai d'Orsay where the Committee is still sitting. The Italians shuffle like fish upon the grass. But in the end the thing is launched off to the Drafting Committee in correct form.

I spend the afternoon translating a portion of the German counter proposals.

May 30, Friday

The Jugo-Slavs lunch with us en bande. I sit between Popovic and Smodlaka. The former is chauvinistic, the latter reasonable. I test them with my Albanian scheme. Popovic screams and yells at the thought of losing Djakova. Smodlaka considers it a good idea.

Philip Kerr comes round and we draft a telegram to Belgrade to tell the Serbs they must stop fighting in Carinthia.

A dinner in the evening to discuss the formation of an Anglo-American Institute of Foreign Affairs, with an annual register or year-book. Lionel Curtis, who conceived the scheme, explains his purposes in a really

admirable speech. A discussion follows. General
Bliss, Bob Cecil, Crowe, Eustace Percy, Coolidge,
Headlam Morley, Latham are there. Crowe makes a
speech criticising the scheme. Bob Cecil supports it.
He said one true thing. He said, ' There is no single
person in this room who is not disappointed with the
terms we have drafted. Yet England and America
have got all that they want, and more : far more. Our
disappointment is an excellent symptom : let us perpetuate it.' In the end we decide to appoint a committee of six to draw up a plan and report. The
general idea is to create a centre of authoritative
opinion, in touch with the League of Nations and the
permanent officials, whose authority shall be such as
that of the General Medical Council. I am deeply in
favour of it.

May 31, Saturday

In the morning down to the Crillon to talk to Day
about Albania. I have received full authority from
A. J. B. to come to some agreement with the Americans
and the French. Day is inclined to keep the existing
frontier in the North and East. He argues that whatever frontier one draws, *some* Albanians will have to
remain outside, and that the little one gains by extending the Northern zone is lost by the unpalatable
element of partition. As regards the Scutari Railway
he feels that we should differentiate between senti-
mental conceptions and economic necessities. The
French on the other hand want Scutari to go to the
Slavs. Day will think it all over.

Lunch with the Forbes-Adams. Weizmann there.
He is exactly like Lenin.

In the afternoon accompany Crowe and Allen Leeper
to a plenary session (a ' secret plenary ') at the Quai
d'Orsay. It is held in order to give the Smaller Powers
an ' opportunity ' of discussing the Peace Terms to be
handed to the Austrians on Monday. I went as a
tourist and out of vulgar curiosity. This was lucky,
as I was wanted.

Bratianu, dandified and querulous, raised objections
to the Minorities clauses and contended that the Great
Powers should not be accorded the right of interference in the internal affairs of Rumania. Clemenceau
who has been fingering an ivory paper cutter in his
lavender gloves, flings it down petulantly. ' Voyons ! '
he shouts. ' Est-ce ici une conférence ou non ?
Admettez-vous l'autorité ici, ou non ? Il y a des
puissances dont l'histoire nous impose des garanties ! '
This reference to the Rumanian treatment of the Jews
causes Bratianu to flush to the roots of his hair. For a
moment I expect him to burst into flames. He recovers himself, pouts, shrugs his shoulders, resumes
his seat. On sitting down he continues to shrug his
shoulders like a vain and self-conscious schoolboy.
Clemenceau turns behind him to Dutasta, upon whose
wretched head he discharges the surplus of his ill-
temper. Paderewsky gets up. He gets to look more
and more like Swinburne every day : that columnar
neck. His speech is tactful and sonorous. He implies
that Poland, while accepting the Minority clauses,
would prefer to have the League of Nations as her
guardian rather than the Great Powers. Kramarsh,
when his turn comes, is clearly alarmed lest he provoke
another tigerish outburst. He makes a somewhat oily
speech asking for certain rectifications. Trumbic

makes a sullen elocution upon the Treaty, but as he
has got the wrong text his remarks are quickly disposed of. Meanwhile Clemenceau's wrath has continued to simmer, expressing itself in growls and
snarls at Dutasta. Then President Wilson rises. He
appeals to the smaller Powers to accept the authority
of their elder brothers who won the war. It is admirably done, admirably conceived. Calm is restored to
the troubled waters. Scarcely has Wilson finished
when Clemenceau snarls, ' Quelques autres observa-
tions ? ' (Does any idiot *dare* to make a further remark ?) ' La séance est levée—la prochaine séance
aura lieu lundi à St.-Germain-en-Laye.'

We adjourn to the next room and have a drumhead
meeting of the Czech committee to discuss Kramarsh's
objections. We rule out two of them but accept a
rectification at Gmünd. Cambon trots off humming
to himself in order to inform the Council of IV. I
walk back alone.

June 1, Sunday

A foul day, owing chiefly to my having to spend the
whole morning and afternoon translating German
Notes which descend upon us like leaves in Vallom-
brosa. Philip Kerr comes in while I am changing for
dinner. He says that the Serbs have refused to be
present at St. Germain to-morrow in view of the terms
of the articles dealing with the plebiscite in Klagenfurt.
Allen and I bolt some dinner and then go off to see
Zolger at the Beau Site. Clearly the Jugo-Slavs funk
a plebiscite in this area, since they know it will go
against them. They argue that it is unfair to impose a
plebiscite upon them in areas where they do not want

it, and to refuse a plebiscite in other areas where they desire it passionately (*e.g.* Gorizia and Gradisca).

As a matter of fact the Drafting Committee had received no instructions as to the form the plebiscite was to take and stuck in the Polish form, in which the whole area is taken as a single block and decides by an absolute majority of votes. Were this system applied to Klagenfurt the Austrians would have a clear majority : if, however, the voting takes place by communes the Jugo-Slavs would get at least the southern portion.

We gather none the less that the Jugo-Slavs will go to St. Germain to-morrow. It would be better to defer the thing for future discussion, only this would mean getting the consent of the Three. As we do not leave Zolger till 1.30 a.m. this is not an easy task.

June 2, Monday

Rush round early to the Rue Nitot and get Ll. G. to accept the Klagenfurt voting being by communes, or at least not as a unity. Then on to P. W. who is out. Wait till 11.15, by which time they all leave for St. Germain. Get hold of Hurst and tell him exactly what to do. If he can't get Wilson's agreement in time, then the Klagenfurt part of the Treaty must be torn out before it is given to the Austrians. Hurst leaves for St. Germain and catches P. W. on the stairs. The latter is in a bad temper as he has had a puncture and is late. He refuses to change anything. Luckily Clemenceau sees the point and tears the Klagenfurt part out of the Treaty before handing it to Dr. Renner.

So far so good, and we have kept faith with Zolger.

He also kept faith with us and attended with all his delegation. But it was a tight squeeze.

Round to A. J. B. in the evening. Appeal to him to do something about Konopisht, which the Czechs are trying to filch from the children of the Archduke Franz Ferdinand. A. J. B., who is never red-tapey about those sort of things, promises to ask our Minister or whatever he is at Prague to make private and unofficial representations.

June 3, Tuesday

A foul day. Translate German Notes all the time. Not very pleasant or cheering sort of stuff.

June 4, Wednesday

Allen Leeper rushed all day about the Klagenfurt plebiscite. In the end they compromise. The district will be divided into two zones, one to be treated as a whole and the next by communes. If the first votes Austrian then there is to be no plebiscite in the second, and the whole basin will remain to Austria. A good decision.

Go and see Venizelos in the morning for a general talk. Nothing much new.

P . . . . . . comes. He repeats his old stories about Montenegro being delighted to join with Serbia. They are based on anything but the truth and lead to nothing of value.

Lunch with Laroche, who is in favour of my Albanian scheme. I wish I were. Work all afternoon.

June 5, Thursday

A feckless day—odds and ends of work with nothing that really helps. I yearn to get away and start with the

League of Nations, but I simply cannot. My work will only begin again when the German Treaty is out of the way.

Lloyd George is trying his best to alleviate the terms imposed upon Germany. The French are furious with him, nor does Wilson appear to give him any support. Cannot understand Wilson. Here is a chance of improving the thing and he won't take it. Ll. G. however is fighting like a little terrier all by himself. He wants modifications (1) in eastern frontier. (2) Reparation. (3) Army of occupation. (4) Admission to the League of Nations. The Empire Delegation have authorised him to exert the strongest pressure in order to induce the French to agree.

June 6, Friday

An empty day. The lull before more storms. The ' Times ' attacks Ll. G. for ' weakening ' in face of the German counter offensive.

June 7, Saturday

Valentine Williams of the ' Daily Mail ' comes to see me. I am feeling worn out and irritable. I let loose to him about the iniquity of Northcliffe jingoism. He takes it well. He says nothing, but looks wise. It was unfair to put him in such a position.

They have decided to get rid of Bela Kun, so we shall have the Hungarians here soon. Then the Bulgars. I may not be expected to stay on for the Turks. I might join Eric Drummond by the middle of July.

Czech committee in afternoon to draw up reply to German counter proposals. It doesn't take long.

June 8, *Sunday*

(Letter to my father) :

' I have every hope that Lloyd George, who is fighting like a Welsh terrier, will succeed in the face of everybody in introducing some modification in the terms imposed upon Germany. Now that we see them as a whole we realise that they are much too stiff. They are not stern merely but actually *punitive*, and they abound with what Smuts calls " pin pricks " as well as dagger thrusts. Lloyd George is concentrating upon Silesia, the cost of the Armies of Occupation, and the admission of Germany into the League of Nations. Yet the real crime is the reparation and indemnity chapter, which is immoral and senseless. There is not a single person among the younger people here who is not unhappy and disappointed at the terms. The only people who approve are the old fire-eaters. I have tried, with the help of the Treasury man, who is first class, to water down the Austrian financial clauses, but was told by Sumner to mind my own business. Anyhow I think we shall, provided Ll. G. wins his battle, get the Germans to sign. God help us if we can't ! They will have us at their mercy.'

June 9, *Monday*

Lunch with Colonel Repington at the Ritz. He tells me that General Mangin practically admitted to him that the Rhineland Republic was a creation of his own. But how silly ! The French press are fulminating against Ll. G. for his efforts to moderate the Treaty.

Very little work to do during this interval between the treaties, and this makes me feel tired and restless.

June 10, *Tuesday*

Conseil des Dix again about Bela Kun. Lloyd George is opposed to letting the Rumanians advance,

since he says they behave badly wherever they go.
And how right he is.

June 11, *Wednesday*

Conseil des V in the morning. A. J. B. sulky at
being dragged out of bed. Object of the meeting was
to break to Bratianu and Kramarsh the nature of the
frontiers which had been decided against Hungary.
If they agree, we are going to telegraph to Bela Kun
ordering him, on pain of dismissal, to retire behind the
frontiers thus established. Bratianu as usual sulks and
ogles all in one. Lucky for him that only that old owl
Pichon was in the chair. Kramarsh accepts in principle but asks for a bridgehead at Pressburg and a
rectification on the Eipel. This is all passed on to the
Council of IV, who won't be able to make much of it.

June 12, *Thursday*

Conseil des V in morning. As we expected the IV
have sent back yesterday's report, which has clearly
irritated them. They ask, ' Why was not the Rumanian
frontier previously communicated to M. Bratianu ? '
Yet it was they themselves who expressly forbade the
Smaller Powers to have any cognisance of our decision.
They also ask what Kramarsh really wants, and can we
satisfy him as time presses. We refuse about Pressburg,
and as regards Eipel give him little snippet to keep him
quiet. Meanwhile I have no idea what the IV propose
doing with Kun Bela. I fear they will give way to him,
and I agree that one cannot suppress Bolshevism by
force of arms. The French mutiny in the Black Sea is
evidence enough of this. The whole Bolshevik business is spreading—there are strikes from Winnipeg to

Palermo.   There are rumours that the Italians are negotiating some sort of Treaty with Moscow.

After dinner there is a meeting of the newly formed Institute of International Affairs.   They elect a Council and pass most of the items on the agenda.   It certainly looks as if the thing would materalize and prosper.   I certainly hope so.

All this fortnight I have been exhausted, hopeless and unhappy.   It is chiefly, I suppose, effects of early over-work.   Yet I see nothing but blackness in the future.

June 13, Friday

Attend a new Committee called the ' New States Committee.'   It deals with the juridic constitution of the New States and the question of commercial treaties, public debts, etc.   It also deals with the question of minorities.   Headlam Morley is our repre-sentative.   I argue against imposing upon Greece too stringent minority clauses.

My friend Bela Kun ordered to withdraw behind the new frontiers of Hungary.

June 14, Saturday

A violent attack upon Hankey in the ' Echo de Paris,' which concludes, ' débarassons-nous de ce scribe peu patenté.'   Now this is nonsense.   Hankey is perfect, and the French know it.   The reply to the German counter proposals has been despatched.   Philip Kerr wrote most of the covering remarks.

June 15, Sunday

Spend the day at Versailles at the Villa Romaine. The streets are barred with spile fencing in which the

wretched Germans are caged like criminals. The
French justification is that they ' must avoid incidents.'

June 16, Monday

The reply to the German counter proposals is
handed to them at 6.0 p.m. It had kept the Drafting
Committee at work from 9.0 a.m. on Sunday till 6.30
a.m. this morning.

June 17, Tuesday

The Council of X allow a Turkish delegation to
appear before them. It is outrageous that the Turks
should be allowed to state their case and the Germans
kept behind cages at Versailles.

Desultory work all day. It is maddening having
nothing to do, with so much to be done. I am burning
to get to London and start with the League.

June 18, Wednesday

Still uncertain whether the Germans will sign or not.
It seems certain that Brockdorff Rantzau himself will
not consent to sign. The general view is that there
will be a change of Plenipotentiaries with a change of
Government at Berlin—and that then they will sign.
The less optimistic think they will refuse and that then
we shall advance from the Rhine and they will sign
under pressure. The definite pessimists think they
will do a Karolyi, hand over power to the Bolsheviks,
join up with the Russians and Magyars, and present
us with a Red Mittel Europa. If they do, it will be our
fault for not crushing Bolshevism in Hungary when
it would still have been easy to do so. Also for
insisting on the absurd Reparation clauses. Lords

Sumner and Cunliffe, tweedledum and tweedledee, must be feeling especially uneasy.

June 19, *Thursday*

General pessimism as to the Germans signing. Také Jonescu gives a farewell dinner at the Ritz. The same old gang. Hate dinner parties.

June 20, *Friday*

Round to see Venizelos at the Mercedes. I take with me a Treaty alleged to have been concluded between the Serbs and the Greeks which was communicated in the strictest secrecy by the Italian Foreign Office to our Embassy in Rome. It is chiefly economic in character, but contains a clause stating that both Powers will cooperate to prevent any hegemony in the Adriatic. Venizelos laughs heartily. The thing is a forgery.

News reaches us (1) that the Orlando Cabinet has fallen, (2) that Erzberger and Noske have got rid of Scheidemann and are determined to sign. What a relief!

I long to get away from this place where improvisations flit above the mists of ignorance like dragon-flies above a marsh.

June 21, *Saturday*—June 23, *Monday*

Go to Geneva to look for a house.

June 24, *Tuesday*

Arrive Gare de Lyon early. Find that people are relieved at Weimar Assembly having authorised signature, but rather shamed by the sinking of the German

fleet. It makes us look foolish and worse. After all
we had rather pressed that the fleet should be sunk in
any case. They will now think we did it ourselves.
The Naval people say it was the fault of the politicians
for insisting that the ships should be interned only and
not surrendered. The French think we have betrayed
a trust. In fact we look fools and knaves.

Dine with Smuts. He has at last consented to sign
the Treaty, but under protest and against his conscience.
A splendid, wide-horizoned man—for whom I have
the deepest admiration.

June 25, *Wednesday*

Lunch with the Bibescos. Go and see Orpen's
pictures. Very competent and striking, but not great
works of art. See Edwin Montagu about Turkey.
The Turks have sent in an idiotic Note claiming not
only Eastern Thrace but also Western. I doubt
whether we shall ever sign a peace with Turkey. It
will just drag on.

June 26, *Thursday*

Lunch with Alan Parsons and Clement Jones.
Latter is fussing from table to table collecting every-
body's private seals and signet rings. The Dominion
Plenipotentiaries have been asked to produce their
seals for the Treaty, and of course they have none.
There is a marked disinclination to lend a seal to Mr.
Hughes. After luncheon the Dominion delegates
change their mind. They will buy seals for themselves
and keep them as souvenirs. So out they troop to the
Avenue de l'Opéra.

Dine with Harry White in his rooms at the Crillon.

June 27, Friday

See Corbett of the Smyrna Aidin Railway and prepare a Note for him to hand to Venizelos. Lunch
with Lionel Curtis to meet André Cheradame. Having
invented Mittel Europa he is sorry to see it disappear.
An odd spluttering little man, like a different H. G.
Wells.

A long talk with A. J. B. in the evening about
Italian diplomacy. I say it has been stupid and dis-
honest. He says that each of those expressions 'require
definition.' I say that well at least it hasn't worked.
He says that he is not quite so sure. He is preparing
a paper to hand to Tittoni who has succeeded Sonnino.
It is a bold paper. It says that they must have the
London Treaty or a fresh deal. They cannot have
both the Treaty and *parecchio più*. Thus after six
months we come round to the conclusion from which
we started.

June 28, Saturday

La journée de Versailles. Lunch early and leave the
Majestic in a car with Headlam Morley. He is a historian, yet he dislikes historical occasions. Apart from
that he is a sensitive person and does not rejoice in
seeing great nations humbled. I, having none of such
acquirements or decencies, am just excited.

There is no crowd at all until we reach Ville d'Avray.
But there are poilus at every crossroad waving red
flags and stopping all other traffic. When we reach
Versailles the crowd thickens. The avenue up to the
Chateau is lined with cavalry in steel-blue helmets.
The pennants of their lances flutter red and white in
the sun. In the Cour d'Honneur, from which the

captured German cannon have tactfully been removed, are further troops.   There are Generals, Pétain, Gouraud, Mangin.   There are St. Cyriens.   Very military and orderly.   Headlam Morley and I creep out of our car hurriedly.   Feeling civilian and grubby.   And wholly unimportant.   We hurry through the door.

Magnificent upon the staircase stand the Gardes Républicains—two caryatides on every step—their sabres at the salute.   This is a great ordeal, but there are other people climbing the stairs with us.   Headlam and I have an eye-meet.   His thin cigaretted fingers make a gesture of dismissal.   He is not a militarist.

We enter the two anterooms, our feet softening on to the thickest of savonnerie carpets.   They have ransacked the Garde Meubles for their finest pieces. Never, since the Grand Siècle, has Versailles been more ostentatious or more embossed.   ' I hate Versailles,' I whisper to Headlam.   ' You hate what ? ' he answers, being only a trifle deaf.   ' Versailles,' I answer.   ' Oh,' he says, ' you mean the Treaty.'   ' What Treaty ? ' I say—thinking of 1871.   I do not know why I record this conversation, but I am doing this section of the diary very carefully.   It will amuse Ben and Nigel. ' This Treaty,' he answers.   ' Oh,' I say, ' I see what you mean—the German Treaty.'   And of course it will be called not the Treaty of Paris, but the Treaty of Versailles.   ' A toutes les gloires de la France.'

We enter the Galerie des Glaces.   It is divided into three sections.   At the far end are the Press already thickly installed.   In the middle there is a horse-shoe table for the plenipotentiaries.   In front of that, like a guillotine, is the table for the signatures.   It is supposed to be raised on a dais but, if so, the dais can be but a

few inches high. In the nearer distance are rows and
rows of tabourets for the distinguished guests, the
deputies, the senators and the members of the delegations. There must be seats for over a thousand
persons. This robs the ceremony of all privilege and
therefore of all dignity. It is like the Aeolian Hall.

Clemenceau is already seated under the heavy ceiling
as we arrive. ' Le roi,' runs the scroll above him,
' gouverne par lui-même.' He looks small and yellow.
A crunched homunculus.

Conversation clatters out among the mixed groups
around us. It is, as always on such occasions, like
water running into a tin bath. I have never been able
to get other people to recognize that similarity. There
was a tin bath in my house at Wellington : one
turned it on when one had finished and ran upstairs
shouting ' Baath ready ' to one's successor : ' Right
ho ! ' he would answer : and then would come the
sound of water pouring into the tin bath below, while
he hurried into his dressing-gown. It is exactly the
sound of people talking in undertones in a closed
room. But it is not an analogy which I can get others
to accept.

People step over the Aubusson benches and escabeaux to talk to friends. Meanwhile the delegates
arrive in little bunches and push up the central aisle
slowly. Wilson and Lloyd George are among the last.
They take their seats at the central table. The table is
at last full. Clemenceau glances to right and left.
People sit down upon their escabeaux but continue
chattering. Clemenceau makes a sign to the ushers.
They say ' Ssh ! Ssh ! Ssh ! ' People cease chattering
and there is only the sound of occasional coughing and

the dry rustle of programmes. The officials of the Protocol of the Foreign Office move up the aisle and say, ' Ssh! Ssh! ' again. There is then an absolute hush, followed by a sharp military order. The Gardes Républicains at the doorway flash their swords into their scabbards with a loud click. ' Faites entrer les Allemands,' says Clemenceau in the ensuing silence. His voice is distant but harshly penetrating. A hush follows.

Through the door at the end appear two huissiers with silver chains. They march in single file. After them come four officers of France, Great Britain, America and Italy. And then, isolated and pitiable, come the two German delegates. Dr. Müller, Dr. Bell. The silence is terrifying. Their feet upon a strip of parquet between the savonnerie carpets echo hollow and duplicate. They keep their eyes fixed away from those two thousand staring eyes, fixed upon the ceiling. They are deathly pale. They do not appear as representatives of a brutal militarism. The one is thin and pink-eyelidded : the second fiddle in a Bruns-wick orchestra. The other is moon-faced and suffer-ing : a privat-dozent. It is all most painful.

They are conducted to their chairs. Clemenceau at once breaks the silence. ' Messieurs,' he rasps, ' la séance est ouverte.' He adds a few ill-chosen words. ' We are here to sign a Treaty of Peace.' The Germans leap up anxiously when he has finished, since they know that they are the first to sign. William Martin, as if a theatre manager, motions them petulantly to sit down again. Mantoux translates Clemenceau's words into English. Then St. Quentin advances towards the Germans and with the utmost dignity leads them to the little table on which the Treaty is expanded. There is general tension. They sign. There is a general relaxation. Conversation hums again in an undertone. The delegates stand up one by one and pass onwards to the queue which waits by the signature table. Meanwhile people buzz round the main table getting autographs. The single file of plenipotentiaries waiting to approach the table gets thicker. It goes quickly. The officials of the Quai d'Orsay stand round, indicating places to sign, indicating procedure, blotting with neat little pads.

Suddenly from outside comes the crash of guns thundering a salute. It announces to Paris that the second Treaty of Versailles has been signed by Dr. Müller and Dr. Bell. Through the few open windows comes the sound of distant crowds cheering hoarsely. And still the signature goes on.

We had been warned it might last three hours. Yet almost at once it seemed that the queue was getting thin. Only three, then two, and then one delegate remained to sign. His name had hardly been blotted before the huissiers began again their ' Ssh ! Ssh ! ' cutting suddenly short the wide murmur which had again begun. There was a final hush. ' La séance est levée ' rasped Clemenceau. Not a word more or less.

We kept our seats while the Germans were conducted like prisoners from the dock, their eyes still fixed upon some distant point of the horizon.

We still kept our seats to allow the Big Five to pass down the aisle. Wilson, Lloyd George, the Dominions, others. Finally, Clemenceau, with his rolling satirical gait. Painlevé, who was sitting one off me, rose to greet him. He stretched out both his hands and grasped Clemenceau's right glove. He congratulated him. 'Oui,' says Clemenceau, 'c'est une belle journée.' There were tears in his bleary eyes.

Marie Murat was near me and had overheard. ' En êtes-vous sûre ? ' I ask her. ' Pas du tout,' she answers, being a woman of intelligence.

Slowly the crowd in the room clears, the Press through the Rotonde, and the rest through the Salle d'Honneur. I walk across the room, pushing past empty tabourets, to a wide-open window which gives out upon the terrace and the famous Versailles view. The fountains spurt vociferously. I look out over the tapis vert towards a tranquil sweep of open country. The clouds, white on blue, race across the sky and a squadron of aeroplanes races after them. Clemenceau emerges through the door below me. He is joined by Wilson and Lloyd George. The crowds upon the terrace burst through the cordon of troops. The top-hats of the Big Four and the uniforms of the accompanying Generals are lost in a sea of gesticulation. Fortunately it was only a privileged crowd. A platoon arrives at the double and rescues the big four. I find Headlam Morley standing miserably in the littered immensity of the Galerie des Glaces. We say nothing to each other. It has all been horrible.

And so through crowds cheering ' Vive l'Angleterre ' (for our car carries the Union Jack) and back to the comparative refinement of the Majestic.

In the car I told Headlam Morley of a day, years ago, when Tom Spring Rice had dined with the Prime Minister. He was young at the time, myopic and shy. The other guests were very prosperous politicians. When the women had gone upstairs they all took their glasses of port and bunched around the Prime Minister. Tom was left out. Opposite him was Eddie Marsh, also at a tail-end. Eddie took his glass round to Tom's side of the table and sat beside him. ' Success,' he said, ' is beastly, isn't it ? '

Headlam Morley agreed that success, when emphasised, was very beastly indeed.

Celebrations in the hotel afterwards. We are given free champagne at the expense of the tax-payer. It is very bad champagne. Go out on to the boulevards afterwards.

To bed, sick of life.

INDEX TO BOOK I

373

INDEX TO BOOK II

Not furnished for reasons indicated in text

SIR HAROLD NICOLSON was born in Teheran, Iran, in 1886, the son of Sir Arthur Nicolson, later first Baron Carnock. He was educated at Balliol College, Oxford, and entered the Diplomatic Service immediately after graduation. He served in a variety of posts and, after the close of the Peace Conference in 1919, became first secretary of the Diplomatic Service. In 1927 he was assigned to Berlin and in 1929 he resigned to devote himself to politics, journalism, and writing. From 1933 to 1945 he was a Member of Parliament and during the Second World War he served as a Governor of the B.B.C. In 1953 he was made a Knight Commander of the Victorian Order by Queen Elizabeth II. Among his many published works are: *The Congress of Vienna* (1946), *King George V* (1953), *The Evolution of Diplomatic Method* (1954), and *Diplomacy* (1950).

STUDIES IN REVOLUTION, *by E. H. Carr*

The Ideological Origins of the European Revolutionary Movement

Starting with Saint-Simon — the French aristocrat turned Revolutionary theorist — E. H. Carr goes on to discuss the major revolutionary thinkers of the nineteenth and twentieth centuries, including Marx, Proudhon, Herzen, Plekhanov, Sorel, Lenin and Stalin.

UL 171 $1.65

A WORLD RESTORED, *by Henry Kissinger*

A study of Metternich, Talleyrand, and the Congress of Vienna

In this history of Europe after Napoleon, Henry Kissinger — a leading foreign policy expert and Professor at Harvard University's Center for International Affairs — shows how order was restored to a world shattered by over a generation of war and revolution. The period following the defeat of Napoleon was a crucial one, for out of the settlements reached at the Congress of Vienna was to come a new European balance of power which lasted until the eve of the First World War.

UL 170 $1.95

A SELECTED LIST OF *Universal Library* TITLES